THE THEATRE ROYAL

ENTERTAINING A NATION

GRAEME SMITH

"Ladies and Gentlemen, please take your seats"

GLASGOW

THE THEATRE ROYAL
ENTERTAINING A NATION

Published by
Glasgow Publications
www.glasgowtheatreroyal.co.uk

Designed by
Cameron Smith
www.camerondigital.co.uk

Printed in Scotland
by Bell & Bain Ltd

ISBN 978-0-9559420-0-6

The Barcapel Foundation and the Binks Trust have kindly assisted the book's publication

Contents

CAST LIST OF THEATRES IN THIS STORY
IN ORDER OF APPEARANCE

Milton Collosseum	from 1860	Cowcaddens
Prince of Wales		
Grand		
Scotia/Metropole	1862	Stockwell Street
ROYAL	1867	Hope St. Cowcaddens
Old Royal to 1869		Dunlop Street
Gaiety/Empire	1874	Sauchiehall Street
Her Majesty's/Royal Princess's	1878	Gorbals Main Street
Royalty/Lyric	1879	Sauchiehall Street
Athenaeum	1893	Buchanan Street
King's	1904	Bath Street
Pavilion	1904	Renfield Street
Coliseum	1905	Eglinton Street
Alhambra	1910	Wellington Street
Savoy	1911	Hope Street

With supporting appearances from other theatres in Scotland, Ireland, England, Canada, and the United States of America.

Introduction

From Cowcaddens to the Colosseum, from Hope Street to Hollywood, for entertainment, drama, pantomime, music and song, this is the fascinating story, told for the first time, of the Theatre Royal.

Emerging from Music Halls to an Opera House and the national home of Scottish Opera and The Scottish Ballet, the Theatre Royal is the oldest theatre in Glasgow, opening in 1867. It is also the largest example in Britain of the theatre designs of Charles Phipps.

Pantomime, plays, spectaculars, silent films, circuses, ballet, opera and television grew up with the Royal. Original documents, and some 400 illustrations, trace its life and personalities, from its parentage in the 18th century, the influence of the Glover family here and and overseas, its links with fine arts and the International Exhibitions, all expressing the confidence of Glasgow and the context of its times.

It is also the birthplace of Howard & Wyndham Ltd, one of Britain's major theatre companies, thanks to the Simons fruit businesses in Candleriggs, and the birthplace of commercial television in Scotland, thanks to Canadian Roy Thomson.

For an encore there is a history of the previous Theatre Royal in Dunlop Street.

Let the curtain rise!

James Baylis
Music Hall Millionaire

The son of a bandmaster, James Stevenson Baylis became a bookkeeper in a brewery store and worked in the Singing Saloons, known also as "free-and-easies", and in the early Music Halls. With the help of his wife Christina Ferguson he rose through the ranks and managed Sloan's Oddfellows Music Hall in Argyle Street. In the 1860s he would create three theatres in Glasgow including the Royal, and become a millionaire in today's money.

By the 1850s some public-house owners were adding a room or hall to cater for the ever-increasing influx of workers arriving in the city, providing popular entertainments in the evenings. Walter Freer, who became Glasgow Corporation's halls manager, recalls his own youth:

...... when youngsters like myself haunted the music-halls because they could get neither warmth nor pleasure in their own homes. In the 'fifties and 'sixties people had very few opportunities of listening to good music and hearing accomplished artistes. Public entertainments were nothing like so numerous as they are today, and the few that did happen to be organised in Glasgow, indeed in Scotland, in 1853 were so prohibitively priced that the great mass of the people simply could not attend them.

Broadly speaking if people wanted amusement, they had either to go to some neighbouring public-house or to one of the few music-halls that existed then.

As you went in you paid your entry-money, and the price of refreshment (for drinking in those days was almost as common as breathing) and took your place in the hall beyond. The stage was railed off from the audience, and the owner of the music-hall acted as chairman, announcing each item as it fell due.

Entertainment was always lively, with communal singing at its heart. The hall could be dangerously packed to overflowing with about 200 customers, mainly men and youngsters, enjoying the exertions of instrument-players, comics, ballad singers, ethiopian singers, gymnasts, jugglers, ventriloquists,

OPPOSITE
James Baylis
Creator of the Royal

James Baylis

James Baylis was born in Ireland where his father was in the army, and other siblings were born in England. Young James met his future wife Christina Ferguson when the main industry of Scotland was cotton. Around this time there were 134 cotton mills in Scotland, mostly in and around Glasgow. She was born in Port of Menteith, the daughter of a tenant farmer. As a young girl she wound yarn for weaving in the nearby Deanston Cotton Works owned by James Finlay & Company and built alongside the River Teith. One of the young Baylis men was a cotton carder at Deanston and lived in its model village.

Settling in Glasgow's Saltmarket with Christina he took up work with a brewery, while two of his siblings became clerks to a firm of wine merchants in the city. His photograph and portraits show him in profile, for a very real reason. He had lost an eye after a bottle had been thrown in one of the singing saloons where he worked. Baylis decided then that if he ever ran his own halls they would not serve liquor.

The variety acts at his Scotia Music Hall in Stockwell Street attracted large audiences, but the record was on the 1st November 1865 when almost 5000 working men crammed in to listen to the Chancellor of the Exchequer (and soon to be Prime Minister) William Ewart Gladstone after he had received the Freedom of the City, earlier in the City Hall. It was reported that:

The Scotia doors were announced to be opened at eight o'clock, but owing to the great number of people who had assembled in the street, admission was given by six. By half-past seven o'clock the large hall was filled to its utmost capacity by an audience principally composed of working men. Admission was regulated by tickets, which were allocated by ballot. For upwards of an hour previous to the arrival of Mr Gladstone, the excellent Band of the establishment discoursed musical selections with much acceptance.

magicians and dancers (from Highland to the can-can). Freer continued:

There, naturally enough, the programmes were somewhat coarse and unelevating. Comparing these extraordinarily crude and rowdy entertainment parlours with our palatial modern theatres, I am amazed that they ever won any patronage whatsoever. But they were popular, and I used to sneak in often enough, and enjoy the warmth and fun of Shearer's Whitebait Music-Hall and Brown's Royal Music-Hall, both off Argyle Street, without any qualms of conscience.

The temperance movement started to encourage laws to license the sale of drink and eventually remove drinking and eating from the auditorium. A number of temperance music-halls

Elevation to the West.

Elevation to the East.

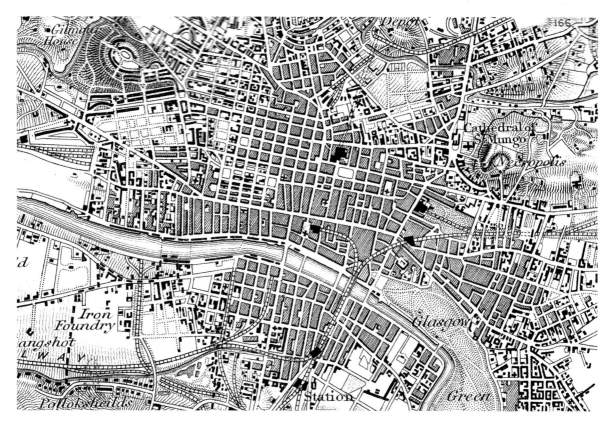

ABOVE
Glasgow
1860s.

opened up, including those of James Baylis.

Firstly in 1860 Baylis, who was then age 30, rented a hall in Cowcaddens above the Milton Arcade at the junction of Stewart Street, Cowcaddens Street, and New City Road and opened it as the Milton Colosseum Concert Hall, running it on "popular prices, good companies, and temperance refreshments." The Arcade at 190 Cowcaddens Street was owned by Alexander Hannay, and contained four shops, the music hall and Baylis family home, and the Cowcaddens Mechanics Institution Public Library and Reading Room (the Mechanics Institution was in adjacent Stewart Street.) The adaptation of the Milton Hall was designed by the architect firm of Clarke & Bell, who also designed bakery buildings probably for the Hannay bakery business.

Business was good and he bought ground in order to build his own music hall in 1862 to a design by architect Robert Black, who was one of the important architects in the early expansion of the town, including Royal Exchange Square. This would be the city's first purpose-built music hall, and many times larger than the earlier singing saloons.

Baylis chose the west side of Stockwell Street near to the Clyde, naming it the Scotia Music Hall (later known as the Metropole), which opened on 29th December 1862. This was also run on temperance lines to encourage more customers and families to come in. He was able to obtain a loan for the building, which was on three floors. The Scotia was about 100 feet long and 60 feet wide, larger than the Theatre Royal which had opened in Dunlop Street. The front facing Stockwell Street had a tower and stairways to the music hall which started on the first floor and was a standard rectangular shape with an upper gallery on three sides. There was a separate door to the ground floor which was used as a private school. At its southern gable – towards the Clyde -was the stage on the first floor, below which were two large dressing areas and three smaller dressing-rooms. The back of the stage had openings allowing scenery and props to be moved up and down from the ground floor. The rear of the building had a public exit door, a door to the stable, dung stores and storage areas; the stage door also gave access to the office and counting-room and a stair up to the family's apartment.

The Dean of Guild Court gave him further consent in March 1863 "to erect an additional storey on the tenement Building fronting Stockwell Street, to erect an Arched Gateway at 116 Stockwell Street and to alter shops and erect a Saloon behind same at 118,120,122 and 126."

Comedian and violinist James Moss travelled with his music hall acts and appeared frequently at the Milton and at the Scotia. His son Horace Edward Moss who was educated in Glasgow and Edinburgh travelled with him when a boy and played piano for the diorama show. When his father took the lease of the Royal Lorne Music Hall in Greenock, remaining a resident of Greenock, young Edward trained as a manager there……….his first steps in founding Moss Empires Ltd in 1899 which became Britain's largest chain of variety theatres.

The Head of Hope Street
Successful in his activities Baylis planned for another new theatre, this time back up at Cowcaddens, where he continued to operate the rented Milton Colosseum. In June 1866 he petitioned the Dean of Guild Court for a building warrant:

> to erect a Music Hall on Ground Bounded on the North by Cowcaddens Street, and on the South by Rutherford Lane.

Much of the land at Cowcaddens had been owned by the Campbells of Blythswood and was feued off to tenement builders, tradesmen and the new businesses springing up. James Baylis bought land at Cowcaddens Street in August 1866 from former Lord Provost Sir Andrew Orr who headed his family business of wholesale stationers in Glasgow, and cleared away the old tenement on it. He bought more land next to North Copenhagen Street (the early name of Hope Street) in April 1867 at a public roup from the Incorporation of Masons who had been left it by the

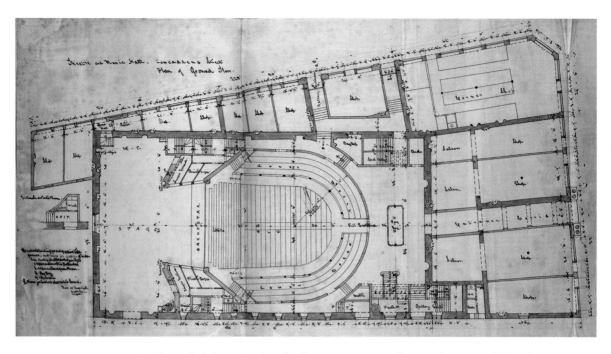

Above
Ground Floor
1867

Below
First Floor
1867

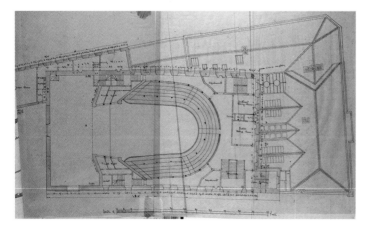

family of Adam Rutherford, mason, active around the 1800s. Rutherford Lane was named after him.

To help pay for this, and then build and furnish what was to be a new theatre, music hall, and shop premises around it, Baylis took out a new loan for £10,000 from a financial institution in 1867 and added another loan of £4,000 the next year to pay his contractors and suppliers who waited for their money, including :

John Morison
(slater and slate merchant)
John Lamb
(builder and wright)
Lachlan Colquhoun
(smith)
James Caird
(plasterer)
John Scott
(timber merchant, Rock Villa Saw Mills, Port Dundas)
John Rae
(glazier)

Building two theatres in quick succession was taking a lot of money. Two of the contractors John Morison and John Lamb drafted a Trust Deed which was signed by James Baylis in September

1869 but the other contractors declined to accept it, by which Baylis would grant rights to the two new theatres (excepting household property and £500 a year) with the profits each year going to pay his creditors.

He applied much the same commercial wisdom at the Royal as at Stockwell Street where the Scotia had four shops next to it which he rented out. His music hall there did not sell alcohol but one of the shops was "The Scotia Vaults" for those who had a drouth. At the intervals patrons who wanted an alcoholic drink were given a brass pass-out check, marked "Scotia Music Hall, Glasgow" which let them back in.

His new theatre faced Cowcaddens Street and he built and rented out shops fronting it and down Baylis Place, Hope Street. The theatre entrance corridor at Cowcaddens Street had two large shops

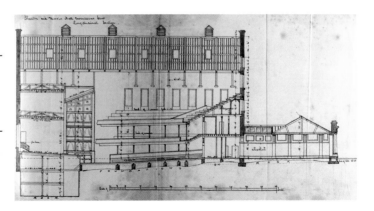

on either side. Above all those he built a new music hall on two levels to accommodate 700 customers, the Alexandra Music Hall. A fifth shop was a very large shop at the corner of Hope Street and it became a public house. Eight smaller shops were built down the side of Hope Street. Theatre dressing rooms, the Ballet Room, and the Green Room for artistes were on the upper floors along Hope Street. Income also came

ABOVE
Theatre Section
viewed from east

BELOW
Front Elevation
from Cowcaddens Street

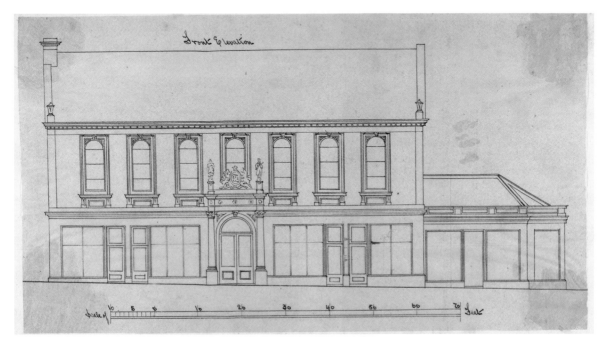

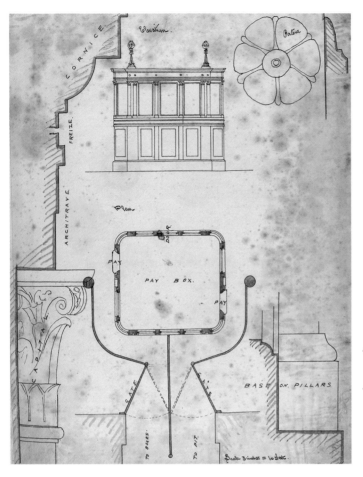

same time inside an Italianate warehouse in the Trongate. He wanted the spaciousness and appointments in order to attract grander productions and keep his audiences coming back. His first hall was called the Milton Colosseum being part of the Milton Arcade. For his new theatre he was next to the Royal Arcade, built in 1852 at the top of Hope Street, and happily called it the **Royal Colosseum & Opera House**. With great celebration he opened for business in November 1867.

The Royal's main door was in Cowcaddens at number 77, its entrance corridor ten foot wide leading to a free-standing Pay Box (where the stalls bar is now). Those going "To the Boxes" and "To the Dress Circle" went to the left after getting their tickets, and those going "To the Pit" to the right after getting their metal tokens – all with attended gateways. Those going to the Gallery, up in the gods, entered from Hope Street past a small pay window and up the winding stairs. For the gallery customers there was also an exit on the other side of the building in Side Avenue (an exit which continues today).

The pit was in the centre with four rows of Court Boxes (later called Side Boxes) raised and curved all round it. In front were seven rows of Orchestra Chairs (Stalls), gated from the pit. The Gallery entrance had started as Hope Street but for the Gallery and its Amphitheatre the advertised entrance became Side Avenue next to the Alexandra Music Hall entrance at number 73. The main entrance at

from property in Russell Street and Rutherford Lane, where the theatre had its stables.

Royal Colosseum & Opera House

Depending on how close you were to the next person, the main theatre held over 3,000 on three levels. Excluding the shops and entrance corridor the theatre was about 150 feet long and 80 feet wide. The stage was 41 feet deep and 74 feet wide with a proscenium opening of 31 feet. All this exceeded his Scotia, and was much larger than the Britannia music hall being developed around the

Cowcaddens continued to be for the Private Boxes, Dress Circle, Stalls, and Side Boxes.

Three Private Boxes, each seating 8 people, were on both sides of the stage at each level, with private stairs connecting them, starting at the stalls. Each series of boxes had a water-closet for their own use. On the stage, one of the boxes at each side was designed as a Singers Entrance. At the Hope Street side a stairway for artistes connected the Singers Entrance with the basement, the stage, the Green Room, and the dressing rooms on the two upper floors.

Refreshment rooms and spacious resting rooms with toilets were on each level. To help the theatre management a system of speaking tubes was installed to allow connection with the upper and lower Flies of the stage, the upper and lower Green Rooms (above the Stage Door), the Pay Box and the Orchestra pit.

The Royal is built with stone quarried on site. It is at the western edge of three quarries used to build much of the early town, the eastern quarry becoming the site of Queen Street Station. The

quarried face can still be seen in the basement below the orchestra pit and in the kitchens of the restaurant.

It was designed by George Bell of Clarke and Bell. He was a founder member of the Glasgow Institute of Architects formed in 1868 and became its President. Other surviving work of Bell includes The Western Baths off Byres Road, the former Fish Market in Bridgegate, Clyde Street and the old Sheriff Court and County Buildings in Wilson Street.

ABOVE
The Royal Arcade
head of Hope Street

Opening the Doors

The Glasgow Herald described *the spacious and well appointed theatre. The internal decorations are designed in a quiet and effective style. The most prominent feature is the proscenium, the arch of which is painted white, the sides being relieved with colour and gilding. The three tiers of stage boxes are hung with red curtains, which contrast finely with the white expanse above. The front of the dress circle is painted in white and green, as is also that of the amphitheatre – the former being decorated with an elegant stencil pattern. In the dress circle the seats are cushioned with red cloth, which combines with the hangings on the stage to impart a general air of warmth and richness to the interior.*

When lighted up by the three gasaliers in the ceiling the house presents an exceedingly pleasing, and we may add imposing, "tout ensemble." Nor is the ornamentation confined to the audience part of the building, for in the grand staircase leading to the boxes is fixed a beautiful transparency, with figures emblematic of Tragedy, Music and Comedy.

The stage also is well provided in this respect. Instead of the usual baize curtain there is a painted scene entitled "The Corsair's Isle", while by way of act-drop we have a pleasingly executed view of the "Lake of Menteith".

James Baylis knew how to pick the best scenic act-drop, his wife Christina Ferguson had been born and brought up in Port of Menteith!

Charging 6d for admission rising to 2/6d per seat for a box (referred to as Her Majesty's Box) Baylis opened the Royal Colosseum on the 28th November 1867. In front of a very large audience the evening started at 7 with the National Anthem followed by the farce *The Laughing Hyena*. An hour was next devoted to singing, sentimental and comic, varied with dancing, and the performances of a German Contortionist. The Glasgow Herald commented:

> The musical resources of the establishment appear to be considerable, but in so large a house more volume of sound from the orchestra would not be amiss.

The main drama was *The Sea of Ice, or the Gold Seeker of Mexico* complete with icebergs. This was known to

OPPOSITE
Inside the Royal
1870s

Baylis' Royal Colosseum Theatre

And Opera House, Cowcaddens.

Sole Proprietor....................... Mr JAMES S. BAYLIS.

———

Mr Baylis has much pleasure in announcing that his New and Magnificent Theatre

IS NOW OPEN,

With Company, Ballet, Band, Entertainment, Artistes, Staff, and Management entirely New to Glasgow.

———

"The Public may rest assured that I shall not be content until they get their Evening's Amusement at a Reasonable Rate. – JAMES S. BAYLIS." – Extracted from a letter in the Daily Mail of Nov. 4, 1867.

———

The Splendid Act Drop

THE LAKE OF MENTEITH

And the New Curtain,

THE CORSAIR'S ISLE - by J. Crawford.

———

The Performances will commence with the Laughable Farce,

THE LAUGHING HYENA.

To be followed by a

MISCELLANEOUS CONCERT,

In which the following Ladies and Gentlemen will appear :-

Madame VALCKENAERE,   Miss KATE HARTLEY.
Miss HOWARD CLAYTON,   Mr ALFRED MILNER, &c.

To conclude with the great sensational Drama, entitled

THE SEA OF ICE, OR THE GOLD SEEKER OF MEXICO.

The Performance will Commence at 7 o clock each Evening, Doors Open Half an Hour previous.

———

PRICES OF ADMISSION -

Her Majesty's Box, each person...	Half-a-Crown.
Private Boxes, each person..........	Two Shillings.
Dress Circle, each person............	One Shilling and Sixpence.
Stall Boxes or Lower Circle, and Front Pit................................ }	One Shilling
Back Seats (Floor of the House)..	Ninepence.
Amphitheatre.............................	Sixpence.

Entrance to Amphitheatre by Side Street, head of Hope Street.

———

Carriage Regulations. - In setting down, to approach by way of Sauchiehall Street, and head of Hope Street, and after setting down at main entrance in Cowcaddens Street, empty Carriages to depart via Renfield Street. In taking up, to approach from Renfield Street, and depart by way of Baylis's Private Street, or otherwise to the West. No Carts at any time to pass either up or down.

N.B - No Smoking allowed in any part of the House.

Strictest order will be maintained.

Stage Manager.........Mr FRANK HUDEPETH.
Prompter.................Mr H. SOMERVILLE.
Scenic Artists...........Messrs J. CRAWFORD and ELLERMAN.
Property Makers......Messrs GEO. HEPBURN & BEN. JONES
Master Carpenter.....Mr MACINTOSH.

Tradesmen are cautioned not to supply Goods to the Theatre without a written order endorsed by the Proprietor.

theatregoers; it was produced in the Theatre Royal Dunlop Street in July 1854, presumably without melting the icebergs.

The theatre advised how carriages should approach and leave, a one way system, and stated "Order Carriages for 10.50pm." To see the seating plan and for booking tickets the box office opened daily from 11 to 3.

Madame Florence Lancia's Grand English Opera Company presented two weeks of opera in December: including *La Traviata, Don Giovanni, Barber of Seville, Il Trovatore*, and *The Bohemian Girl*. The adverts declared "Bonnets allowed in the Dress Circle." That full opera season was the only one Baylis took into his theatre. Other venues in Glasgow performed opera – in 1868 there were 76 performances of 23 different operas.

The first pantomime *Ye Jolly Miller of Dee, or Harlequin*, and *Ye Bluff Hal and Ye Anne Boleyn* opened on 30th December 1867. Its advance advertising described the show as one:

> Which will excel anything yet attempted in Glasgow. The beautiful Scenery, the Burlesque Opening, the Splendid Transformation Scene, and the Comic Scenes for the Harlequinnade, are all original, and that is something original for the Glasgow Public - nothing having been used before at any other Theatre – everything having been invented and manufactured by Mr Baylis's own Artistes for this the

Largest and most Complete Theatre in the Kingdom.

As usual in theatres until the 1880s there were several items on the bills of fare. Often there was a recitation or concert, then the main feature, followed by a burlesque, ballet or farce! The pantomime continued for all of January 1868, preceded each evening by a play or musical such as *Alassandro Massaron*, or from the "Double Pantomime Co" the tale of *The Wife of Seven Husbands*, supported by the theatre's own orchestra and corps of ballet (chorus girls.) For a time the Royal Colosseum adverts had a sentence inserted:

> To prevent Mistakes and Disappointments this Theatre is Situated at 77 Cowcaddens, Head of Hope Street.

Soon the theatre was very busy, and the advertising sub title changed to THE GREAT THEATRE - HEAD of HOPE STREET.

Springtime attractions included Scott's *The Bride of Lammermoor*, concluding each evening with the historical drama of *Mary Queen of Scots*. For many weeks Don Boucicault's anti-slavery play *The Octoroon* was staged, followed by a Grand Ballet Divertissement. *Richard III* took his turn and for March 17th Baylis added a drama of *The Shamrock of Ireland*. The opera *The Jewess*, first performed in Paris in 1835, was a Grand Spectacular Drama on a Grand Scale of

OPPOSITE
Opening Advert
November 1867

ROYAL COLOSSEUM THEATRE AND
OPERA HOUSE
SOLE PROPRIETOR........................ MR JAMES S. BAYLIS.

Grand Production of the New
CHRISTMAS PANTOMIME

Engagement for a Few Nights More of
MR GARDINER COYNE

ON MONDAY EVENING, DEC. 30,
The Theatre will be Closed, to make necessary Preparations for
the Pantomime.

ON TUESDAY EVENING, 31ST DEC,
There will be a Grand
DRESS REHEARSAL OF THE PANTOMIME
To which the Public will be admitted at the usual Prices.

GRAND
ILLUMINATED MORNING PERFORMANCES.

WEDNESDAY (New Year's Day)....	At Two o'clock Each Day
THURSDAY, January 2d..............	Doors Open half-an-hour
FRIDAY, January 3d..................	previous.
SATURDAY, January 4th.............	

The Evening Entertainments will commence at Seven o'clock

On WEDNESDAY EVENING, JAN. 1, 1868,
and during the week,
The Performances will commence with a Favourite Irish Comedi-
etta, in which Mr GARDINER COYNE, the Celebrated Irish
Comedian and Vocalist (who is engaged for a limited number
of nights), will appear, supported by the Company, to be
followed by
THE GRAND, NEW, AND ORIGINAL
Allegorical, Biological, Chronological, Demoniacal, Enigmatical,
Farcical, Geographical, Horological, Ironical, Joeosical,
Knoxmoonical, Luministical, Meteorological, Numeristical,
Omenistical, Physiological, Quizzical, Redundical, Satirical,
Tormentical, Universical, Vocalistic, Whimsical, Xotical,
Ynolistical, Zeological
CHRISTMAS PANTOMIME,
Entitled
YE JOLLY MILLER OF DEE ;
OR, HARLEQUIN, AND
YE BLUFF KING HAL AND YE ANNE BOLEYN!
Or, Witchery, Willany and Wengeance.

NEW AND BEAUTIFUL SCENERY!
Painted and Invented by Mr JOHN CRAWFORD, expressly for this
Theatre only.
New Dresses by Mr JAMES SCOTT and Numerous Assistants; New
Properties by Mr G. HEPBURN; New Comic Scenes in
Harlequinade invented by Mr SAMSON BOLENO; New Overture
and Music by Mr JUKES; New Ballet by Mons. LAVIGNE. The
Opening – Written, Invented, and Produced under the
immediate superintendence of Mr HARRY BOLTON, late Stage
Manager of Theatre-Royal, Marylebone, London, on a Scale of
Splendour and Completeness never before attempted in the
City of Glasgow.

SYNOPSIS OF SCENERY:
MUSHROOM SWAMP (Moonlight – Crawford).
CHAMBER IN WINDSOE CASTLE.
VIEW OF THE RIVER DEE AND FARM OF THE JOLLY MILLER.
(Crawford.)
SUDDEN CHANGE FROM SUMMER TO WINTER.
In this Scene will be Produced one of the Greatest Effects ever
witnessed in the Provinces.
Grand Morris Dance , arranged by Mons. Lavigne.
Snow Storm
RETREAT OF THE FAIRY QUEEN
HAUNT OF THE NYMPHS IN THE BOWERS OF CORAL, SEAWEED,
AND SHELLS OF THE OCEAN (Crawford).
Fairy Fays by a numerous Corps de Ballet.
The Arrival of Puck – The Affairs of the Nation.
GRAND FAIRY BALLET!
Arranged by Mon. Lavigne. Principal Dancers, Mdlle. Lavigne
and Miss Fortesque.
WIZARD'S OAK AND DELL.
THE WITCHES' RAVINE AND MORASS. (Crawford).

TRANSFORMATION!
The Forest of Flowers and Descent of Fairy Fays – The Land of
Jewels – Throne of Sapphire in the Glittering Bowers of
Tranquil Delight – Vineyard of Fruit and Dias of Glory –
Revolving Pillars of Crystal – The Home of Brilliance in the
World of Light.

HARLEQUINADE
Harlequin – Signor LAVIGNE.
Columbines – Mdlle. LAVIGNE and Miss JENNY DEARDREW.
Pantaloon – Mr ROBERSTON.
Sprites –The CROSBY FAMILY.
Merry Clown – Mr SAMSON BOLENO.

The Performance will commence at Seven o'clock.
Doors Open Half-an-Hour previous.
Stage Manager, Mr George Blythe. Conductor of the Orchestra,
Mr Jukes.
Box Office Open at the Theatre Daily from Eleven till One,
where Tickets and Places may be secured.
For Particulars, see Small Bills.

Magnificence, with Hungarian dancers from the famed Kiralfy family. Other productions included *Oliver Twist*, and a Burlesque by Brinkley Sheridan.

Towards the summer, Baylis presented the national drama of *Wallace*; and evenings with Arthur Lloyd, the Grand Comique well known in Glasgow. In June patrons were entertained "with entirely new scenery, dresses, properties, music, dances, reels etc in the Grand National Burlesque of *Tam o'Shanter, or the Brig o'Doon*." In some of these evenings the spectacle of the recently won Abyssinian War was staged, when the band of the 25th Regiment King's Own Borderers played overtures at the end of the evening. For July the drama unfolded of *Aladdin or the Wonderful Lamp* – Baylis claiming it as the first time in Glasgow in 25 years.

During the recess the stage was enlarged, with *Henry IV Part I* christening it, and David Fisher playing the part of Falstaff. On musical evenings guest sopranos were hired, including Annie Adams from London, who is considered one of the first female star artistes of the Music Halls. The play *Catherine Howard* by Alexander Dumas was popular "watched by upwards of 3000 on Saturday night" and Shakespeare lovers saw Henry Talbot in *Hamlet*. Guest actors came from the Theatres Royal in Newcastle and Edinburgh, one of the plays being *The Ticket-of-Leave Man*. And Monsieur *Blondini*, the hero of Niagara Falls, showed off his tightrope skills and trapeze acts.

In December James Baylis opened

LEFT
Arthur Lloyd
grand-comique

his second pantomime *Let Glasgow Flourish, or, The Fairy of St Mungo* written by William Lowe. Ticket prices were Dress Circle 3/-, Pit Stalls 1/- and Amphitheatre 6d. Running for three months, one of its theme tunes sung by leading lady Margaret Thorne was

"Here's to the Bird, and here's to the Bell,
And here's to the Bonnie Green Tree,
The Fish and the Ring, their praises we'll sing,
Let Glasgow Flourish, say we."

Baylis headed his programmes "Royal Colosseum Theatre" - "The Great Theatre". They had many advertisements, including a full page which amounted to a history of the Singer Sewing Machine. The American company had started assembling sewing machines in Glasgow that year, moving to a factory in Bridgeton and then relocating to

OPPOSITE
First Pantomime Advert
December 1867

COWCADDENS IN THE 1860S

The district of Cowcaddens was annexed to Glasgow in 1843. Its original name in 16th century documents is Kowcaldens and variations of it, meaning the home or dens of unkind goblins (kow) and nothing to do with the later habit of the city`s kye (cows) being driven from the High Street up to the farm pastures each day. Meikle Cowcaddens farm sat to the west of Cowcaddens Street and became the property of the Campbells of Blythswood, while Lytle Cowcaddens farm sat to the east, and became the property of the Bell family who provided a number of Provosts and Baillies of Glasgow, and are also remembered by the name of Bell Street at Glasgow Cross.

The Bells of Cowcaddens opened up three quarries, known as Black Quarries, which produced a greyish brown stone when excavated but turned black soon after. This was used in the early buildings of Glasgow and Cowcaddens; the edge of the western quarry called Cowcaddens Quarry is where the Theatre Royal sits.

The village of Cowcaddens grew on the south side of Cowcaddens Street. Silk mills and cotton mills were set up on the north side, giving the name Mylton (or Milton), to use water from the Pinkston Burn flowing westwards to Kelvinbridge. The Milton Arcade was built on the site of an old silk mill. The Forth and Clyde Canal Company opened its cut to Port Dundas in 1777 with its construction of basins, stores and granaries, quickly followed by whisky distilleries and chemical works. The Phoenix Iron Works was opened around 1786 by Thomas Edington, after whom Edington Street is named. Other iron works, foundries and engineers` shops sprung up together with flour mills, sugar mills, timber yards, glassworks and potteries.

The first teacher training college in Britain was promoted by David Stow and established in 1836 at Dundas Vale by the Church of Scotland as the Normal School for the Training of Teachers. Just after the Disruption of 1843 he helped create the Free Church of Scotland`s college for teacher training in Cowcaddens Street, known as the Free Church Normal school (Stow College). Cowcaddens was a bee-hive of industry into which came more people, displaced by the City Improvements Act around Saltmarket and High Street, giving rise to overcrowding for many years north of Renfrew Street.

Clydebank to what became the largest factory in Europe.

In the spring *Tam o'Shanter* was followed by *The Miller of Fife*; and the ever popular Julie Sleaman from London in the tragedy of *Leah the Forsaken*. Baylis ran the national drama of *Rob Roy*, "with new scenery on over 10,000 yards of canvas painted by Brunton and Eduard," for over a month until Saturday 22 May 1869 which was the final day of the theatre as the Royal Colosseum and Opera House. For the final night there was a special feature in *Rob Roy* of "Mr William Glover of the Theatre Royal in his Great Sword combat with Mr Brunton."

Cowcaddens or Bath Street?

Theatre and music hall owners knew they would likely have to move from the old congested centre of the city around the High Street and Glasgow Cross, or see many customers move away. But should they move to the New Town areas west of George Square, with terraces of elegant townhouses stretching over Blythswood Hill, Woodlands and Park Circus, or to already populated areas like Cowcaddens? In the 1860s the time for decisions came with the arrival of railway lines over the Clyde to St Enoch Square. Baylis had already identified his site in Cowcaddens and built his new theatre there.

In Dunlop Street, former actress Mrs Edmund Glover continued as head of the respected Theatre Royal. One of her elder sons William Glover had returned from theatre in Dublin in

LEFT
Miss Annie Adams
who went on to tour the USA

1860 to help the family businesses of the Theatre Royal, and the Prince's Theatre-Royal at 100 West Nile Street facing along West Regent Street. He thought Cowcaddens "was too far north for a fashionable theatre" but the Theatre Royal had to move. In August 1866 the newspapers reported he had secured a site in Bath Street which would have "audience accommodation three or four times greater than the present Royal." Glover applied to the Dean of Guild Court in 1867 and again the next year for a warrant "to erect a Theatre in Bath Street." for which he received funds from the British Linen Bank. The architects for the proposed theatre were Clarke & Bell, the same firm used by James Baylis. The site he would buy for a new theatre was on the south side of Bath Street between West Nile Street and Buchanan Street, but it would never be built.

Theatre Royal and the Glover Inheritance

James Baylis reflected on his new theatres and decided that being a property owner had fewer risks than being a showbusiness operator. In the spring of 1869, he leased the Royal Colosseum & Opera House, to **William Glover** (a trustee of his late father **Edmund Glover**) and **George Francis**, the building being renamed **Theatre Royal**.

The Glovers had built a good name in theatre, from a start that was far removed from acting. The story of the Glover Inheritance can now be told.

Edmund Glover, actor/manager, scenic artist and father of William Glover, helped set the standards of the Glasgow stage in the 19th century. On his death in 1860 the newspapers wrote Testimonials, acknowledging that theatregoing had become more acceptable. Some extracts are shown here:

Glasgow Herald

Mr Glover was a talented, accomplished and versatile actor. In tragedy he was fervid and classical; in melodrama, chastened and effective; in comedy, humorous and quaint.

The deceased was a model manager, and spared no effort or expense to please the public. As a director of stage business he was hardly surpassed in Britain, especially after the emigration of Mr James Wallack (to New York). In putting a play upon the stage his endeavour was to heighten the effect, and his scenes, properties, and dresses were always in good taste, and got up with suitable splendour. He was unrivalled in his spectacular productions, as witness the magnificent illustrations given in Dunlop Street of the Crimean War, and the Indian Revolt. The pantomimes and burlesques in Glasgow were also noted for their gorgeous scenery and elaborate mechanism. Mr Glover kept a good stock-company and brought a regular succession of "stars" of the first magnitude to Glasgow. The theatrical presentations were interspersed by seasons of Italian and English opera.

Glasgow Sentinel

The Theatre Royal has sustained under Mr Glover's management an unblemished reputation….

Endowed with a refined taste, a sonorous voice, and an emphatic delivery Mr Glover rarely failed to make

OPPOSITE
William Glover

THE GLOVER INHERITANCE

The Glover family hailed from Birmingham and became very wealthy in the Industrial Revolution. In the 18th century their standing was recognised by **Joshua Glover** and his son **Samuel** being appointed High Bailiffs of the Manor of Birmingham. Based in Cannon Street, the Glovers were hardware merchants which included "Birmingham toys" and jewellery. "Toys" meant small decorative objects made from silver, bronze, steel and other materials, from buttons, buckles and boxes to caddy spoons and candelabra. They sold to Holland, the German States, Austria, France, Spain, Portugal and North Africa. They also became involved in copper and tin mining in Cornwall and ventured into operating iron furnaces and a wireworks in South Wales. The works supplied wire to the Lancashire cotton industry. In changed circumstances in the 19th century it was Julia Betterton Glover, a young actress, who would save her family from penury.

ABOVE
Abercarn Ironworks

Joshua Glover and his partners ran Abercarn Ironworks in Ebbw Vale from around 1760 – and one of the partners Samuel Garbett also founded Carron Ironworks in Falkirk. Father and son established a pit coal forge in Abercarn in 1782 and a charcoal-fired wireworks. Samuel owned all this outright when his father died in 1786, and five years later purchased Abercarn estate, house and minerals, for the princely sum then of £27,000. He also leased and operated Hirwaun Ironworks in Rhondda for seventeen years to 1803. In that year he sold land at Rhymney for £8,000 to a Benjamin Hall who became owner of the Union Ironworks there.

The French Revolution affected their trade because of ships and their goods and bullion being plundered by French privateers. (No electronic transfers of money in those days.) It was greatly harmed by the Napoleonic wars which followed. The final straw may have been Napoleon's closure of the continental ports to British trade.

Around 1807 he became financially embarrassed and had to make arrangements with his creditors to pay his debts. To help, he sold his estate of Abercarn in the same year to Hall's family for £51,000. Young Benjamin Hall later became a Member of Parliament, where he was known as "Big Ben". He was also the Chief Commissioner of Works overseeing the building of the new Houses of Parliament, where the famous clock was given his nickname.

Samuel Glover junior lived the rich life. At age 26 he married a young actress **Julia Betterton** age 19 at a ceremony in London in 1800. Young actresses marrying rich men is not new! However unknown to her he was busy squandering his father's wealth. "Betterton" was not her real name, despite her father's promotion of the fiction. She was born Julianna Butterton in Newry, Ireland, the daughter of the town's theatre manager William Butterton. His venture failed and he decided there would be financial benefit to him if her name were changed to "Betterton", claiming links to a famous actor and long dead Thomas Betterton. With this deception he and his family travelled round the theatres and the young Julia was acclaimed as an infant acting prodigy in York, the West Country, Bath and elsewhere. At age 9 she made her debut in Scotland at the Dumfries Theatre Royal in 1790, and at age 16 she made her debut on the London stage in 1797.

Samuel Glover senior passed away in 1808 and his widow Phillis and Samuel junior were summoned to appear at the Court of Chancery, England's court of debt and misery so well described by Charles Dickens. Agreements were made and remade to try to pay off creditors. Another son was evicted from the house and lands of High Meadow near to Abercarn. The widow Phillis could return to her native Cornwall where her family had been sailing masters in Falmouth but her son still aspired to continuing the high life. Her daughter-in-law Julia had an income from her acting but it is unlikely the two women had anything to do with each other. Acting was not a respectable occupation and it was held that young Sam had married below his station. In correspondence with Mathew Boulton (business partner of James Watt) his father mentions his son's very inappropriate marriage. However it would be Julia Betterton Glover who saved the family from oblivion.

Julia Betterton Glover and her family

When the Glover trade money finally ran out in 1808 her husband Samuel would appear backstage at the end of her appearances holding out his hand for money, which he would spend on drink and other pursuits. He even took the London Drury-Lane Theatre Committee to court in 1818 to recover ten weeks salary amounting to £100, due to his wife, upon which he felt as a husband he had a call - "to save himself from the walls of a prison." In future, he said to the court, they should pay him £6 per week of her salary and give to her the remaining £4. The theatre countered...... "Mrs Glover is our labourer, and we shall pay her the salary." The court awarded Samuel Glover one farthing.

The family would travel with Julia and fellow actors to towns and cities. One daughter Phillis became an actress in her short life, and two sons made their way in acting and music. Two portraits of her are in the National Portrait Gallery, London. In his Diary her son Edmund describes his father as "a confessed deceiver" and after a business meeting with a fellow actor and actress he describes "their delightful villa with three acres of land. Just what poor dear Mother ought to have if she had not kept on working all her life." Samuel Glover always styled himself "Gentleman" even when he moved in and out of debtors' prisons. He died in 1832 in Marshalsea Debtors Gaol, Southwark, London.

Edmund Glover was her eldest son and started as a "panorama operator" for the stages where she appeared. Becoming an actor and then a producer he was able to rebuild some of the financial standing which the family once had. He is the man who helped put the earlier Glasgow Theatre Royal firmly on the map. The Theatres Royal in the city before the 1860s, including Edmund Glover's extensive activity, are described in the Encore chapter of this book.

ABOVE
Edmund Glover

Edmund's half-brother **Howard Glover** taught music and opera singing for a while in a school of music and drama his mother started in London. He came to Glasgow as music director for his brother for a year in 1849, then became music correspondent of the Morning Post (Daily Telegraph). He also composed operas, pianoforte, romances and partsongs. His overture cantata *Tam O'Shanter* was conducted by Berlioz in front of Queen Victoria on Saturday 23rd January 1858. To this day the family say that Berlioz complained of parts being difficult to play but contend he then copied it in some of his own music. *Ruy Blas: A Grand Opera* based on Victor Hugo's drama was performed at Covent Garden in 1861. Finally, in 1868, he moved to America to become a composer and arranger of musicals at Niblo's Garden Theatre on Broadway, including *White Fawn* which ran for 176 performances and was the successor to the Niblo's *Black Crook* which is considered to be the first Broadway musical spectacular. He died in New York in 1875.

an impression in the part he chose to appear in.

Glasgow Citizen

His practical skill as a painter, and admirable knowledge of artistic effect, imparted a propriety and splendour to many of his presentations…………

Caledonian Mercury

He exhibited the best qualities of a man of business. In his hands the character of the stage was raised mightily in the western metropolis.

Greenock Herald

He had a high sense of his mission which was to make the West of Scotland a school for the development and appreciation of poetry and art. In Glasgow on one occasion when he had lavished large sums on gorgeous representations of the Shakespearian drama, and spectacular exhibitions, he was railled by a friend on what he called the **waste**. Edmund Glover replied:

Venice was mercantile, and if you give me time, I shall give Glasgow the taste to appreciate what is good.

In Greenock one of his pantomimes at its Theatre Royal did not take as well as might be expected. "It is too much of a novelty as yet", said Glover, "when they understand this sort of thing they will like it."

By the Royal Letters-patent held by the family, William Glover transferred the Royal name from their Dunlop Street theatre which had now closed under compulsory purchase to make way for the railways across the Clyde, curving in at high level to St Enoch. In May the same year Baylis leased the Scotia to his wife's brother-in-law, John Stevenson, for what turned out to be three years. This kept it within the family circle. Ironically the railway bridge over Stockwell Street left the Scotia untouched.

Glover knew that his father's wealth was tied up in the Edmund Glover Trust

OPPOSITE
Juliet Glover
Hamlet
1807

RIGHT
Theatre Royal
Dunlop Street
1860s

for the lifetime of his widow and he had no extra capital of his own to be able to buy, but was happy to take a lease. A dispute continued over the use of Baylis equipment and props and James Baylis started a court action in September 1869 against Glover and Francis. Part of Baylis's inventory after his death is the full detail of props and a valuation of £500 being "Machinery property, fittings and other moveable effects in the Theatre Royal Cowcaddens."

For the new Theatre Royal Glover would bring from Dunlop Street many of the existing company of the old Royal. The core numbers were 19 management, design and stage; 17 of an orchestra; and artistes of around 60 people. The orchestra composed of:

1st Violins
2nd Violins
Violo
Violoncello
Contra bass
Oboe
Bassoon
Flute
Clarinet
Horns
Cornet
Trombone
and Tympani

The management included the:

Manager and treasurer
Stage manager
Scenic artists

Master carpenter
Costumiers
Modeller and property men
Librarian
Music librarian
Gas engineer
Box book-keeper
Prompter
and Call-boy

The Theatre Royal opened under Glover and Francis in June 1869, bringing to it the productions and high standards from the renowned old house in Dunlop Street. The Dean of Guild granted them consent in July "to make certain alterations to the Boxes, Gallery and Pit sittings and deepening the Stage of the building." And Glover painted a new drop scene, a view of Ben Venue and Loch Katrine.

From the word go Glover and Francis increased their trade around the site by becoming wine and spirit merchants, firstly at 85 Cowcaddens right at the Hope Street corner calling it the "Theatre Royal Vaults" – next door to number 83 the boot and shoe maker William Quarrier - and secondly at 288 Hope Street next to Rutherford Lane and close to Renfrew Street. The other shop tenants were R&J Dick bootmakers at 81 Cowcaddens, Robert Smart general drapers at 79, and T&S Wilson hatters at 75.

Both managers stayed close to the theatre and the takings, Glover at 86 Bath Street at the corner of Hope Street and Francis at 144 Renfrew Street. The theatre manager Edward Knapp

transferred with them from Dunlop Street to the new Royal.

In early 1870 James Baylis decided to refinance the cost of building and fitting out his two theatres by selling them for a combined sum of £23,000 to his lenders the Scottish Heritable Security Co Ltd and leasing them back, with an option to buy back one or both of them within a 14 year period. The finance company agreed to apply all rents from the theatres and adjacent properties

ABOVE
Programme Cover
March, 1878

MRS CHRISTINA BAYLIS

Based at the Scotia the widow of James Baylis became the doyen of variety theatre.

She helped the career of many entertainers including Harry Lauder and Charles Coburn, real name Colin McCallum, who became a national star with songs such as "The Man Who Broke the Bank at Monte Carlo" and "Two Lovely Black Eyes." On her retiral H. E Moss (of Moss Empires) paid special tribute and recorded the esteem in which she was held.

Their surviving children were girls, and understandably Christina Baylis doted on her grandson Tom Colquhoun, who helped her in the Scotia. The family recall that she spoiled Tommy and used to give him "bags of gold" to go to the races at Longchamps in Paris. She later encouraged him to become manager of the Tivoli theatre at Anderston Cross and the Queen's variety theatre, Watson Street at Glasgow Cross. However he did not have his own Midas touch, and by the 1930s had become doorman at the New Grand cinema on Cowcaddens, the very site of his grandfather's Milton Colosseum. Dallas's well known departmental store in Milton House eventually expanded into the space of the music hall turned theatre turned cinema.

On her passing in 1898 the newspapers could look back at over thirty years of achievement:

It was the ability and enterprise of James Baylis and of Mrs Baylis that the townsfolk of Glasgow during the past generation have been chiefly indebted for healthy music hall recreation. Many of us recollect the early days, or rather nights, of the Scotia. In that glittering temple, to the tune of blithesome music, our eyes would eagerly follow the movements of the young sylphides of the corps de ballet in such gorgeous spectacles as "The White Dove", "Scotland and her Shires", "The Gathering of the Clans", and "As Good as a Pantomime".

The music at her funeral was provided by a band drawn from the orchestras of the Glasgow theatres. Among the floral tributes was one from Sir Thomas Lipton. During her lifetime Mrs Baylis would not allow her eldest daughter, also named Christina, to marry as she was her mother's right-hand woman; which is why the daughter married at age 40! When she was a young woman one of her suitors was Tommy Lipton, which always drew the remark from Mrs Baylis that "you cannot marry a wee grocer." Lipton continued to expand his international tea and grocery businesses, and remained single.

TOP
Christina Baylis

BOTTOM
Scotia Variety Theatre

towards the option of buying back if that was taken up.

At curtain up time in the evening of 1st November 1870 James Baylis died suddenly age 41 at his home in the Scotia building, at 116 Stockwell Street. Christina Baylis succeeded her husband as owner of the Theatre Royal and of the "Scotia Variety Theatre", through the Baylis Trust.

The Scotia was rebuilt in 1875 following a fire, the designs by architects Campbell Douglas and James Sellars making it the largest variety theatre in Scotland that century. It was wide and high, accommodating about 3500 people. The arrangement of the galleries was now similar to the Royal with the galleries in horse-shoe shape, and the upper galleries recessed back from the line of the first gallery. At its re-opening in December 1875 the Glasgow Weekly Herald reported:

This gives the Scotia a lightsome and airy appearance. The stalls in the front of the area are roomy and comfortably finished in leather, the first circle being similarly appointed. Four handsome private boxes have

been fitted up in the stage ends of the respective galleries and these are furnished with crimson velvet. The decoration of the theatre is Pompeian in style………

She continued to direct the Scotia until retiring in 1892, residing at her home Newark House in Pollokshields. It was not uncommon for wives and widows to be prominent in the theatre business. Of the fifteen women managing proprietors then in Britain she was the longest reigning.   Her musical director for many years was Bob Singleton whose family went on to develop their own chain of cinemas. H E Moss took over the Scotia by agreement with her and it was later renamed The Metropole.

Theatres in Britain had an average life of only 12 years due to fire, until gradually, over decades, there was improvement through the use of electric light, better building regulations, fire resistant material, larger street frontages allowing for better and more numerous exits, improved access for fire brigades, and more vigilant management. But all that was in the future.

THEATRE  ROYAL

HEAD OF HOPE STREET, GLASGOW.

SOLE LESSEES and MANAGERS ... ... (BY ROYAL LETTERS PATENT) ... Messrs GLOVER & FRANCIS

LAST FOUR NIGHTS
OF
ITALIAN OPERA
GRAND
MORNING
PERFORMANCE
THIS DAY, SATURDAY

2nd November, 1872. (Doors open at 2, commencing at 2.30,)

On which occasion Meyerbeer's celebrated Opera, **LES**

HUGUENOTS

Will be performed with the following unprecedented Cast :—

Raoul de Nanges	Signor CAMPANINI
Il Conte de St. Bris	Signor AGNESI
Il Conte de Nevers	Signor MENDIOROZ
Marcello	Signor POLI
Urbano	Madame TREBELLI BETTINI
Margherita di Valois	Mdlle. ILMA DI MURSKA
AND	
Valentina	Mdlle. TITIENS

THE INCIDENTAL DIVERTISSEMENT
Will be supported by Mdlle. BLANCHE RICOIS and the CORPS DE BALLET.

This Evening, SATURDAY, 2nd NOV., 1872,

Rossini's admired Opera,

IL BARBIERE
DI
SIVIGLIA

Il Conte Almaviva	Signor BETTINI
Il Dottore Bartolo	Signor BORELLA
Figaro	Signor MENDIOROZ
Don Basilio	Signor AGNESI
Fiorello	Signor RINALDINI
Ufficiale	Signor CARABONI
Marcellina	Mdlle. BAUERMEISTER
AND	
Rosini	Mdlle. MARIE MARIMON

Who will introduce in the Lesson Scene,

MATON'S POLONAISE.

THE BAND, CHORUS, & BALLET
Will be considerably strengthened by Members of HER MAJESTY'S OPERA.

Principal Danseuse - - - - - - - Mdlle. BLANCHE RICOIS

Director and Conductor, ... Sig. LI CALSI

Leader ... ... Sig. ADELMANN

Stage Manager, ... Mr RANOE

Suggeritore, ... Signor RIALP

Monday, Nov. 4—FAUST
Tuesday, Nov. 5—MARTA
Wednesday, Nov. 6—(LAST NIGHT of ITALIAN OPERA)—
BENEFIT OF MDLLE. TITIENS
IL DON GIOVANNI.

SPECIAL LATE TRAINS
THE CALEDONIAN RAILWAY COMPANY will run Special Trains each evening at 11.15 to Coatbridge, Hamilton, Paisley and Greenock. All these Trains will call at Intermediate Stations.

A Late Train will also leave Buchanan Street Station This Evening, and Wednesday, Nov. 6, at 11.15, for Wishaw.

The NORTH BRITISH RAILWAY COMPANY will run Special Trains each evening at 11.15 to Helensburgh, Balloch, Coatbridge, and Airdrie, calling at Intermediate Stations.

CROSSHILL & LANGSIDE.
BLAIR'S OMNIBUSES will leave Opposite Theatre-Royal for CROSSHILL and LANGSIDE Every Evening at the conclusion of the Performance.

MONDAY, Nov. 12th (for Twelve Nights only) the eminent Tragedienne

MISS BATEMAN

PRICES OF ADMISSION—

Private Boxes .. £5 5s, £2 10s, £2	Amphitheatre Stalls (Unreserved) 5s
Dress Circle and Stalls .. 10s 6d	Pit 3s
Side Boxes (Unreserved) .. 7s 6d	Gallery 1s

Seats may be secured for all the Operas at the Box Office of the Theatre this Day, Saturday, from 10.30 till 12.30.

Doors Open each Evening at 7-30, the Opera Commencing at 8.

AUTHORISED BOOKS OF ALL THE OPERAS to be had at the BOX-OFFICE.

Principal Scenic Artist ... ... Mr WILLIAM GLOVER

Acting-Manager ... ... Mr R. L. KNAPP

GILCHRIST, Printer, 94 Howard Street.

THEATRE ROYAL,

HEAD OF HOPE STREET, GLASGOW.

SOLE LESSEES and MANAGERS ... ... (BY ROYAL LETTERS PATENT) ... Messrs GLOVER & FRANCIS

NEW-YEAR HOLIDAYS!
GRAND ILLUMINATED
DAY PERFORMANCES
OF THE
"ROYAL" PANTOMIME
WILL BE GIVEN ON

WEDNESDAY,	Dec. 31st,	-	at **2** o'clock
THURSDAY,	Jan. 1st,	at **12 & 3** o'clock
FRIDAY,	" 2nd,	at **12 & 3** o'clock
SATURDAY,	" 3rd,	at **12 & 3** o'clock
MONDAY,	" 5th,	-	at **2** o'clock

AND EVERY EVENING TILL FURTHER NOTICE.

At Half-Past SEVEN o'Clock precisely, and on SATURDAYS at SEVEN o'Clock, THE GORGEOUS COMIC PANTOMIME, ENTITLED, THE

SEVEN
CHAMPIONS
OR HARLEQUIN
ST. GEORGE AND THE DRAGON

Written expressly for this Theatre by W. H. LOGAN, Esq.

THE MAGNIFICENT SCENERY BY MR WM. GLOVER

1. **KALYBA'S CAVERN.**
2. BORDERS OF FAIRYLAND.
3. **THE AZURE LAKE.**
4. THE UNKNOWN COAST.
5. **HARBOUR NEAR UNKNOWN COAST.**
6. EGYPTIAN HALL.
7. **GRAND PALACE**
IN THE
VALLEY OF THE SBBUDESOOG
GORGEOUS EGYPTIAN & ETHIOPIAN PROCESSION.
8. AVENUE OF THE SPHINXES.
9. **THE DRAGON'S HAUNT.**
10. THE DISMAL WOOD.
GORGEOUS TRANSFORMATION TO THE
HALL OF A THOUSAND LIGHTS
APOTHEOSIS OF ST. GEORGE.
"HONI SOIT QUI MAL Y PENSE."
GRAND PROCESSION OF 100 KNIGHTS.

THURSDAY, 25th December, being
CHRISTMAS-DAY,
The THEATRE will be **CLOSED**

LATE TRAINS
TO BE RUN DURING THE NEW-YEAR HOLIDAYS:

From Wednesday 31st December, to Saturday 10th January, inclusive—at 11 p.m. from Glasgow (Buchanan Street) to Carstairs, Lanark, and Intermediate Stations.

From Thursday 1st, to Monday 5th January, inclusive—at 11 p.m. from Glasgow (Buchanan Street) to Ferniegair, Larkhall, Ayr Road, Newarthill, Bellside, Shotts, and Fauldhouse.

From Thursday 1st, to Wednesday 7th January, inclusive—at 11 p.m. from Glasgow (Buchanan Street) to Stirling, calling at Cumbernauld, Greenhill, Larbert, and Bannockburn.

Nightly from Glasgow (South side) to Hamilton, at 11 p.m., calling at Intermediate Stations.

On Wednesdays at 11.15 p.m. from South side to Uddingstone, and Intermediate Stations.

From Wednesday 31st December, to Saturday 10th January, inclusive—at 10-45 p.m. from Glasgow (Bridge Street) to Greenock and Intermediate Stations.

Private Boxes for seating 8 Persons £2 10s; for seating 4 Persons, £1 5s and £1 1s.—Orchestral Chairs, 4s—Circle 3s.—Pit, 1s 6d. Amphitheatre, 1s—Gallery, 6d.

Children under Ten Years of age—Circle, 1s.—Pit, 1s.—Amphitheatre, 6d.

 # NOTICE

To avoid the crowding at Pit and Amphitheatre Doors, the Principal Entrance in Cowcaddens Street will be open at 6-30 Each Evening, Except SATURDAYS, when it will be opened at 6 o'Clock, and parties admitted at the following Prices:—

PIT, - - - - **2/**		**CHILDREN, 1/6**
AMPHITHEATRE, 1/6		**CHILDREN, 1/**

NO SECOND PRICE.

The BOX OFFICE opens Daily at the Theatre Royal, from 11 until 3, for securing Seats—No Charge for Booking.

NOTICE. ENTRANCE to the Private Boxes, Dress Circle, Stalls, and Side Boxes by the MAIN DOOR, adjoining Howard Street, St. Cowcaddens Street ...

REFRESHMENTS CAN BE OBTAINED AT THE VARIOUS SALOONS WITHIN THE THEATRE.

Principal Scenic Artist ... ... Mr WILLIAM GLOVER

Musical Director ... ... Mr JOHN ROSS

Acting-Manager ... ... Mr R. L. KNAPP

GILCHRIST, Printer, 94 Howard Street.

Royal Performing

The Royal exuded confidence and from 7th June 1869 onwards presented its annual banquet of music and drama, starting with Offenbach's comic opera *Grand Duchess*, which he wrote for the Paris Exhibition two years before, and ending 1869 with the pantomime *Harlequin and the Forty Thieves or, the Good Fairies and the Naughty Children in the Wood*. This was designed by William Glover and his assistant Eduard, with over 300 performers, for which the jewellery, costumes and armour were selected in Paris by G.D. Francis.

In the four years 1872 to 1875, for which much detail remains, about 300 separate plays, comedies, operas and panto-mimes were staged. The 1872/73 pantomime was *Blue Beard, or The Mystic Chamber and the Magic Key* written by WH Logan, and produced, directed and designed by William Glover. As its adverts said it was "Written in Rhymes, to suit the Tymes" enjoying a cast of 200 performers in addition to the regular company. William Hugh Logan was a banker, poet, and dramatist as well as an author on Scottish banking and theatre. William Foster was the theatre's musical director, who had come from Dunlop Street, succeeded later by John Ross.

The Italian Opera Company came in 1873 and 1874, as did the English Opera Company. Prices always went up for opera. Plays abounded and the pantomime seasons sold out. When the Italian company were in, the theatre presented the Italian Singers in a *Sacred Concert of Handel's Messiah* at 8pm on the Fast Day of 23rd October 1873, and again in April 1874.

Alfred Young's Holburn Theatre Company had a long season. In September 1873 Miss Marie Litton's London Court Theatre Company pre-sented a comedy and burlesque *Happy Land* with the sanction of WS Gilbert, and other plays during 1874. *Meg Merrilees* was produced, based on Sir Walter Scott's work and written for the stage by composer Henry Leslie and William Glover.

Starting in December 1873 the season's Gorgeous Comic Pantomime was written by WH Logan and designed by Glover, depicting the *Seven Champions* of Christendom versus the Infidels and Supernaturals, starting on the Borders of Fairyland, with ten scenes .....moving to its finale in the

OPPOSITE
Playbills
1872 & 1874

THEATRE  ROYAL,
HEAD OF HOPE STREET, GLASGOW.
SOLE LESSEES and MANAGERS ...... (BY ROYAL LETTERS PATENT) ...... Messrs GLOVER & FRANCIS

GREAT SUCCESS OF
SIR WALTER SCOTT'S
LADY OF THE LAKE
POSITIVELY THE
LAST SIX NIGHTS
SPECIAL ENGAGEMENT OF
MR A. D. M'NEIL
(LESSEE OF THE PRINCESS'S THEATRE, EDINBURGH)
AS "RODERICK DHU."
AND MISS
PHYLLIS GLOVER
AS "BLANCHE OF DEVAN,"
HER FIRST APPEARANCE HERE SINCE HER RETURN FROM AMERICA.
THE MAGNIFICENT SCENERY
PAINTED FROM SKETCHES (FROM NATURE) BY
MR WILLIAM GLOVER
Mr FISHER, Mr SMYTH, and Assistants.
THE MUSIC selected from the works of some of our Greatest Composers, and in part specially composed by the late W. M. FOSTER.

On MONDAY Evening, 30th Aug., 1875,
AND DURING THE WEEK,
The Play, in Four Acts, Dramatised by CHARLES WEBB from Sir WALTER SCOTT'S

LADY
OF THE
LAKE

King James V. of Scotland (otherwise James Fitzjames, the Knight of Snowdoun) ...... Mr EDWARD COMPTON
Herbert ...... Mr GEORGE
Lufftoun { Two Gentlemen of his Suite } ...... Mr DANVERS
James Bothwell (Earl of Douglas, an Outlawed Exile) ...... Mr GEORGE BLYTHE
Malcolm Græme (a young Chieftain, his Friend) ...... Mr CHANTERIE
Roderick Dhu (Chief of the Clan "Vich Alpine ") ...... Mr A. D. M'NEIL
Brian (the Weird Outcast Monk—a half-crazed Monk supposed to be gifted with supernatural power) ...... Mr TATE
Red Murdoch ...... Mr C. JOHNSTONE
Malise { Henchmen to Roderick Dhu } ...... Mr WEIR
Norman (a young Bridegroom) ...... Mr DANVERS Young Angus (of Duncragan) ...... Mr WEIR
Archibald ...... Mr WILLIAM NOBSON
Sandie { Two Gillies of Roderick's in attendance on Margaret } ...... Mr BOYD
Allan Bane (an aged Minstrel, and faithful follower of the House of Douglas) ...... Mr EDWARD L. GOFTON
John O'Brent (a Soldier of Fortune, in the pay of King James) ...... Mr WILLIAM NOBSON
Robin Hood ...... Mr TATE Little John ...... Mr BOYD
Friar Tuck ...... Mr ALFRED W. WALMISLEY
1st Soldier ...... Mr REDGE
Lady Margaret (Mother of Roderick Dhu) ...... Mrs HENRY COURTIE
Blanche of Devan (a Maniac) ...... Miss PHYLLIS GLOVER
The Widow of Duncan of Duncragan ...... Mrs DUGARDE
Ellen Douglas (The Lady of the Lake) ...... Miss FANNY PITT
Maid Marion ...... Miss CHARLTON
Mattie

PART FIRST.
THE CHASE—THE TROSACHS.
THE ASCENT—LOCH KATRINE BY SUNSET.
APPEARANCE OF THE LADY OF THE LAKE—THE MEETING—AN AUGURY.
PANORAMA
Of the PASSAGE of ELLEN'S SKIFF with the stranger Knight from the TROSACHS to ELLEN'S ISLE, with Views of
BEN VENUE from the LAKE—LOOKING UP THE LOCH—BEN-ENION—BEN-AN—ELLEN'S ISLE and Entrance to the ENCHANTED HALL (Douglas' Retreat)—The GLOAMING on the LOCH—ELLEN'S ISLE from the SILVER STRAND (Moonlight)—The Landing on ELLEN'S ISLE—INTERIOR of the HALL—SLEEPING APARTMENT OF FITZJAMES—terminating with A View of
THE LAKE FROM ELLEN'S ISLE.
THE TROTH-PLIGHT—ARRIVAL OF SIR RODERICK—THE RIVALS.
PART SECOND.
The INCANTATION—PASS OF BEALA-NAM-BO.
THE PASSAGE OF THE CROSS—HALL OF DUNCRAGGAN—THE CORONACH.
PASS OF ACHRAY
The False Guide—Blanche of Devan—The poor Maniac, in warning Fitzjames, falls a victim to the treachery of Red Murdoch.
THE DEATH OF BLANCHE OF DEVAN,
AND VOW OF FITZJAMES TO AVENGE HER DEATH ON RODERICK DHU.
PART THIRD.
THE PROPHECY—WOOD BY LOCH VENNACHER.
Roderick's Vigil—Fitzjames and Roderick's Chivalrous Resolve.
THE MOULDERING LINES OF BO'CHASTLE—BRIAN'S PROPHECY.
Watch with the boldest fearless Eye.
THE HILL SIDE NEAR LANRICK.
COILANTOGLE FORD—The Goal achieved—THE COMBAT.
PART FOURTH.
THE REVELS
STIRLING CASTLE FROM THE KING'S PARK.
THE GUARD ROOM
RODERICK'S PRISON & DYING COUCH—THE MINSTREL-SEER'S VISION OF BATTLE
DEATH OF RODERICK
A GUARD ROOM.—EXTERIOR OF STIRLING CASTLE.
FINAL TABLEAU—"AND NOW 'TIS SILENT ALL."

MONDAY First, 6th September—Engagement of the Celebrated Tragedian, Mr
WM. CRESWICK

Doors open at Seven, Performance to commence at Half-past Seven.
On SATURDAYS—Doors open at Half-past SIX, Performance to commence at SEVEN.
PRICES:—PRIVATE BOXES (to seating 8 Persons, £2 10s; for seating 4 Persons, £1 5s and £1 1s.
DRESS CIRCLE and ORCHESTRAL CHAIRS, 4s; SIDE BOXES, 2s 6d; PIT, 1s 6d; AMPHITHEATRE, 1s; GALLERY, 6d.
Children under TEN Years of Age—Circle and Stalls, 2s; Side Boxes, 1s 6d; Pit, 1s; Amphitheatre, 6d.
NO SECOND PRICE.
The BOX OFFICE open Daily at the Theatre Royal, from 11 until 3, for securing Seats.—No Charge for Booking.
NOTICE.—ENTRANCE to the Private Boxes, Dress Circle, Stalls, and Side Boxes will be from the MAIN DOOR, CONCLUDERS, in the Head of HOPE STREET; ENTRANCE to Pit, Amphitheatre, and Gallery, winding Premise No. 2 Cowcaddens; Gallery, in Cowcaddens.
REFRESHMENTS CAN BE OBTAINED AT THE VARIOUS SALOONS WITHIN THE THEATRE.
TRADESMEN are respectfully cautioned not to supply Goods to the account of Theatre-Royal, unless by Printed Order, signed by the Manager of the Theatre.
Principal Scenic Artist ...... Mr WILLIAM GLOVER
Acting Manager ...... Mr JOHN ROSS
Principal Musical Director ...... Mr E. L. KNAPP

THEATRE  ROYAL,
HEAD OF HOPE STREET, GLASGOW.
SOLE LESSEES and MANAGERS ...... (BY ROYAL LETTERS PATENT) ...... Messrs GLOVER & FRANCIS

Messrs GLOVER & FRANCIS have the honour to announce a Series of ITALIAN
OPERAS
WITH THE FOLLOWING DISTINGUISHED ARTISTES OF
HER MAJESTY'S OPERA
FOR SIX NIGHTS ONLY
MDME. CHRISTINE NILSSON
MDME. TREBELLI-BETTINI MDME. DEMERIC-LABLACHE
MDME. ROSE MDME. BAUERMEISTER
AND
MADLLE. VARESI
SIGNOR GILLANDI SIGNOR GALASSI
SIGNOR PALADINI SIGNOR DEL PUENTE
SIGNOR RINALDINI SIGNOR COSTA
SIGNOR GRAZZI SIGNOR ZOBOLI
SIGNOR BRIGNOLI SIGNOR CASTLEMARY
AND
HERR BEHRENS
Musical Director and Conductor ...... SIGNOR LI CALSI
Stage Manager ...... Mr A. HARRIS Assistant do. ...... Mr PARRY
THE BAND & CHORUS
Will be considerably strengthened by Members of HER MAJESTY'S Opera

On THURSDAY Evening, Nov. 25, 1875,
VERDI'S OPERA
RICOLETTO
Il Duca ...... (His Third Appearance in Glasgow) ...... Signor GILLANDI
Rigoletto ...... Signor DEL PUENTE
Sparafucile ...... (His Second Appearance in Glasgow) ...... Signor CASTLEMARY
Monterone ...... Signor COSTA
Borsa ...... Signor RINALDINI
Marullo ...... Signor ZOBOLI
Maddalena ...... Madame TREBELLI BETTINI
Giovanna ...... Madame BAUERMEISTER
AND
Gilda ...... (Her Second Appearance in Glasgow) ...... Mdlle. ELENA VARESI

On FRIDAY Evening, Nov. 26th, 1875,
VERDI'S OPERA
TROVATORE
Manrico ...... Signor BRIGNOLI
Il Conte di Luna ...... Signor COSTA
Fernando ...... Signor RINALDINI
Ruiz ...... Madame TREBELLI-BETTINI
Azucena ...... Madame BAUERMEISTER
Inez ......
AND
Leonora ...... (Her Third Appearance on the Stage in Glasgow) ...... Madame CHRISTINE NILSSON

On SATURDAY Evening, Nov. 27th, 1875,
MOZART'S OPERA, IL
DON GIOVANNI
Don Ottavio ...... Signor BRIGNOLI
Leporello ...... Herr BEHRENS
Masetto ...... Signor ZOBOLI
Il Commendatore ...... Signor COSTA
Don Giovanni ...... Signor DEL PUENTE
Zerlina ...... Madame TREBELLI-BETTINI
Donna Elvira ...... (Her Third Appearance in Glasgow) ...... Mdlle. ELENA VARESI
AND
Donna Anna ...... Madame MARIE ROZE

SPECIAL LATE TRAINS
From South-Side Station at 11-15 p.m., for Barrhead, Kilmarnock, and all Intermediate Stations, on Friday, Nov. 26th, and Wednesday, Dec. 1st.
A Special Late Train will leave Bridge Street Station at 11-15 p.m., for Greenock, on Friday.
A Late Train will leave Bridge Street Station at 10-30 p.m., on Thursday and Friday, for Paisley, Port-Glasgow, and Greenock.
A Late Train will leave South-Side Station at 11.30 p.m. on Saturday, for Hamilton and Intermediate Stations.
A Late Train will leave Buchanan-St. Station at 10.30 p.m. on Saturday, for Carstairs and Intermediate Stations.
A Late Train will leave Bridge Street Station at 10.45 p.m. on Saturday, for Greenock and Intermediate Stations.
A Late Train will leave South Side Station at 11-0 p.m. on Saturday, for Hamilton, and Intermediate Stations.

MONDAY, Nov. 29th,	WEDNESDAY, Dec. 1st
FAUST	BENEFIT OF
TUESDAY, Nov. 30th,	MDLLE. CHRISTINE
MARTHA	NILSSON
	LES HUGUENOTS

Private Boxes £5 5s, £2 10s, £2
Stalls ...... 15s Amphitheatre Stalls (Unreserved) 5s
Dress Circle ...... 10s 6d Pit 3s
Side Boxes (Unreserved) ...... 7s 6d Gallery 2s
Seats may be secured for all the Operas at the Box-Office of the Theatre from Eleven till Three daily.
Doors Open Each Evening at 7-30, Opera commencing at 8.
AUTHORISED BOOKS OF ALL THE OPERAS TO BE HAD AT THE BOX-OFFICE.

IN ACTIVE PREPARATION, THE "ROYAL" GRAND
PANTOMIME
Entitled, JACK AND THE BEAN STALK.

Principal Scenic Artist ...... Mr WILLIAM GLOVER
Musical Director ...... Mr JOHN ROSS
Acting Manager ...... Mr E. L. KNAPP

Hall of a Thousand Lights beyond the Avenue of the Sphinxes.

In the winter of 1874/75 the Grand Comic Pantomime was *The Invisible Prince* - with King Furiband the Bad and the Three Magic Roses. Starting with Father Time in Cloudland it moved through seven scenes. After the interval there was ballet, harlequins and clowns, finishing with a Tableau "Britannia's Glory" which ended with ....Who'll Man the Fleet? and a Grand Naval Review. In the spring there was Wilson Barrett's London Company dramas (the same name of company would emerge sixty years later.) The 29th March 1875 was *Volunteer Night* when the Lord Provost presented prizes to the 1st Lanarkshire Engineer Volunteers. The band of the 64th Regiment gave a concert, and two comedies completed the evening. The adverts invited the audience - "Officers and Volunteers are requested to appear in Uniform"

Two weeks of the Italian Opera Company brought the magic of *Norma, Rigoletto, Il Talismano, Der Freischutz, Faust*, and *Martha*. Operas were sung mainly in Italian, but also German and French with the audience buying a libretto to follow the score and the plot. The first Wagner opera sung in Glasgow was *Lohengrin* in 1875, but was sung in Italian by the Italian Opera Company. The Italian Opera Company also introduced *Il Talismano* – the Walter Scott influence was everywhere- and in 1870 a Parisian company gave an Offenbach season, which drew criticisms of the can-can and its immorality.

Glasgow, then as now, had a great love of opera. In just over eleven years, since the theatre opened, 83 different operas were performed in the city, 64 of them in the Royal.

The box office opened daily from 11 to 3, with no charge for booking. Seat descriptions would change over time, but the best seats would remain the dearest! Hotels, public houses, and country patrons could have the Theatre Royal Programmes sent to them regularly by the publishers Messrs Wilson & Company of North Coburg Street.

For the shows coming out in the late evening, trains were advertised from Queen Street Station, from South Side Station (before St Enoch's Station was opened), from Bridge Street Station (before Central Station was built) and from Buchanan Street Station (on whose railway yards Glasgow Caledonian University now stands.) Andrew Menzies's horse drawn Tartan Buses and his new Glasgow Tramway Co were expanding their routes, while for those in far flung Crosshill and Langside the management advertised "Blair's Omnibuses will leave opposite the Theatre Royal every evening at the conclusion of the performance." Over the New Year holidays special trains were organised for 11pm.

1875 to 1877 were equally productive years. Customers in the spring of 1878 enjoyed Gilbert & Sullivan's *Sorcerer* and *Trial by Jury*, and *Engaged* written by WS Gilbert the year before. This comic play inspired Oscar Wilde to write *The Importance of Being Earnest*.

OPPOSITE
Playbills
1875

THEATRE  ROYAL,

HEAD OF HOPE ST., **GLASGOW.**

SOLE LESSEES AND MANAGERS — Messrs GLOVER & FRANCIS

GRAND REVIVAL

OF THE GREAT NATIONAL DRAMA OF

ROB ROY

SPECIAL ENGAGEMENTS!

MISS EMMELINE COLE

MDME.

GERALDINE WARDEN

MR EDWARD COTTE

MR JAMES HOUSTON

MR HENRY COURTE

AND

MR A. D. M'NEIL

The Original Scenery

(SKETCHED FROM NATURE) BY

MR WILLIAM GLOVER

Mr J. BRUNTON, and Assistants.

The OVERTURE, SCOTCH AIRS, ENTR' ACTES, and OTHER MUSIC,
Composed and Arranged by the late **Mr W. M. FOSTER.**

On MONDAY Evening, 10th MAY, 1875,

And FOLLOWING EVENINGS (at 7-30),

ROB ROY

OR, AULD LANGSYNE.

Helen Macgregor			Miss FANNY PITT
Diana Vernon			Miss EMMELINE COLE
Mattie	Miss LAURA SAKER	Martha	Miss HODGKISS
Jean M'Alpine			Miss J. WALMISLEY
Sir Frederick Vernon			Mr J. MORTON
Rashleigh Osbaldistone			Mr HENRY COURTE
Francis Osbaldistone			Mr EDWARD COTTE
Rob Roy			Mr A. D. M'NEIL
Owen			Mr A. W. WALMISLEY
Bailie Nicol Jarvie			Mr JAMES HOUSTON
Dougal "Cratur"			Mr WILLIAM DOBSON
Major Galbraith			Mr A. LEFFLER
Captain Thornton	Mr E. COMPTON	M'Stewart	Mr BOTEWELL
Jobson	Mr BEDDOS	Sergeant	Mr M'PHERSON
Robert and Hamish, Rob Roy's Sons		Misses	MINA CHARLTON & SANSOM
Saunders Wylie	Mr WEIR	Willie	Master ARCHIBALD
Lancie	Master MURDOCH	Andrew Fairservice	Mr CHARTERIS

IN THE COURSE OF THE DRAMA WILL BE SUNG:—

CHORUS—"Born the Sun will gang to rest"   DUET—"Though you leave me now in sorrow," ... Miss EMMELINE COLE and Mr E. COTTE
SONG—"My Love is like a red, red Rose," ... Mr E. COTTE
BALLAD—"Home Sweet Home," ... Miss E. COLE   QUARTETTE—"Hark! from Saint Mungo's Tower" ...
SONG—"Bonnie Prince Charlie," ... Miss E. COLE   DUET—"Forlorn and Broken Hearted," Miss EMMELINE COLE and Mr E. COTTE
SONG—"A famous one was Robin Hood," Mr LEFFLER   CHORUS—"Roy's Wife"
SONG—"Auld Langsyne," ... Mr E. COTTE   FINALE—"Rob Roy Macgregor"

Messrs HUGH CAMPBELL & RODERICK M'LEOD ... HIGHLAND PIPERS
Messrs R. BRAND & A. RAMSAY ... HIGHLAND DANCERS

ACT I.—ON THE BORDERS.

Library of Osbaldistone Hall—Chamber in the House of Bailie Nicol Jarvie.

OLD GLASGOW BRIDGE BY NIGHT

INTERIOR OF THE TOLBOOTH

ACT II.—COLLEGE GARDENS.

JEAN M'ALPINE'S CHANGE-HOUSE.

The Bailie's Little War—General Engagement.

Clachan of Aberfoyle.

CAPTURE OF ROB ROY BY RASHLEIGH'S TREACHERY.

ACT III.—PASS OF LOCHARD.

BATTLE BETWEEN THE ENGLISH AND SCOTCH.

GREAT COMBAT

BY MR J. BRUNTON AND MR WILLIAM GLOVER.
LAMENT, and ESCAPE OF ROB ROY.
HIGHLAND REJOICING, HIGHLAND DANCING, & SCOTCH REEL.

THE LONE ISLAND

JEAN M'ALPINE'S HUT. Scene the Last—VIEW OF THE HEAD OF

LOCHLOMOND by Moonlight

From ROB ROY'S CAVE. Death of Rashleigh—TRIUMPH of the GREGARACH!

MONDAY, May 17th

MRS W. H. LISTON'S

LONDON OPERA-BOUFFE COMPANY.

GIROFLE-GIROFLA, LES CENT VIERGES,
and LA FILLE DE MADAME ANGOT.

Doors open at 7, to commence at 7.30.   SATURDAYS—Doors open at 6.30, to commence at 7.
PRICES—Private Boxes for seating 8 Persons, £2 10s; for seating 6 Persons, £1 5s and £1 1s.
Dress Circle and Orchestral Chairs, 4s; Side Boxes, 2s 6d; Pit, 1s 6d; Amphitheatre, 1s; Gallery, 6d
Children under the Years of Age—Circle, 2s.—Pit, 1s—Amphitheatre, 6d   **NO SECOND PRICE.**

The BOX OFFICE open Daily at the Theatre-Royal, from 11 until 3, for securing Seats.—No Charge for Booking.

NOTICE. ENTRANCE to the Private Boxes, Dress Circle, Stalls, and Side Boxes will be from the MAIN DOOR, Cowcaddens; the Pit, Head of HOPE ST. Amphitheatre SIDE AVENUE, adjoining Premises No. 79 Cowcaddens; Gallery, as before.

REFRESHMENTS CAN BE OBTAINED AT THE VARIOUS SALOONS WITHIN THE THEATRE.

Principal Scenic Artist — Mr WILLIAM GLOVER   Musical Director — Mr JOHN ROSS
Acting-Manager — Mr R. L. KNAPP

1875 PRICES

1875 PRICES		PLAYS & PANTOMIME	OPERAS
Private Boxes for	8 persons	£2 10s	£5 5s
	4 persons	£1 5s, £1	£2 10s, £2
Dress Circle and Orchestral Chairs		4s	10s 6d
Side Boxes (unreserved)		2s 6d	7s 6d
Ampitheatre Stalls (unreserved)		1s	5s
Pit		1s 6d	3s
Gallery		6d	2s

Books of all the Operas are to be had at the Box Office.

Refreshments can be obtained at the various saloons within the theatre.

Opera Glasses are on hire from the Programme Boys.

Two nights in May were devoted to a *Grand Amateur Performance* by the 79th Queen's Own Cameron Highlanders, with the proceeds going to the Glasgow Royal Infirmary. A season of plays included the *Vicar of Wakefield*; while for four nights there was the first appearance in Scotland of Hall's *New York Minstrels* complete with Quintette, Grand Orchestra, Ten Great Comedians, Full Corps of Singers and Chorus....... with the Latest New York Successes. They had sailed in from New York and played Greenock, Glasgow and Dublin.

Minstrel shows and spectaculars mushroomed now that the American Civil War was over.

Scott's *Guy Mannering* followed. Two weeks of summer entertainment came from the magicians and pantomimists known as the *Majiltons* – Charles, Marie and Frank. Autumn heralded *Jeanie Deans and the Heart of Midlothian* produced by Glover; Italian and English Opera companies played, as did John L. Toole's company usually with two comedies each evening.

ABOVE
Ticket prices
1875

OPPOSITE
Playbill
1875

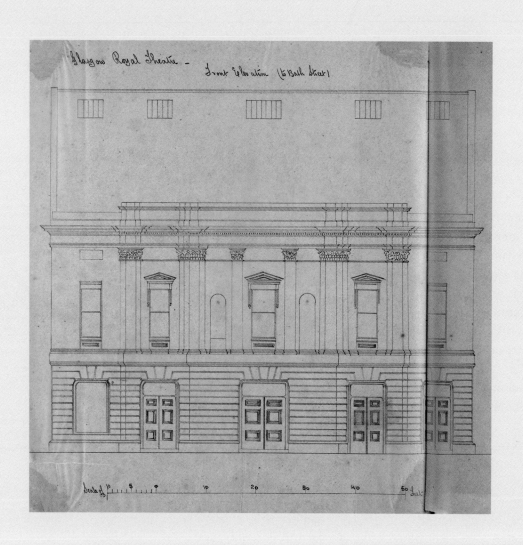

Glasgow Royal Theatre — Front Elevation (to Bath Street)

Scale of

Theatre All Around

As well as directing the Theatre Royal, William Glover and George Francis extended their business interests to Newcastle. They became the lessees and managers of the prestigious Theatre Royal with its classical frontage in Grey Street for the years 1871 to 1878, five years before James Howard and Fred Wyndham became managers of it. Its interior had been designed by Charles Phipps in 1867.

In 1875 Glover and Francis also opened and managed the New Theatre at the foot of John Finnie Street, Kilmarnock, for over two years. Known also as the Operetta House it was a large building seating 1,050 in two tiers, designed for a syndicate of local owners by James Ingram, who had designed the town's Corn Exchange Concert Hall – now known as the Palace Theatre. Thirty years previously Glover's father had operated the wooden-built theatre in the town's Langlands Brae.

Glover still hankered after a new theatre in Glasgow, in his own name. He found encouragement in William Gilchrist, letter-press printer in the city, who did all the printing for the old Theatre Royal and the new one, a friend and trustee of his father Edmund Glover. Reviving their earlier plans for Bath Street, Glover and Francis got a further cash credit in 1875 for £6,000 from the British Linen Bank on security of land to be purchased on the south side of Bath Street near West Nile Street. In June 1876 William Glover bought the property from William Gilchrist and the architects' drawings for a ROYAL THEATRE were brought out. It would be a large well-equipped theatre, with a classical frontage to Bath Street, and three galleries. In September 1877 the Bank loaned William Glover more money, £565, and in November Andrew Yuille loaned £1,200, all secured over Bath Street. But the theatre was still not built.

The Baylis Trust decided it would again advertise the Theatre Royal and neighbouring properties for sale, but no offers came during 1876. At the public roup on 30th January 1877 it was sold for £38,000 to Andrew Yuille, Practical Chemist and Oil Merchant. With the knowledge of the trustees there was a secondary agreement by which John Rae, glass merchant, and a trustee of Baylis until November past, took half ownership at £19,000 and Yuille the

OPPOSITE
Bath Street Theatre Royal
unbuilt

WILLIAM GLOVER

TOP
William Glover

MIDDLE
Winter Scene *by William Glover*

BOTTOM
Sea Painting *by Edmund Glover*

William Glover was born in 1836 the second son of Elizabeth and Edmund Glover. His parents travelled the theatres in Scotland and he and his brothers were boarded out for their schooling, including a time in Rothesay with the family of actor Edmund Kean. His father apprenticed him to William Beverley the chief scene painter at the Lyceum and Covent Garden theatres, London. It was in his early days that he first met Charles Dickens. He had been painting scenery for a sketch that the novelist was producing when Dickens insisted that the painter should go and see the areas and conditions of the London he was writing about to capture the true essence of the images. He also took some small acting roles, including with McCready in Greek drama but remarked the great actor "Very good, my boy, but you have a fearfully Scotch accent for a Greek". In 1855 he took his first salaried engagement, in Dublin's Theatre Royal rising to £4 a week, continuing there to 1860. He was a founder member of the bohemian Savage Club in London in 1857, along with Dickens.

He was highly creative and sociable, but often to the detriment of his family. Just before he left to return to Glasgow he married Emily Kohler, daughter of a German tailor in Dublin, by whom he was to have 12 children. After her passing he soon married Agnes Brown in 1882, daughter of a Glasgow journalist, and had more children. He had a seaside villa at Kilmun, where the family would stay for the summer months, and he would join them when he could, taking the steamer down the Clyde. On the return to the Broomielaw his horse and carriage would await. He enjoyed a glass or three of Scotland's national drink but the horse always knew the way home.

Landscape painting was a leisure interest and he exhibited for over 40 years from 1861; after his own bankruptcy in 1879 the sale of paintings became more important. He opened his commercial studios, designing and making sets for theatres, in a building at Port Dundas next to one of the flour mills. When painting and then transporting cloths to the theatres his staff had to clear off the flour dust!

In his studios he engaged scenic artists as well as a joiner and chargehands. One such artist was William Page Atkinson Wells, whom Glover "strongly advised to go out and paint from nature." Wells was educated in Glasgow, the Slade Academy of Art in London, and studied further in Paris. He became one of the painters of the Barbizon school and an acquaintance of the Glasgow Boys. Glover brought into the business three of his artist sons, described as scenic artists, engravers and theatre property masters – Harold Glover, who is thought to have gone to South Africa in his twenties; Ernest K Glover who also made a name for himself in American scenic art; and William F Glover who continued in Glasgow.

The Glover studios had a business life of 80 years from their founding in the 1880s. Commentators writing in the Edwardian years justifiably stated "William Glover has the distinction of being the finest scenic artist ever known in Scotland." In 1916 he took his final bow at his home in Garnethill.

other half, £19,000. The sale at £38,000 cleared all long term loans of Baylis over both his sites, and gave his trust an additional free £15,000 (in today's money over £3m.) The Baylis Trust had more than doubled its value since his early death, and easily gave Yuille & Rae a £3,000 loan secured over the theatre.

Andrew Yuille was "a wholesale tea merchant, manufacturer of chocolate and coffee essence, practical chemist and oil merchant" with premises in the Trongate and a house in the west-end to where he had moved from 1Sauchiehall Street. For a number of years he had been buying and selling property using very large loans, mainly around Cowcaddens and occasionally in Gorbals and Calton. John Rae was the head of a substantial firm of glass merchants, stainers and embossers based in Montrose Street and Ingram Street, who had glazed the theatre buildings for the Baylis family.

On the day of its purchase, and by prior agreement, Yuille sold on his half share of the theatre to the three partners of McClures & Hannay, lawyers, but would continue to be involved as a property agent for them. William Glover continued to be the lessee, with Edward Knapp his manager. Stormy times lay ahead.

For many years Glover had also been a landscape artist, with a private studio at 40 West Nile Street. He continued to exhibit successfully at the Royal Glasgow Institute of the Fine Arts, of which he was a founder member, the Royal Scottish Academy, and the Royal Scottish Society of Painters in

ABOVE
Theatre Royal
Newcastle

Watercolour, of which he was also a founding member in 1878.

Royal Charter for Newcastle

In the management of Newcastle's Theatre Royal Glover and Francis held the Royal Charter in their names. They produced their own successful pantomimes and introduced Newcastle's citizens to the works of the aspiring Arthur Sullivan and W S Gilbert (in that order in the programmes) with D'Oyly Carte as stage manager, and presented Shakespeare's plays with Henry Irving and others. Henry Irving had learned his craft as a member of stock companies in particular that of Edmund Glover. Years later when Irving was knighted the newspapers recalled the early days when the practically unknown Irving was better known as one of the Edmund Glover Boys.

Unfortunately the financial pressures of theatre caused George Francis to be declared bankrupt in England in 1878, resulting in his breakdown and retiral, returning that year to Glasgow

WILLIAM GILCHRIST and the West Nile Street Circus Proprietors

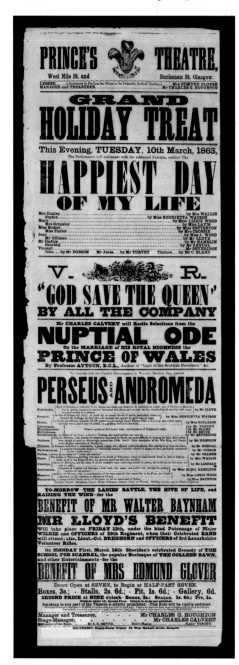

William Gilchrist was the printer for the Glover family's theatres, and other theatres including Charles Bernard at the Gaiety (Empire). Throughout his business life "he was a man greatly beloved. Endowed with a large body, he had a still larger heart. He was shrewd and always prudent. His selection of type for posters was strikingly large and varied, and no office in the city produced more unique bill work."

He became as prosperous as his old friend Edmund Glover and was able to lend the Glasgow Institute of the Fine Arts a large sum towards the building of their first gallery in Sauchiehall Street. He had a long list of customers and organisations for whom he worked at his Letter-Press in Howard Street. Fortunately over 400 of the Glover playbills from his press for the Prince's, the old Royal and the new Royal theatres are well preserved and accessible in Glasgow University Library.

He was a trustee of the Glover Trust from 1860 for almost twenty years. He and four other business people created a joint-venture in 1866 called "**The West Nile Street Circus Proprietors**", which purchased property on the east side of West Nile Street up to Bath Street from the late Lord Provost and stationer James Lumsden for £15,000. Part of this included the Prince's Theatre now leased to **Hengler's Circus**.

The Hengler family came from Germany and was well established in the circus business in England by the 1840s. Charles Hengler first came to Scotland in 1861 to Glasgow Green, before leasing the Prince's Theatre. Each year the circus came to town for the winter season of about six months. Crowds came to Hengler's Grand Cirque or Circus which was renowned for its equestrian acts set to music including themes of exploration, battle and dance. High-wire artistes, clowns, water spectaculars (including mermaids and water pantomimes) and minstrel choruses alternated with shooting competitions and skating shows. When the circus moved to Wellington Street in the 1880s the West Nile Street Circus Proprietors sold the building for £31,700 to the Glasgow City & District Railway Company to become stables for railway carters, and carriage hirers.

where he died age 59 at his home 231 St George's Road in 1883. He was the son of an organist but never used his father's surname, Lynas - no doubt the organist would not have approved of his son's career choice.

It was announced that the Royal pantomime starting on 16th December 1878 would be the first appearance in Glasgow of *Puss in Boots, or the Orge, the Cat, and the Miller's Son*. Even although the shadow of the City of Glasgow Bank failure was widespread life went on. To aid the City of Glasgow Bank Relief Fund for the support of the besieged shareholders the Lanarkshire Volunteer Officers Dramatic Society presented for three nights at the end of November the appropriately named play *The School for Scandal* by Sheridan. Tickets could be had at principal restaurants and music sellers and at the offices of the Lieutenant Secretary of the Society. Just before the pantomime opened the Baillie magazine wrote:

> Mr Glover's benefit has been fixed for Friday. His programme for the evening includes the comedietta of the *Happy Pair*, the farce of *The Two Polts*, *Trial by Jury* and the burlesque of *Bombastes* - by members of the Pen and Pencil Club. Surely a merrier bill of fare was never submitted to the approval of the public. The audience, I believe, will be crowded and fashionable.
>
> It is some time since Mr Glover took a benefit – six years at least I

may say – and if he ever deserved one it is at the present moment. Perhaps he is just now the hardest worked man in Glasgow, having the whole management, stage management, and everything else up on his own shoulders.

The Baillie printed an ode to THE PEOPLE's WILLIAM:

> For Glover's benefit on Friday,
> "Bombastes Furioso" played,
> By "Pen and Pencil" Club, with ladies
> Professional to give their aid,
> Should make a "house" from floor to ceiling,
> Of all the season's nights THE night –
> The Pencils all with point for "drawing",
> The ladies with the Pens all right
> And scenes successive that discover
> The genius, palette, taste of Glover

The manager Edward Knapp could not be forgotten. On Wednesday 29th January 1879 the Baillie was pleased to note:

> Friday week, the seventh of next month, has been set aside for the benefit of Mr E. L. Knapp. Of course the Theatre Royal will be crowded on the occasion. We have few better-known or better-liked townsmen than Mr Knapp, and his troops of friends make an invariable point of rallying round him on the

occasion of his annual benefits.

This new year was soon to be different. The day after the pantomime closed fire brought the theatre to its knees. But his friends rearranged his benefit for that Friday, taking place in the New Halls, the first name for St Andrew's Halls in Granville Street. "There was a capital audience and the entertainment was peculiarly tasteful and elegant." The show must go on! More than that Knapp

was snapped up quickly and became manager of Her Majesty's Theatre built and owned by Morrison and Mason, building contractors, and newly opened in Main Street, Gorbals.

A meeting of the Theatre Royal company and its employees took place on Friday, 19th February, in the Balmoral Hotel when Knapp submitted a statement showing how he had distributed the funds collected among his private friends for the benefit of sufferers of the fire - not all the company could find work, and their equipment was lost. He also suggested how the sums to be raised from the two performances next day by Frederick McCabe in the Circus, West Nile Street should be dealt with.

William Glover was declared bankrupt as will be explained later, but was still much in demand by the public. In the first week of March advertisements announced a:

GLOVER TESTIMONIAL
At a Meeting of Gentlemen, held in the rooms of the Scottish Society of Water- Colour Painters, on Wednesday 19th February, it was resolved to form a Committee for the purpose of organizing a GLOVER TESTIMONIAL. The recent distressing occurrence of the total destruction of the Theatre Royal by fire has precipitated, though it does not constitute, the sole motive for such a step.

The eminent services rendered to Dramatic and Scenic Art by the

BELOW
Programme Cover
December 1878

Glover Family for a long series of years – services tending invariably to the elevating and refining of those important factors of every-day life – constitute a claim to which, the Gentlemen present believed, the Public would not be slow to respond. In furtherance of this object, the Committee resolved, in addition to the issuing of Subscription-sheets, to arrange a SERIES of DRAMATIC PERFORMANCES in the PRINCE of WALES THEATRE, which the Committee are able to do by the kindness of Mr John Coleman, who besides giving his services, has generously offered to place the Theatre at the disposal of the Committee.

ABOVE
Pit Token

The performances began on Monday 10th March for the whole week. Monday and Tuesday was *Rob Roy*; Wednesday and Thursday, the modern play *Caste*, Friday the *School for Scandal*, and the Saturday finale was *Macbeth*, six tableaux of the Life of Mary Queen of Scots, and an Act from the *Corsican Brothers*. Glover designed some of the scenery. The Subscriptions and proceeds of the entertainments were placed in a Trust to help Glover return to work, and not to be available to his creditors. Of the business men and artists on the committee two are of special note.

Michael Simons, fruit merchant, was an active supporter of arts and theatre; and Alexander Wellwood Rattray, an exhibiting artist who had studied in Glasgow and Paris, was joint secretary of the testimonial. He was a member of the wealthy family of Charles Rattray & Co, clothing manufacturers and ware-housemen. Another kinsman, but not on the committee, was David Rattray, secretary of the Central Halls Co which was building commercial premises and a Hall in Sauchiehall Street, to which would be added a new theatre.

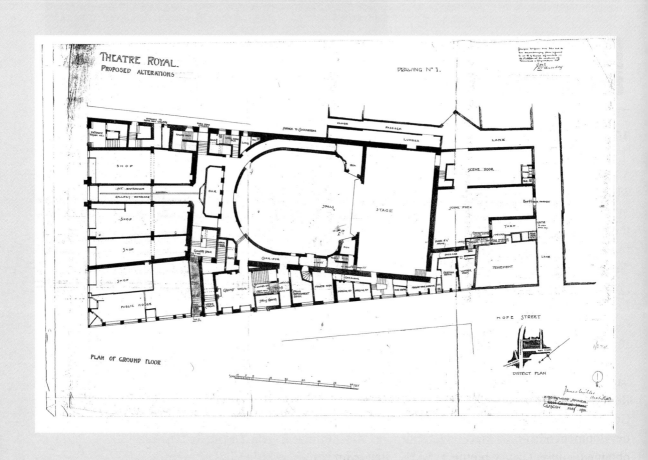

THEATRE ROYAL.
PROPOSED ALTERATIONS.

DRAWING Nº 1.

PLAN OF GROUND FLOOR

DISTRICT PLAN

HOPE STREET

The Visit From Vulcan

Late in the night of 2nd February 1879 fire broke out and gutted most of the main building. As well as being a spectacle for the citizens, it drew Glover's tenure to an end. The two public houses in Hope Street and Cowcaddens managed by Glover were taken over by Samuel Dow. The Alexandra Music Hall and shops underneath were not affected.

Andrew Yuille and Robert Rae, age 24, the son of John Rae who had died in 1878, now invited Charles Phipps the country's leading theatre architect to design a new auditorium. For this, Yuille and Rae should have a memorial plaque in their honour at the present Royal. The Dean of Guild Court gave consent to the works to start in July 1879 at a value of £15,000.

Another competitor appeared in Sauchiehall Street at the corner of Renfield Street when the Central Halls Company in the course of building their development of shops, offices and a hall obtained consent in September 1879 to add to their 1878 plans, and build a Theatre to the designs of a young Frank Matcham. The race was on, and their Royalty Theatre won. The hall became the Dramatic Lodge of Masons, which was one of the first "theatrical" lodges in Britain and where Harry Lauder was initiated in the 1890s when its Master

was Edward de Banzie, the Royal's orchestra leader.

By October 1879 Knapp was appointed the first lessee and manager of the Royalty Theatre now nearing completion. He took on a number of former staff from the Royal including Edward de Banzie the musical director, Robert Smyth as scenic artist, but not his old boss Glover.

During the months of the Royal's rebuilding, the Prince of Wales Theatre was very busy with its own programme and with extra customers from the Royal. Its 1879 pantomime was

ABOVE
Signatures *of Andrew Yuille and John Rae*

OPPOSITE
Ground Floor
1880

CHARLES PHIPPS

Originally from Bath, Charles John Phipps qualified as an architect in 1857 and after a few years set up his practice in London, (as well as designing scenery for productions at the Gaiety Theatre there in the 1860s.) He designed offices, blocks of flats, and later the

Devonshire Club for Liberal Party supporters in St James. He exhibited frequently at the Royal Academy in London. In his 34 years of theatre work till his death in 1897, age 62, he designed or remodelled over 70 theatres. He was only surpassed in number by his younger rival Frank Matcham who totalled around 150 theatres in 47 years, until his passing in 1920. While Matcham's styles were exuberant and sensuous Phipps excelled in a dignified and classical manner.

Edwin Sachs, himself an architect and founder of the British Fire Prevention Committee, wrote in his "Modern Opera Houses and Theatres" around the time of Phipps death in May 1897:

> With his departure we have lost a man who excelled in his speciality to an extent that can scarcely be understood by an outsider. He had been able to satisfy the requirements of the typical theatrical speculator, who primarily

ABOVE
Charles Phipps
Architect

demands the greatest accommodation in a limited space at as low a cost as possible, and what is more, he enjoyed full confidence, since no one had cause to fear any inclination on his part to incur expenditure merely in the interests of art.

In Newcastle Charles Phipps had designed the Theatre Royal, managed by William Glover. In Scotland he had already co-designed Her Majesty's Tivoli Theatre Aberdeen in 1872, designed the Theatre Royal Edinburgh in 1873, and remodelled the Theatre Royal Dumfries and the Theatre Royal Dunfermline in 1876. The Theatre Royal Glasgow is the largest surviving example of his theatre design in Britain.

designed by Glover. The new Royalty opened on 24th December 1879 with Offenbach's comic opera *Madame Favart*, and Knapp soon filled it with a full programme of plays, opera, Gilbert & Sullivan, all the favourites of the Royal patrons. It could accommodate around 2000 people. The owner of Her Majesty's in the Gorbals, which Knapp had left, renamed his theatre The Royal Princess's that December to counter the publicity surrounding the new theatre.

The main entrance now became Hope Street where one of the large shop spaces was converted to a vestibule and a new main staircase was built for the Dress Circle. The Cowcaddens entrance also continued to be used. Inside, Phipps applied his designs, adding a huge gallery third tier; the dress-circle is a serpentine shape and the upper tiers are horseshoe shape. A total of 18 boxes elaborated in moulded and fluted columns framed the proscenium opening, and the arch over it was painted with allegorical figures representing the arts of drama. The stage boxes are set between giant Corinthian columns. He incorporated nine boxes at the rear of the balcony dress-circle, each for six people and curtained off; and decorated the whole auditorium in the French Renaissance style, which continues today. On the ground floor the orchestral stalls were separated from the three rows of pit stalls behind them, and in turn the pit stalls were separated from all the pit benches behind them. There were wooden stairs and a corridor beneath the stalls to let patrons of the private boxes cross the theatre without mingling with the pit.

Dressing rooms continued to be along the length of Hope Street at first floor level. Likewise on the second floor along Hope Street were two very large Wardrobe rooms above the new main door and its staircase, with the Property Room above the stage door area, and the Painting room above and at the rear of the stage.

All the floors and passages were now of concrete with inner walls of brick and fire-proof cement. The roof terminated in a coved ceiling with a sun-burner in the centre. The ceiling colour was of light cream upon which were painted eight panels of elaborate ornaments in gold and colours.

The stage was rebuilt with the usual traps, doors and bridges, and apparatus for the working of the scenery; and the scene-dock was below the stage. Phipps used Glasgow tradesmen for the building work and his London tradesmen for the internal decoration and finishing. The patrons in the dress-circle and orchestra stalls had the extra comfort of sitting on folding chairs invented by the architect, and made in Bath.

The Glasgow Herald reported its opening on 26th October 1880, under the management of Marie Litton:

While at one end (Cowcaddens)
there was a large crowd eager
to obtain admittance, a regular
stream of carriages flowed past
the doors on the other side (Hope

DAVID RATTRAY

After serving an apprenticeship in warehouses in Glasgow, David Rattray went south to represent Young`s Paraffin Company, and also Walter MacFarlane & Company of architectural and structural engineers. On his return to Glasgow he became a chartered accountant with his brother in Rattray Brothers & Smith (in the 1930s it merged with Cooper Bros. nationally) He was especially adept in turning round the fortunes of businesses to become profitable. He created a large firm of hotels, made up from individual establishments which were ailing, including the major hydros in Kilmalcolm, Peebles, Callander, Oban, Gairloch and Skye as well as Forrester & Ferguson Ltd, better known as F & F, restaurateurs and caterers of Buchanan Street. He was also a director of Daniel Brown`s restaurants. The Baillie said of him "he is the guide, philosopher and friend of the Central Halls Company, owners of the Royalty theatre."

EDWARD L KNAPP

Originally from Surrey he had been in business in London, but trade was dull and he also lost deposits in the collapse of the Birmingham Banking Company. His interest in the stage and his friendship with many artistes of the time encouraged him to a new start - this time as the manager of the travelling company of Henry Leslie, author, actor and journalist. He then assisted George D Francis at the old Theatre Royal in Dunlop Street and moved with Glover and Francis to the new Royal.

Street), and this, too, for well nigh an hour before the ringing up of the curtain. Spacious as the house is it was crowded to excess; not a seat was vacant, nor was a bit of standing room unoccupied; and the magnificent audience, many of the number in evening dress, were as enthusiastic as the most hopeful management could have wished. Without a doubt Mr Phipps has given us a most admirable theatre..........the sweep of the three tiers of galleries is exceedingly graceful, there is chasteness in the elaboration of the ceiling and in the decoration of the walls, while the rich cream colour and gold, in which the prominent features of the house are treated, blend very effectively with the crimson hangings and cushions.

The Royal had room for over 3,000 people comprising the

Ground Floor Stalls	100
Pit, behind the stalls	1000
Balcony Dress Circle	312
Upper Circle	300

Amphitheatre	300
Gallery, behind it	1000

The stair landing of the main stair before entering the Dress Circle was described as the Crush Room (one hundred and twenty years later it is the Circle Cafe.) Each floor had greatly enlarged refreshment Saloons and on each level starting at the Dress Circle each Saloon had a doorway connecting to its own Smoking Room complete with its own fireplace. The splendid original Pay Box moved to the Side Avenue entrance, with a smaller pay box in its former place at Cowcaddens (to allow for a larger bar.) The Glasgow Herald`s reporter also remarked:

> First nights are always a terror to theatrical managers – especially when to the ordinary hazards of productions are added the mechanical difficulties inseparable from a new theatre. Audiences, especially those of their number who get nearest the ceiling, do not sufficiently appreciate these difficulties. On the contrary they are rather disposed to regard the occasion as one on which more license than usual may be taken in the way of amusing themselves in a manner that is not provided for in the programme.

The Ordnance Gazetteer book of 1883 describes the Theatre Royal reopening:

with a company, including Miss Marie Litton, Mr Hermann Vezin actor, and Mr Lionéll Brough jester (and a journalist by day). There is no architectural display outside, and no room for it, but inside the structure is worthy of the city. The stage is 74 feet wide and 56 feet deep, while the proscenium is 31 feet wide and 36 feet high. The auditorium, which contains accommodation for about 3200 persons, consists of three tiers of galleries and the pit. Behind the orchestra are rows of stalls, the door to which enters from Hope Street. The balcony, which contains seven rows of seats, is also entered from Hope Street, and so is the upper circle. The pit and amphitheatre are entered from Cowcaddens. The outer vestibule is paved with tesselated marble of various colours and graceful designs, and the interior is handsomely and beautifully fitted up and decorated. There are a number of private boxes, and the usual refreshment and other rooms. The opening was celebrated with great éclat, but the fortunes of the house have not as yet been very prosperous.

1877 to the early 1880s was a time of recession in many trades in Britain made worse by the consequences of the financial collapse of the City of Glasgow Bank in 1878 bringing further hardship to more families and businesses. It was a period of varying fortunes for those

COWCADDENS COMPETITION AND MR HANNAY

In Cowcaddens James Baylis met instant competition from his former landlord there, **Alexander Hannay**, who appears from correspondence to have been annoyed and probably jealous at Baylis's progress. In 1866 he decided upon legal action alleging that wood taken from him, without permission, was used by Baylis in the building of the new Royal. Hannay writes "Baylis had no cash when he opened the Scotia Hall."

Alexander Hannay's father was a baker with premises at 110 Cowcaddens Street, and offices at no.188. The young Hannay was also a baker but became a portioner, the old word for a man of property, who made more from property owning and renting than from baking. He bought in Cowcaddens Street, Stewart Street, Maitland Street and William Street. He redeveloped numbers 186 to 194 Cowcaddens Street creating new tenements and shops with an entrance-way through to his theatre in place of the Milton Colosseum, which he had already renamed the Prince of Wales by 1867. To redesign it he chose William Spence, the architect of the Theatre Royal Dunlop Street. This was the New Prince of Wales Theatre, built in 1869 with the help of a loan from James Thomson, shipbuilder and engineer. The Thomson brothers were successful at their Clyde Bank shipyard in Govan, and amassed a huge fortune in building steam-ships and machinery for the Confederate Navy during the American Civil War.

When James Baylis died suddenly in 1870 Hannay showed interest in buying the

TOP
The Grand Theatre
Cowcaddens

BOTTOM
Cowcaddens Cross
looking towards Hope Street

Royal and its adjoining property, valuing it in his own hand at £12,000, but an acceptable offer was not made to the Baylis Trust. In any event the Baylis family was not impressed with Hannay.

The Prince of Wales was popular, although in the 1870s it had a series of lessees, some ending with Hannay threatening litigation. A number of managers took to "large amounts of drink." Times were becoming difficult for all theatres. He wrote about "the considerable competition." He even advertised it for sale in the Glasgow Herald in 1877. After a fire in

February 1879 (the same month as Vulcan visited the Royal) it was rebuilt and opened as the more luxurious Grand Theatre. The Carl Rosa Opera Company became frequent visitors there.

Always looking for an opportunity, Hannay prepared a Limited Liability company in 1889 with the intention of it leasing the Grand Theatre from him for twenty years. This would be "The Glasgow Empire and Grand Theatre of Varieties Ltd" if it had got support. On his death five years later the family considered selling all the Cowcaddens property as one lot, but it was November 1898 when the Hannay Trust sold the theatre for £5,000 to its existing manager Ernest Stevens, who also ran the Lyceum Theatre, Govan, where productions by the Carl Rosa Opera Company were equally enjoyed.

"Diamond Hannay"

Hannay's sons entered business on the back of the family property and theatre. One became a Baillie in Glasgow Corporation. Another son James Ballantyne Hannay found fame in chemistry and diamonds, by his inventions and manufacturing in chemicals, oils and paint. He became a Fellow of the Chemical Society and demonstrated to them how he had managed to synthesise a diamond, becoming known thereafter as "Diamond Hannay". Reportedly he was offered money by the Amsterdam diamond merchants to cease his researches. To this day hard elongated crystals found in Australia are called Hannayite, in honour of "Diamond Hannay." His family home Cove Castle was gifted to the Scottish Youth Hostels Association in the 1940s.

involved in theatre. By the middle of the 1880s the economic slump was ending and international trade expanded again. Glasgow became the eighth largest city in Europe and the Second City of the Empire in industrial power and commercial influence. In population the Second City was actually Calcutta.

In opening such a large and well-appointed theatre as the Royal the Baylis family attracted competition. The nearest was the Prince of Wales Theatre across the street in Cowcaddens, built by Alexander Hannay on what had been the Milton Colosseum. The second competitor was the Gaiety Theatre opened in 1874 by Charles Bernard on Sauchiehall Street at the corner of West Nile Street. It was a variety theatre, with stars such as Vesta Tilley and Marie Lloyd, and also staged drama, opera, and pantomime. At the end of the century it became the Empire Theatre.

1   *Milton Colosseum*

2   *Royal Colosseum / Theatre Royal*

3   *Royalty*

4   *Prince's*

5   *Theatre Royal, Dunlop Street*

6   *Scotia*

Money, Managers & Musical Chairs

Illiam Glover would have celebrated the opening of the St Andrew's Halls at Charing Cross in 1877 as a sign of the city's continuing growth but in his heart he must have known that by 1878 he was running out of money by operating so many theatres.

In January he borrowed £3,333 more from Yuille & Rae, secured over his Bath Street site for a Royal theatre. In June his old friend William Gilchrist and the West Nile Street Circus Proprietors had to sell off that site to help Glover pay back the loans from the British Linen Bank and others, now totalling around £12,000. The dream of a new Glover Royal theatre in Bath Street had gone. (Its site is now the Albert Chambers, a red sandstone office block with shops on the ground level.) Much of the money had gone South to pay 15/- in the £ to his creditors connected with the Newcastle Theatre Royal. However he was able to borrow from two supporters of the arts to let him move his family to a new home in Landsdowne Crescent in the West End. One of the lenders was Benjamin Simons, fruit merchant in the city.

The fire at the Theatre Royal in February 1879 had put him out of business. There was nothing for him to lease or manage. A week later he was sequestrated, and at his bankruptcy examination his creditors asked him to explain how he had arrived at this situation. His statement and replies are in his own words:

I started business in 1869 in partnership with George Francis. I put in £1000 of the stock I got from the Union Railway Company and a bank credit of £3000 from the British Linen Bank on my own property in Bath Street. And a bond of £1,500 (possibly from his mother) making in all £6,000.

When George Francis went bankrupt (in England in 1878) I offered to pay my creditors in full. I have paid 15/- in the £. In order to pay the balance and other creditors not on the list I had to realise all my property in Bath Street and the whole of my interest in the Theatre Royal, the patent, effects and goodwill. I then entered into an arrangement to be sole lessee of the Theatre for three years. That was brought to a termination by the fire. The effect of the fire has been practically that it has destroyed my goodwill for the three years.

OPPOSITE
Locations *of linked theatres*

THE BUCHANANS · LINENS AND LOANS

Mrs Margaret Anderson had returned from Melbourne, Australia where her late husband had been a landscape painter. Her mother was a Buchanan of the tobacco, linen and cotton families – after whom Buchanan Street is named. The loan of £13,000 in 1876 is equal to some £3m in today's money. Sadly Margaret Anderson died in November 1878 age only 54 at her new home *"Mie-Mie"* in Auchingramont Road, Hamilton, the result of an alcohol overdose.

Allan Buchanan, who loaned £5,000, had been a partner in the firm of George Buchanan & Co, linen and cotton calenderers in Candleriggs, and was related to Margaret Anderson. He already owned property in Cowcaddens. His daughter was the wife of lawyer James McClure, senior partner of McClures & Hannay. The law firm and their families were well established and presumably wanted to buy the Royal because of an interest in the artistic and social side of an iconic theatre - as well as having eyes on the development potential of its additional buildings. James McClure's own daughter Grace had married John White of the Shawfield Chemical Works, becoming Lady Overtoun when White got his peerage. After starting in soap and soda manufacturing the Whites developed new chrome chemicals for the textile and other industries. They made fortunes from the noxious chemical processes of the day (the Works being the largest of its kind in the world) and had a hypocritical attitude of working on Sundays. They were interested in the arts, but above all they donated widely to evangelical and social causes including the building of the Christian Institute and YMCA in Bothwell Street, and seaside homes providing fresh-air holidays for children and their families.

David Hannay (no business connection with Alexander Hannay) moved on to his own law firm, and was Clerk to the General Council of Glasgow University from 1872 to 1887, the period when the University was settling in at its new site on Gilmorehill.

At that time I had myself acquired since the sale to Yuille & Rae things I bought for the pantomime and music for the pantomime.

The price (I got to pay my creditors) for the goodwill of the Theatre Royal and the whole of the business in 1878 was £2,400. As a going concern I think that a very insufficient price. I was forced into the sale…………….. they had the power of breaking the lease. The principal losses to the Theatre Royal were through the Newcastle and Kilmarnock theatres. In 1874 the Theatre Royal stood well. It paid into the bank …… all the credit account was paid clear.

The property in Bath Street (for a new theatre) which I realised in 1878 brought £12,000. I now know that Mr Binnie surveyor for the

British Linen Bank had valued it at £23,000. I had no knowledge there was such a large surplus.

Since then I have been dependant on the success of the business as a going concern..............."

Unfortunately the going concern had burned down. He said, unjustly, that Knapp his manager had not kept the books in order. But the books had not survived! After settling with his lenders over his house in Glasgow and in Kilmun he still had liabilities to suppliers and others of £2,702 and his remaining assets amounted to £219. A payment of 1/6d in the £ was paid to his creditors.

When Andrew Yuille (for the firm of McClures & Hannay) and John Rae made their offer of £38,000 for the Royal and its buildings they funded it by £9,300 of their own money and £28,700 from long-term loans secured over the property. Within a year repayments were not being made, and interest rates soared. At a time of national financial uncertainty, and the closure of the City of Glasgow Bank in October 1878, investors everywhere checked and rechecked their assets. Legal writs flew. The loans for the Royal buildings were:

Yuille & Rae still owed money to the lenders and to the building contractors. In 1879 Yuille was sequestrated, and he signed an arrangement to pay what he could to his creditors. For Andrew Yuille this was not new. In 1856 he was buying and selling cigars as a business and became financially embarrassed; in September that year his premises burned down and he was able to receive £180 from the insurance company, he was sequestrated and paid only a small part of his debts. He was sequestrated again in 1871, owing money to the bottle manufacturers who supplied his chemist shop.

Margaret Anderson's cousin, Alexander Buchanan Dick-Cleland, a soap manufacturer in Cowcaddens and a major landowner, was appointed as her trustee and the **Mrs Margaret Anderson Trust** asserted its right in January 1879 to own the buildings (being the largest lender.) Dispute raged, but the Anderson Trust's ownership was confirmed and the rebuilding continued to the Charles Phipps drawings commissioned by Yuille & Rae. The insurance company settled the fire claim, with £5,859 of it reducing the Trust's loan.   The Anderson Trust now owned all the property apart from the Alexandra Music Hall and the shops

£13,000 from Mrs Margaret Rowan Waddell Anderson, Glasgow

£5,000   from the trustees of Allan Buchanan, calenderer, Glasgow

£3,200   from the trustees of Charles Cunningham, merchant, Glasgow

£3,000   from the trustees of William Gibson, merchant, Glasgow

£3,000   from the James Baylis Trust

£1,520   from Mrs Mary Thomson Wright, widow, Edinburgh

under it, which became the property of the Allan Buchanan Trust and the other lenders.

Alexander Buchanan Dick-Cleland appointed the theatre's new manageress and lessee **Marie Litton**. When the Royal did reopen in October 1880 it was with a performance of William Shakespeare's *As You Like It* which she had first performed that spring in the Imperial Theatre, London (formerly the Aquarium). She was a favourite actress of Gilbert and Sullivan usually at her Royal Court Theatre in the metropolis. Her husband Wybrow Robertson assisted. He had taken the lease of the Aquarium Theatre attached to the gothic National Aquarium, which had very few fish in it and soon closed. Its site became the present Methodist Central Halls, Westminster.

By the 1870s resident companies were disappearing from theatres, the railway companies offered cheap fares to touring companies, and customers enjoyed the freshness they could offer. Curiously Marie Litton reintroduced a resident company to the Royal (a novelty for a while, but not lasting.) Marie Litton was not unknown in Glasgow - she had produced six plays at the Royal in the 1870s. The resident manager was now the actor Walter Baynham, a president of the Athenaeum Dramatic Club, who had also stage-managed at the old Royal in Dunlop Street. *As You Like It* and the redesigned theatre proved popular, with the comedy play running for over a month.

Following its first week of reopening,

the Baillie magazine carried a letter from its diarist:

My Dear Baillie, Everybody – save a few croakers – is in raptures with the new Theatre Royal. It is comfortable – always the first necessity in a place of entertainment, it is excellently lighted, and the acoustic properties are first-rate.

The Baillie also praised the tidiness of the stage and behind-the-scenes, noting:

The Green Room seems the equal of the *Theatre Francais* in Paris. Disposed along the walls are drawings, some in ink and some in pencil, by the caricaturist George Cruickshank; in the middle of the room is a table, the centre of which is occupied by a bouquet of flowers, while books and magazines and newspapers are heaped here and there in admirable confusion; and round the table are chairs and sofas of the latest and most comfortable construction.

That winter her pantomime was *Pretty Bo-Peep and Little Boy Blue*, with upwards of 300 performers and scenery by William Glover and others. Four weeks of *Grand Popular Concerts* were held in February when Litton was producing at the London Gaiety. The Royal Concerts as they became known were mainly Italian concerts and opera

ABOVE
Alexander Buchanan Dick-Cleland

recitals with a band of sixty performers conducted by Signor Tito Mattei, a chorus of fifty, and solo vocalists led by Signor Foli, the Irish-American bass who had trained in Italy. The whole pit was turned into a level promenade – an attraction in its way to many - by constructing a carpeted wooden platform over it and erecting a new area for the band. The auditorium was yellow and gold and the stage red and olive. Each evening had a new programme. There were Ballad Nights (the best attended), Oratorio Nights (not so well attended), and one evening was of British Army Quadrilles played by a band and pipers of the 74th Regiment. The enterprise was said to have the merits of both novelty and boldness, but prices had to be cut in the last week. Plays ran throughout the spring of 1881, and the Baillie effused:

LEFT
Marie Litton
a favourite of dramatist W.S.Gilbert

> Under her management our Theatre Royal has taken a position which is unique in contemporary theatricals. Miss Litton has dared to give Glasgow a resident company. Unawed by the success of perambulating tragedians, regardless of the charms of opera bouffe, she has set herself to the task of organising a company with whom you shall laugh in comedy and cry in tragedy..... The company is called Her Majestys Servants..... This clever and energetic lady..... brings the best people together, and spares no pains to provide these people with adequate accessories in the shape of beautiful scenery, rich stage appointments, and an all together intelligent and satisfactory system of stage management.

In May that year Litton advertised the Royal as not only the "Most Fashionable Theatre in the Provinces" but also the "THE CHEAPEST." Prices were Gallery 6d, Pit 1s, Boxes 1s6d, Pit Stalls 2s, Dress Circle 3s Balcony and Orchestra Stalls 5s and 6s, and Private Boxes from half-a-guinea. The repertoire became stale and not demanding enough for the Glasgow audiences. She closed the theatre in June and returned to London, taking up management of the Globe Theatre.

Charles Bernard stepped forward on the 1st December 1881 as the next lessee and manager of the Royal. He was well known as the owner of the Gaiety Theatre at 31 Sauchiehall Street, presenting fare which competed with the Royal, and branching out to a number of theatres in England.

His stage debut was in 1846 at London's Stand theatre and he worked his way up through singing and drama to become a theatre promoter. He owned, conducted and sang in his black-face company The Queen's Minstrels – "the original and legitimate Christy's Minstrels" - which he advertised with the royal coat-of-arms, as the only minstrel company to have the patronage of the Royal Family. Most likely this was through young Edward Saxe-Coburg-Gotha and not his mother Queen Victoria who preferred concerts and circuses! However he had sung for the Queen and advertised himself as "The Queen's Favourite Baritone."

In the 1860s he leased the Choral Hall near the corner of West Nile Street and in 1872 he was able to purchase it and the houses fronting it to Sauchiehall Street. Taking ideas for a new theatre there from the *Gaiete* and the *Theatre-Lyrique* in Paris he opened his luxurious Gaiety Theatre in 1874, designed by the architect William MacIlwraith. Its stalls, balcony and gallery could accommodate 1400 and for the stalls and balcony it had newly patented tip-up chairs upholstered in yellow and red satin. Bernard's wife became manageress, and his wife's sister funded his expansion in Manchester.

The artistic example of the Glover family was in front of him and he succeeded William Glover as lessee of Newcastle's Theatre Royal in 1878. Contemporaries there write of the five good pantomimes he produced,

appearing in two of them *Robinson Crusoe* and *Dick Whittington*. Pantomimes ran for the same length in Newcastle as in Glasgow, usually around 11 weeks. He brought to the town the early Savoy operas of *HMS Pinafore*, *Sorcerer*, and the *Pirates of Penzance*, and had started his own Comic Opera Company (which toured as far south as Eastbourne.)

Adding to the plays and pantomimes in his Gaiety theatre, which he advertised as "a musical bijou for Glasgow, where the most respectable of both sexes can witness good music and other popular entertainments", he presented the D'Oyle Carte Opera Company and the Carl Rosa Company in each of 1880 and 1881. In 1881 he introduced to the Gaiety the very seductive Sarah Bernhardt who "attracted the lovers of fashion and the lovers of art."

Charles Bernard opened at the Royal with a pantomime in December 1881, *Dick Whittington and his Cat, or the harlequin – The Faithful Cat and the Demon Rat*. His nearest competition in pantomimes came from the Prince of Wales now called the Grand Theatre. Towards the end of January he was reducing his prices. He put on plays on occasional weeks. The contrast between the Royal and the Royalty was clearly marked in March - Bernard presented the *Uncle Tom's Cabin Company* with Freed Slaves, Negroes, Octoroons and Jubilee Singers , while at the Royalty Edward Knapp had the musical drama of *Rob Roy*, always a huge money-maker.

In April 1882 a series of *Promenade*

Concerts was being promoted and conducted by him at popular prices: Dress Circle 2/6d, Upper Circle 1/6d and Gallery 6d. "The most Marvellous Sixpennyworth known in Glasgow" said Bernard before he staggered to a halt. What the public did not know was he had expanded too far. His progress came to an end when he was sequestrated in Glasgow in July. At his bankruptcy examination Charles Bernard said:

I have been on my own account since 1869...... I bought the Gaiety in 1872 for £12,500. I continued there till May 1882.....profits were £1000 a year.

I took Theatre Royal Newcastle in May 1878 for four years lease...... profits were around £1000 a year.......Then I took up Princes Theatre Manchester August 1879 on a ten year lease....profits made there being £2000 a year. The smaller Her Majesty's in Carlisle was not profitable.

I took the Theatre Royal on 1st December 1881 for seven years lease at a rent of 6½% upon the receipts with a guaranteed minimum to be paid of £1500 per year. It was not profitable to date. I believe I have lost £3,500 at the Theatre Royal besides the amount of stock, altogether between £7,000 and £8,000.

In reply to questions about his own

LEFT
Charles Bernard
conducted the Queen's Minstrels

performing companies and music material Bernard said:

I paid £1500 each for the copyright of *Les Cloches de Corneville, La Petite Madamoiselle* and *Sharon's Sceptre*. My Comic Opera Company made small profits with these, but my Childrens' company lost a lot of money.

Asked why he was not benefiting from the copyright investments of £4500 he simply replied "...... popularity changed". Gilbert and Sullivan's new style of entertainments swept the country. At the time of his bankruptcy he still owned the Gaiety, which had loans of £15,000 upon it. It was sold for much less than that. In all the theatres

he had furniture and theatrical properties belonging to him. To his suppliers and lenders he owed £9574. More than half of this was at the Gaiety, over one fifth at the Princes Theatre Manchester, over one tenth to his sister-in-law, and only £303 at the Theatre Royal Glasgow.

What happened was that he had paid out substantial money for long term copyrights, paid money for new stock and covering costs at the Theatre Royal and his suppliers elsewhere ran out of patience waiting for their money. At the final counting he had assets of £3,200 and combined debts of £15,000. Payments totalling 3/9d in the £ were made to his national list of creditors. A few years later he made a small comeback, managing the Palace Theatre in London.

Meanwhile the builders of the new Phipps auditorium and its improvements throughout the theatre wanted

to be paid their final bills. In August 1881 Robert Rae, still in his twenties but who must now have felt nearer 70, signed over his £4,400 personal share of the ownership of the Royal in favour of Henry Tosh, ironmonger, George Ross, wright and William Stevenson, brickmaker and builder. A few months later the Anderson Trust intimated to Yuille & Rae that the loan was to be called in and fully settled. Mrs Anderson's trustees advertised the theatre for sale in 1882 in the Glasgow Herald and other papers almost on a weekly basis from June through to the beginning of August, all to no avail.

The builders now knew that the prospect of being fully paid was getting slimmer. Seven of them created The Glasgow Theatre & Opera House Co.Ltd in October 1882 to buy and manage the theatre. It never owned the building, and it never traded. The Royal opened occasionally for panoramas and concerts, and in October the Italian actress Madame Adelaide Ristori, supported by Walter Bentley and his actors, headed a week of plays.

At a public roup in 1883 the Anderson Trust finally received one offer. This was for £9,750 from Robert MacDougall, but the sale was never finalised.

Macdougall was an accountant, bank agent, and an established property agent. The property was thought to have been "bought" and a registered lease survives which shows MacDougall "renting" the Theatre Royal to Edward Garcia of the Alexandra Theatre, Peter Street, Manchester for five and a half years to

1889 at £1,500 a year. Fortunately none of this was valid, because it emerged that not all of the earlier lenders had been repaid. Garcia ran his Manchester music hall, which could only seat 800, for almost twenty years and renamed it the Folly Theatre of Varieties. One reviewer writes "Garcia was as familiar with the chapters of bankruptcy laws as with the texts of the plays he put on." The same "tenant" may have been a relative of Michael Garcia, a partner in the fruit businesses of the Simons family.

The Royal now opened only when a hire was made of it. The veteran T.D. Fenner based in Liverpool, who started in Sam Hague's Minstrels in the USA in 1866, took up the month of January 1884 and staged the *Great American Star Minstrels* describing it as the Grandest Programme of Negro Novelties. The variety programme was changed weekly, sometimes "Plantation Pastimes" and other times "The Pirates of the Clyde." Ticket prices boasted – "No charge for Programmes or Cloakroom."

Under the patronage of the Lord Provost the theatre hosted the *Panoramas of Hamilton's New-World Excursions* during March and April. These were on a revolving loop with special music and lighting effects, one week would be the Eastern world, the next the Egyptian world, another a week on Warfare.

At the end of 1884 **Fred Sydney,** who previously ran the Prince of Wales Theatre, took up the lease and presented *Aladdin and the Wonderful Lamp!* for five weeks into January – his daybills

announcing "72,356 persons have already seen it in 4 weeks." He followed with plays to March 1885.

After six years Edward Knapp's lease of the Royalty Theatre came to its end. The partnership of J B Howard and F W Wyndham announced they would commence management of the Royalty on 24th December 1884. It was thriving in contrast to the Theatre Royal. They honoured the bookings made by Knapp for the coming months and retained him as their theatre manager. J.L Toole and Company opened with comedies, and the D'Oyle Carte Opera returned in February 1885. In the New Year Howard and Wyndham advertised their first pantomime in Glasgow would be *The Forty Thieves* "to be produced in early December 1885". They added that, during the summer, alterations would be made to the building, decoration,

THE GLASGOW THEATRE & OPERA HOUSE CO. LTD

"Phantom of the Opera"

The shareholders of this new venture in 1882 each held shares of £5, with the publicised plan of a shareholding of £20,000 by issuing shares to others. The company's Prospectus declared it's intention:

> to purchase the Theatre, adjacent buildings, and vacant ground, the Royal Letters-Patent, scenic properties, wardrobes and other theatrical appurtenances, furnishings and equipment requisite and necessary in the representation of stage plays and other entertainments for the amusement of the public and the engagement of actors and others.

It planned to buy the Theatre Royal and manage it; the dividends from profits going to the seven shareholders and replacing the £4,400 ownership right granted to them by Robert Rae in August 1881.

The seven founder shareholders were tradesmen and contractors involved in the recent rebuilding:

Henry Tosh	*Ironmonger*	99 Hill Street
John McCormack	*Wright*	22 Canning Place
George Ross	*Wright*	13 West Gordon Street
John Rose	*Cabinet Maker*	13 Sauchiehall Street
James Robinson	*Draper*	66 Rose Street
Henry Morrison	*Slate merchant*	31 India Street
Daniel Stewart McKie	*Measurer*	167 St Vincent Street

J. Morrison & Son, were the slaters and concrete builders; George Ross & Son, carpenters and joiners; Chalmers and Tosh, gasfitters; W.Stevenson & Sons were the masons and bricklayers; McGregor, Gilmour & Co and Stevens, ironworkers; W. Bremner, plasterer; Alexander Rae, plumber. The company never got off the ground, and it remained a "Phantom of the Opera."

and comforts; which they did to a revised design by Frank Matcham, reducing its capacity to 1400, and still with manager Knapp. The planned pantomime, designed by William Glover, went instead to the Grand Theatre.

Edward Lee Knapp must have wanted to be his own boss again. He proudly announced his move to the Theatre Royal, commencing 24th

December 1885. "The Theatre has been redecorated and furnished," he said. The Royal was technically as advanced as the Royalty and it was much larger. The Royal could hold twice as many, and its rent was now only £500 a year. He started in 1885 and was able to bring back with him some of the earlier Royal staff including its musical director Mr de Banzie.

Knapp reopened at the Royal with a musical comedy *In Camp*, followed in January with Robert Arthur's production of *Guy Mannering*. Plays and comedies took up much of February and March, with Marie de Grey in *Jane Shore* early in April, but gaps were appearing and he ran out of money.

By June 1886 he was bankrupt. The landlords wanted payment of rent outstanding, and forced him into sequestration. At his bankruptcy examination Edward Knapp said:

The reason for my bankruptcy was owing to the badness of the season 1885/86; it seemed a bad year all round for amusements. The weather was exceedingly unfavourable. The Theatre had been closed for some time before I took it, and the fact of opening a place where the public had not been for some time was against me. The Theatre was in bad odour with the public.

I borrowed £100 from Sir William Pearce (chairman of the Fairfield Shipbuilding and Engineering Co.) when I opened the theatre first.

There were no speculative debts of any kind.

He had no assets, and no payment was made to his creditors. Interestingly Knapp superintended Her Majesty's Italian Opera Company led by Colonel J H Mapleson in the Royal near the end of 1886 after almost eight years absence from Glasgow, with 10 operas in two weeks. Still with Knapp as a manager, Carl Rosa Opera opened in March 1887 for four nights only, when Wagner's *Flying Dutchman* was sung in Glasgow for the first time; the other operas were F H Cowen's *Pauline* and Beethoven's *Fidelio*. Presumably the bookings were beneficial to the owners.

Mrs Margaret Anderson's daughter, Mrs Elizabeth Richmond, age 29, and her husband now took the place of the Anderson Trust, the family trust becoming the Richmond Trust from October 1886.

In 1887 **William Thomas Rushbury** took up the lease after the summer. He was also the lessee of the Theatre Royal, Greenock, still owned by the Glover Trust. Rushbury was a music teacher who had moved into theatre and occasionally published his arrangements of comic opera. New dramas from America and Britain were staged by Walter Bentley & Co and ran in October and November, accompanied as all were with incidental music. His advertising emphasised the Safety of the Theatre building, quoting the Evening News: "The Royal can, without fear, claim to be the safest Theatre in the City." His

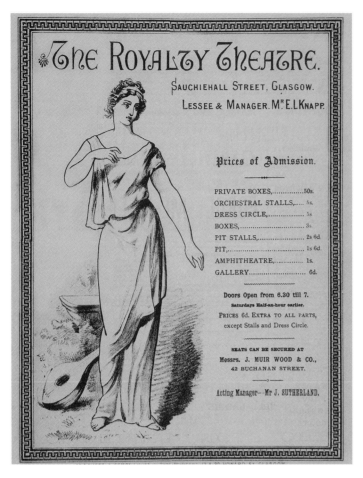

The Royalty Theatre.

SAUCHIEHALL STREET, GLASGOW.

LESSEE & MANAGER. Mr E.L KNAPP.

Prices of Admission.

PRIVATE BOXES,..............50s.
ORCHESTRAL STALLS,...... 5s.
DRESS CIRCLE,.................. 5s
BOXES,............................ 3s.
PIT STALLS,..................... 2s 6d.
PIT,............................... 1s 6d.
AMPHITHEATRE,............. 1s.
GALLERY........................... 6d.

Doors Open from 6.30 till 7.
Saturdays Half-an-hour earlier.
PRICES 6d. EXTRA TO ALL PARTS,
except Stalls and Dress Circle.

SEATS CAN BE SECURED AT
Messrs. J. MUIR WOOD & CO.,
42 BUCHANAN STREET.

Acting Manager—Mr J. SUTHERLAND.

ABOVE
Royalty Theatre
*programme
1882*

programmes boasted of the six modernised exits, adding:

> In all parts of the theatre are hosepipes fixed to fire hydrants. Oil lamps have also been provided.

The programmes also advertised neighbouring restaurants including Thomson's Theatre Royal Dining Rooms at 85 Cowcaddens (previously the corner public house) for Fish, Tripe and Other Suppers; Purveyors for Marriages etc.

Her Majesty's Opera Company planned a visit again but it was postponed

(due to Mapleson's own financial difficulty in America and Britain).

The first three days of December welcomed the 1st Lanark Rifle Volunteers Amateur Dramatic Society presenting *Guy Mannering* in aid of the City Charities, and the rest of the month was a revival of *Uncle Tom's Cabin*, complete with its Jubilee Singers.

The Royal's New Year production of *Meg Merrilees* included "a powerful Band and Chorus," with more drama staged at the end of January 1888. The Royal continued to emphasise the theatre's safety while the Royalty retaliated describing itself as "the Premiere Theatre of the City" - both the Grand and the Royal Princess's would dispute that. Attendance at the theatre must have dwindled, forcing Rushbury to advertise a melodramatic thriller presented in a cabaret setting, written by Augustin Daly of Broadway fame:

"Gigantic Success of the Reduced Popular Prices"
"Under the Gaslight"
A sensational drama in four Acts
Note the Further Reduction of Popular Prices

Gallery & Amphitheatre	3d
Entire Pit, Best in Scotland	6d
Family Circle, Select	9d
Dress Circle and Stalls, Marvellous	1/-
Single Seat in Private Boxes, Luxury	1/6d

That was the end of Mr Rushbury. In March 1888 he too was sequestrated, having liabilities of over £1000, more than half being due to his printer John

Horn of Glasgow, and few assets of worth. No payment was possible to his creditors.

William Rushbury picked up again and ran concerts in halls from Forfar to Maybole with his Grand Concert Company, as well as staging the trans-Atlantic drama *Shadows of a Giant City*. Madam Rushbury - presumably his second wife (the daughter of a missionary)—appeared in holiday revues at the Princes Theatre, Rothesay.

On 15th February 1888 the Royalty Theatre under Howard and Wyndham announced their stage and auditorium (including passages and staircases) "will be entirely LIGHTED BY ELECTRICITY tonight by the Anglo-American Brush Co, looked after by Professor Sir William Thomson." – soon to become Lord Kelvin. During the year they proclaimed the benefits of electricity "thus ensuring Pure Air and Cool Atmosphere, and most important of all reducing the possibilities of Accidents to the minimum." Howard and Wyndham continued to tour with their special productions including *Lady of the Lake*, as far south as Liverpool.

In Glasgow the International Exhibition 1888 was about to open, attracting six million visitors to Kelvingrove Park. The Theatre Royal could hardly be allowed to lie idle in the heart of the city.

Michael Simons and his father Benjamin were fruit brokers, whose

LEFT
Theatre Royal
*programme
1886*

firm Simons, Jacobs & Co was the largest fruit importers and produce brokers in Britain with its auction hall and warehouses in Candleriggs and Brunswick Street, branches in Liverpool, London and Southhampton, and agencies overseas including New York and Boston. They were keen on theatre, drama and music. Baillie Michael Simons had been elected to Glasgow Corporation and was one of the promoters of the International Exhibition, as well as the convener of its Refreshments, Music and Entertainments committee. The Simons family would now move centre stage at the Royal and remain centre stage for over 50 years, creating one of the largest groups of theatres in the country, Howard & Wyndham Ltd.

Michael Simons creates Howard & Wyndham Ltd

Michael Simons reached Glasgow as an infant in the 1840s when his father Benjamin decided there was a better life to be had than being one of the many traders selling fruit from a wheel barrow in Covent Garden, where his forefathers had arrived from Spain or Portugal in the 1700s. Benjamin walked with his fruit barrow the length of the country from London up the eastern side, selling as he went, settling a while in Newcastle and then Edinburgh. In his own words, he noted the grass was still growing in its markets and he moved west to the burgeoning city of Glasgow. He set up business in Candleriggs, forming the firm of Simons, Jacobs & Co and became the largest fruit importers and brokers in Britain.

The two Simons and their families had three main social interests outside of business   - involvement in the congregational activity of the small Jewish community, fine art and theatre. They attended the old Royal in Dunlop Street and the new Royal in Cowcaddens as well as attending the Royalty Theatre in Sauchiehall Street.

When Edward Knapp rejoined the Theatre Royal in 1885 he was succeeded at the Royalty (to be later known as the YMCA Lyric) by James Howard, based in Edinburgh, and Fred Wyndham based in Newcastle. The Royalty had opened to the public under Knapp in 1879 in the new Venetian-style block of shops and offices on Sauchiehall Street at Renfield Street owned by the Central Halls Company Ltd. and designed by Glasgow's most commercially successful architect James Thomson. The theatre in it was by young Frank Matcham, one of his earliest designs in Britain.

Michael Simons did not own shares in the Central Halls Company (interestingly Knapp held twenty shares) but saw the management ability of Mr Howard and Mr Wyndham in its theatre. Similar to the Glasgow Public Halls Company Ltd, which began in the 1870s with public shareholders and created the St Andrew's Halls, the Central Halls Company was formed to buy over and

OPPOSITE
Interior c1920s
with Appollo and the nine muses above the opening by Ballard, and the act drop by T F Dunn

Michael Simons - Fruit Merchant

After leaving school, Michael Simons was apprenticed to Syme, Simons & Smith, seedsmen, nurserymen and fruiterers in the Argyll Arcade (who had their glasshouses and nurseries at Kennishead, near Pollokshaws) and then joined his father Benjamin Simons' business of fruit merchants and auctioneers in Candleriggs. He learned the skills of auctioneering in the Glasgow salerooms and of buying in Spain, Canada and the United States. By the early 1870s he was in partnership with his father and others in Glasgow, London, Southhampton and Liverpool as fruit importers, brokers and merchants.

The fruit trade was being revolutionised by lower rail freight charges in Britain and the Continent and by the introduction of steamers equipped to carry perishable cargoes using the latest refrigeration technology. Journey times were also greatly reduced, putting Glasgow on an even footing with London as a market for the national distribution of fruit and vegetables.

The scale of activity is reflected upon in the Dictionary of Scottish Business Biography. The firm became pre-eminent in the United Kingdom in the marketing of Spanish and Portuguese oranges, importing them from Valencia, Seville, Opporto and Lisbon. Based on this success they broadened the range of imported and domestic produce......lemons, melons, nuts, olives, onions and pomegranates were imported from Spain and Portugal. Glasgow became the first UK market for Almeria grapes. Apples and pears were imported in great volume from New York, from where he also introduced consignments of coconuts. Links were established with Egypt, Jaffa, Malta and the West Indies. Across the Atlantic came fruit and vegetables from California. Eggs came, largely from Canada in the winter

ABOVE
Simons fruit warehouses
(left to right)
Candleriggs, Brunswick Street, Montrose Street.

months.

Vegetables were brought from the Continent, and tomatoes from Valencia. Simons also encouraged the establishment of tomato growing in the Clyde Valley….. the tomato had been an unknown fruit in Glasgow in the 1880s. To a House of Lords committee in 1894 Michael Simons stated "it would be utterly impossible to satisfy the demands for fruit which exists all over the country if we depended altogether on home growers." The Baillie magazine commented in 1880 that "Fruit is no longer a luxury in our city….. it is a daily

▼

LEFT
Michael Simons

RIGHT
Benjamin Simons

complete a development initiated in Sauchiehall Street. The company's objectives were:

The establishing, maintaining and utilizing of Halls or Assembly Rooms in the City of Glasgow and neighbourhood, the conducting of Concerts and Public Entertainments, the acquiring, fitting out of Houses, Shops, Warehouses , Offices………

Its secretary and eventually its senior director was David Rattray, of Rattray Brothers, chartered accountants. David Rattray impressed Michael Simons and would feature in Simons' new venture as it unfolded.

The Richmond Trust, the family successor to Mrs Margaret Anderson, now exposed their Theatre Royal to sale at a public roup on 31st October 1888. There was only one offer made, and that was for £7,500 from Howard and Wyndham who had started a lease of it in July. The guiding hand of Michael Simons was at work. Howard and Wyndham started managing the theatre right away and followed a private written agreement with Simons.

Simons and the Richmond Trust got together in the Exhibition year 1888. The purchase of the Theatre Royal was financed by a loan of £4,000 from Michael Simons and colleagues, and a loan of £3,500 from the Richmond Trust. The Royal and its adjacent buildings including the original Alexandra Music Hall, described as the "empty Music Hall at 73 Cowcaddens" and shops under it, were now owned by a Trust created by Michael Simons, 206 Bath Street, Paul Rottenburg, Dowanhill Gardens, and

△

article of food within reach of all, and it is to the Simons that we are indebted to this."

He encouraged retailers to develop and provided loans to people such as (Sir) Malcolm Campbell to expand their chains of fruit shops and railway kiosks. Bananas were imported from the Canary Islands after Malcolm Campbell shops displayed the ones grown in the Duke of Hamilton's greenhouses. Michael Simons received a knighthood from Spain for his services to the Spanish fruit trade.

Premises were expanded at the ports and city markets. In Glasgow the firm built extensive warehouses and auction salerooms in Candleriggs and Brunswick Street, with additional warehousing in Montrose Street. Simons commissioned the design and building of the most advanced cold stores in Britain, erected in George Street in 1896 and later sold to the meat-trader Lord Vestey.

MONS. TREWEY.
(COMIC, SHADOWGRAPHIST AND WELL ILLUSTRATED)

TOP
Henry Irving
MIDDLE
Phyliss Broughton
BOTTOM
Monsieur Trewey

James Woodburn, doctor and dentist, 197 Bath Street.

Howard and Wyndham sail the good ship Theatre-Royal

Howard and Wyndham's regime at the Theatre Royal, where they retained manager Frank Sephton, started on 10th September 1888 to a packed house, including the Lord Provost Sir James King and members of the city council. A Commemoration Supper was held afterwards in the Central Hotel. The opening night featured Henry Irving and Marion Terry in the drama *Faust*, followed the rest of the week by plays from Wilson Barrett and His London Company. The Carl Rosa Opera Company "with Full Band, Chorus and Ballet" returned in November, being conducted by Carl Rosa just a few months before his sudden death. He was born in Hamburg and became a violinist especially interested in opera. The operas over two weeks were *Maritana*, *The Jewess*, *Carmen*, *Bohemian Girl*, *Faust*, and *Mignon*.

The first pantomime by Howard and Wyndham could now take place, and the Baillie reported:

The *Forty Thieves* begins its run at the Theatre Royal. Mr Howard and Mr Wyndham recognise that the Royal is essentially a pantomime house and they are determined that the public shall recognise this also.

The plot was invented by Mrs Howard (who had written many of the pantomimes when at Newcastle Theatre Royal), directed by Mr & Mrs Howard and Mr Wyndham, the stage director being Mr Howard and the dresses were under the supervision of Mrs Howard. Music was by Thomas Smyth. Principal Boy was actress and dancer Phyllis Broughton. A special attraction was Monsieur Trewey, billed as "The Prince of Prestidigitataeurs." He was a humorist, juggler and shadowgraphist, who helped introduce Cinematographe-Lumiere to Britain in 1896. Howard & Wyndham pantomimes would last for a record of over 70 years. Fred Wyndham produced

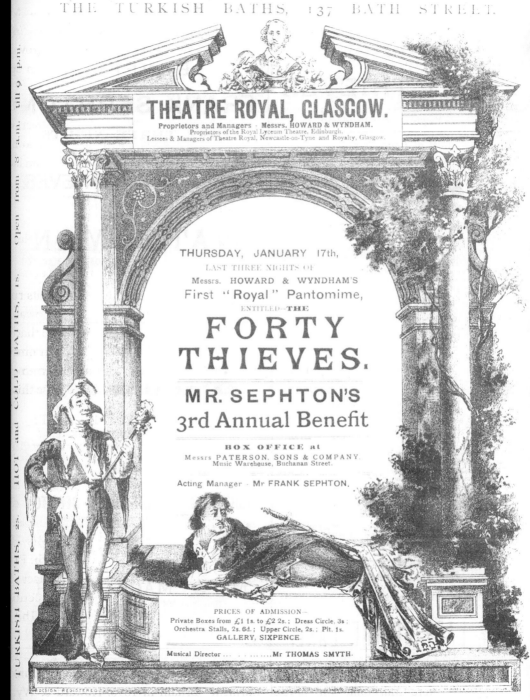

THEATRE ROYAL, GLASGOW.

Proprietors and Managers - Messrs. HOWARD & WYNDHAM.
Proprietors of the Royal Lyceum Theatre, Edinburgh,
Lessees & Managers of Theatre Royal, Newcastle-on-Tyne and Royalty, Glasgow.

THURSDAY, JANUARY 17th,

LAST THREE NIGHTS OF

Messrs. HOWARD & WYNDHAM'S

First "Royal" Pantomime,

ENTITLED—THE

FORTY THIEVES.

MR. SEPHTON'S
3rd Annual Benefit

BOX OFFICE at

Messrs PATERSON, SONS & COMPANY,
Music Warehouse, Buchanan Street.

Acting Manager - Mr FRANK SEPHTON.

PRICES OF ADMISSION—
Private Boxes from £1 1s. to £2 2s.; Dress Circle, 3s;
Orchestra Stalls, 2s. 6d.; Upper Circle, 2s.; Pit, 1s.
GALLERY, SIXPENCE.

Musical Director ... ... Mr THOMAS SMYTH.

TURKISH BATHS, 2s. TOLL and COLD BATHS, 1s. Open from 8 a.m. till 9 p.m.

MR HOWARD AND MR WYNDHAM

James Howard was born in Ireland in 1841 under his real name Michael Hoban and came as a boy to Liverpool where he first trod the boards. When a young man he joined the company of the Royal in Dunlop Street as a comedy actor, moving in 1866 to London and the Theatre Royal Drury Lane. He then toured with his actress wife Sara Nathan.

Howard became the manager of Edinburgh's Theatre Royal in 1876 in partnership with Robert Wyndham, who was a close friend of Edmund Glover. When Robert Wyndham, and his actress wife Rose Saker, retired to Sloane Street, Chelsea in 1883 he joined with Wyndham's son Frederick in theatre management. Only a few months after Michael Simons formed Howard & Wyndham Ltd in 1895 James Howard died suddenly at the age of 54.

RIGHT
(left)
John Howard
(right)
Fred Wyndham

Fred Wyndham was born to a theatre family and christened Frederick William Phoenix Wyndham. His father Robert trained as an actor in London, made his Scottish debut in 1844 at the Adelphi Theatre on Glasgow Green with his wife-to-be, and settled in Edinburgh. Young Wyndham was born in 1853 in the Adelphi Theatre, Edinburgh where his father had become the lessee. A week later the building burned down and his father added the name "Phoenix", theatres often rose from the ashes! He worked in a shipbroker's office in London until he decided to follow in the family footsteps. Fred Wyndham and his wife Louisa Hudson acted on a number of stages, moving into production and theatre management. With the help of a loan from old man Wyndham, Mr Howard and Mr Wyndham built a new theatre in 1883 in Edinburgh, the Royal Lyceum designed by Charles Phipps.

all the pantomimes into the 1920s apart from 1908 to 1910, when Robert Arthur was in charge. They extended their pantomimes to Edinburgh from 1895 onwards.

Shakespearean plays and a revisit by Wilson Barrett's company in February 1889 were followed by *The Lady of the Lake* with William Glover's scenery and James Howard as Roderick Dhu.

However the theatre was not yet opening in all weeks in contrast to the Royalty. The Carl Rosa opera season started, and the ever-popular *Rob Roy* opened in August, including in a main role the opera singer Durward Lely (real name James Lyall from Arbroath). He was a principal singer for D'Oyly Carte, Gilbert & Sullivan, and an opera star in America, after which he toured the world with his wife in a lecture recital of "Scottish Song and Story." Plays and opera took the year to December when *Robinson Crusoe* landed on the stage with Glasgow's own Marie Loftus as Principal Boy. She had been discovered by Christina Baylis at the Scotia in Stockwell Street, and was enjoying the same national acclaim as Vesta Tilley.

In 1890 the Royal staged an evening of Tableaux to raise funds for the newly formed Scottish Artists Benevolent Association. The Pen-and-Pencil Club (whose members included Michael Simons and Henry Irving) and the Glasgow Society of Musicians "furnished the human material" which was shaped by William Glover into picturesque groups such as "The Judgement of Paris", "Cleopatra before Caesar", "Burns and Highland Mary." It was 1891 by the time all weeks settled into a pattern. Some productions of burlesque or opera would interchange with the Royalty a few months later. To buy tickets in advance the Royal's box plan could be seen at Paterson's music store in Buchanan Street and at the Royalty, but not at the Royal.

Many of William Glover's achievements were money making successes such as *Rob Roy*, *Old Mortality*, and *The Lady of the Lake* which was originally dramatised by Henry Webb of Queens Theatre, Dublin. These were now presented in association with Howard and Wyndham. Glover's scenic success continued with a new production - *Marmion*. In order to get the local colour right he spent months in the Border countryside,

MARIE LOFTUS,

AN IDEAL PRINCIPAL BOY,

Now appearing with enormous success as

"Robinson Crusoe,"

THEATRE ROYAL, GLASGOW.

ABOVE
Marie Loftus

making sketches, getting the correct atmosphere, and discovering new inns. This was the first stage play anywhere of Sir Walter Scott's *Marmion*, and was adapted by the Glasgow born poet and playwright Robert W Buchanan. John Howard directed, and both Howard and Wyndham acted in it, as did Mrs Wyndham. The *Marmion* overture and incidental music was composed

PAUL ROTTENBURG

ABOVE
Paul Rottenburg

Paul Rottenburg was born in Danzig in 1846 and came to Glasgow as a chemical merchant, becoming President of the Glasgow Chamber of Commerce. He was an associate of the Society of Musicians formed in 1884, a convener of the 1888 International Exhibition, and a founding benefactor of the Glasgow Grand Opera Society. Around this time there were over a 1000 Germans living and working in the city, including Otto Phillipi managing director of threadmakers J&P Coats, the largest industrial company in Britain, and Henry Dübs head of one of the largest British locomotive builders.

A founder member of the **Glasgow Society of Musicians** was Julius Seligmann, its first President, who came from Hamburg where he was principal violinist in the private orchestra of the Duke of Brunswick. He became the conductor of the Glasgow Choral Union a few years after its start in 1843, and founded the St Cecilia Musical Society. Another founder was William Mackie Miller the tonic sol-fa pioneer, and Hamish McCunn, composer and conductor. Members included Sir Frederic Cowen, composer, conductor of the Scottish Orchestra and an exponent of Beethoven; and Sir Charles Grove who had been an engineer in Glasgow working at Napier's engineering and shipbuilding company before becoming secretary to the 1851 Great Exhibition in London, and then compiler of Grove's Dictionary of Music and Musicians. Alfred Carpenter, music director to the Howard & Wyndham theatres in Glasgow, became a member in 1904 and Vice President in the 1920s, and Philip Simons, lawyer brother of the Royal's chairman, became Vice-President from 1913 but declined the Presidency.

by Professor Alexander C Mackenzie, the Principal of the Royal Academy of Music in London from 1888 to 1924. During the opening evening in April 1891 telegrams were read out by Mr Howard:

> Every success to-night, my dear Howard, with Marmion. You will beat your record even with Rob Roy and the Lady of the Lake. My heartiest remembrance to Glasgow friends. — HENRY IRVING.

> Wishing you big success for Marmion. Just home from Australia.

Kindest regards to all Glasgow friends. Shall be ready to play Rob Roy next season on a kangaroo.— JOHN LAURENCE TOOLE.

Glover always meant to follow up the *Marmion* success with Scott's *Lord of the Isles* and the libretto was actually written by a Glasgow man, but it has never been produced.

One of the plays in 1892 was *The White Star*, a new melodrama written by Tom Craven, "with a wonderful mechanical scene illustrative of sinking an American liner in Mid-Atlantic." Vesta Tilley's Burlesque Company appeared for six nights in October and she came back in the pantomime *Dick Whittington*. Sarah Bernhardt was the summer attraction in July 1894, with queues at all the doors.

Glasgow's wealth and population kept increasing, as did the sizes of the theatres. The Gaiety became linked with Moss Empires and advertised itself in 1891 as "The City's Foremost Variety Theatre, and the only one lit by electricity in Scotland." It had plans to double in size. In 1894 the Royal got modern – and went electric. The Baillie magazine liked what it saw:

> The interior of the Theatre Royal has been newly decorated by Thomas Lawrie & Co. The entrance hall presents a harmony of buffs and blues. On the upper portion of the walls leading to the circle are a series of heads of the poets painted on a buff ground linked by festoons. The auditorium is lavishly decorated with festoons and figure ornaments on ivory white and gold ground, and the general effect when seen under the electric light is brilliant and pleasing.

At Simons' suggestion a combined annual dinner each winter was started for the staffs of the Royal and the Royalty, toasts held, and speeches made by the directors about the year coming. The theatre was hired by organisations in the city. Once, when Prime Minister Gladstone came in July 1892 to give an important speech at the height of the

Irish Home Rule debate, there were no public halls available. Walter Freer, the Corporation's Halls manager came to the rescue. He arranged for the Royal to be used, and the tickets at 5/- each were sold out very quickly by the Liberal committee, with the result there was no room for the newspaper reporters – who all decided to boycott the speech unless they were accommodated. Freer contacted the leading editor, and long before the meeting started the reporters were admitted through the stage door and dropped from the stage into

ABOVE
Pen-and-Pencil Club
Tableaux
1890

DAVID HEILBRON

David Heilbron was born in Breda, Holland in 1844 and came to Glasgow when age 16 to join the business run by his uncle. But instead of entering the drapery trade he became

an importer of cigars, and his wife Fanny an importer of cordials. With his young family he stayed for a time at Holland House, 6 Rose Street, Garnethill, moving later to India Street. He expanded into the whisky business with his firm David Heilbron & Sons becoming distillers, blenders, bottlers and brokers. The malt distilleries were in Brora, Campbeltown, Tullibardine, Glenlivet and Skye. He was an active member of the Jewish community and a founder of Garnethill Synagogue. In 1893 Heilbron and Simons founded the Jewish Literary and Social Society.

His son **Granville Heilbron** joined him in the theatre, wines and whisky businesses, succeeding his father as a managing director of WH Chaplin & Company, in Gorbals, known for its Long John whisky. Granville

TOP
Granville Heilbron
RIGHT
David Heilbron
BOTTOM
Vivien Heilbron

was a member of the Music and Entertainments committee of the Empire Exhibition 1938, while Eric de Banzie the journalist son of the Royal's music director was on its Press Club committee. Another Heilbron son was the distinguished chemist Professor Sir Ian Heilbron. They would all have been pleased to know that a great-grand-daughter Vivien Heilbron would become an actress of the stage, television and film – including the Theatre Royal. As did her sister Lorna.

the orchestra pit. The Grand Old Man's speech was widely read.

In his love of theatre Simons was joined by the Heilbron family. David Heilbron was a wine merchant who became a whisky distiller, and was one of the founders of Garnethill Synagogue. His uncle's young daughters were also attracted to the limelight. In 1865 two

of the ladies in the Glover Company of artistes at Dunlop Street were Esther, age 21, and Rose Heilbron, 17. For a number of years in the 1870s a third cousin Dinah Heilbron was an actress and theatrical dancer at the Royal in Cowcaddens. In 1878, when age 25, she had a daughter. The father's name was not put on the birth certificate, but the baby's name given was Florrie Glover Heilbron.

Simons and Heilbron had a common interest with Robert Crawford who was in the whisky trade in Leith, and had become chairman of Edinburgh's Theatre Royal. Michael Simons outlined his plans for theatre on a grander scale.

Howard & Wyndham Ltd

In many cities the public were now being invited to invest in theatre businesses by buying shares to be quoted on the Stock Exchanges. Michael Simons and his colleagues put their heads together. However the first off in Glasgow, in January 1895, was Glasgow Empire Palace Ltd which brought together the Gaiety and Scotia theatres. The money raised paid for the Gaiety's demolition and its rebuilding as the Empire Palace, designed by Frank Matcham.

In February Simons unveiled his new venture. Showbusiness was big business. Members of the public were invited to buy shares, which could be traded on the Glasgow Stock Exchange and on the Edinburgh Stock Exchange, in a new company – Howard & Wyndham Ltd. It would continue for 100 years.

The company set out "to carry on the businesses of theatre proprietors, lessees, or occupiers, agents and box-office keepers; to produce or arrange for the production of stage plays, operas, pantomimes, concerts, and generally of every description of theatrical, musical, spectacular, or other entertainment. And to act as caterers for public enter-tainments, exhibitions or amusements

... Madame Sarah Bernhardt ...
Appearing at the Theatre Royal on Wednesday at one Matinee only
Born, 23rd October, 1844.   Height, 5ft. 6½in.   Weight, 9 stone 4 lbs.
Earns £2,000 per week during the Season.

of any kind; to organise companies or combinations; to arrange and conduct tours; to enter into engagements with actors, artistes, musicians, and other persons."

Its launch was well received and the promoters Michael Simons, chairman, David Heilbron, and Robert Crawford were joined on the board by John Howard and Fred Wyndham as joint managing directors. The secretaries ap-pointed were Carter, Greig & McEwan, chartered accountants, Edinburgh; and the auditors were Rattray Brothers & Cairney, chartered accountants,

ABOVE
Sarah Bernhardt
in Glasgow

Robert Crawford

Robert Crawford was a whisky manufacturer and stayed at New Bank, Trinity Road, Leith. He was the son of Thomas Crawford, master baker and part of William Crawford & Sons, biscuit manufacturers of Leith and Liverpool. In 1875, at the age of 36, he bought what had

Above
Encore *water jug*

been Bernard & Co's distillery in Leith. By 1890 his firm was described as "distillers, methylated spirits and British wine manufacturers." His whisky was named *"Encore"* which used the advertising slogan *"they ask for it Again and Again."* It was a double distilled whisky and its newspaper adverts had medical endorsements attached, with The Lancet calling it a "very wholesome and pleasant whisky."

Edinburgh Theatre Royal Ltd was formed in 1875, after a fire that year, to rebuild the theatre in Broughton Road, using the architect Charles Phipps. It had another fire in 1884, requiring Phipps' services again. Robert Crawford bought a share in the company in 1883 and progressively became its chairman and largest shareholder a few years later.

The wider family business of William Crawford & Sons opened their new headquarters and biscuit factory at 40 Elbe Street, Leith in 1913 in what had previously been a bonded warehouse, presumably of Robert Crawford who died the year before. Their large range of biscuits, and assorted shortbread in the round tin, was of course strictly teetotal.

Glasgow. Both firms would continue with the new company for decades to come.

Over the previous five years the average profits of the theatres managed by Howard and Wyndham (two in Glasgow and one in Edinburgh) were £7,356 a year, being the total for three. The existing manager of the Edinburgh Theatre Royal did not make his books available but it was considered that a reasonable profit could be earned from it from 1895 onwards. (By way of an aside, the Glover family at the old Theatre Royal, Dunlop Street, in the 1860s made profits of between £2,000 and £3,000 a year.) For their interests James Howard and Fred Wyndham were paid £60,000 in total, half being shares in the new company and half by cash. Payment of the cash element had to be delayed for almost a year, because of the breakout of fire at the Royal and the need to have the architect and contractors on site without delay.

Fire brigade again

Electric light had been introduced

in the Royal at the end of 1894 when Glasgow Corporation provided electricity for private users in the city's central area and the theatre gaslights became redundant. Indeed, Baillie Simons had switched on Glasgow's supply of this new energy. However on the evening of 28th February 1895 fire destroyed the stage, auditorium and roof of the main building ....occurring about 5.30pm when gas from an unused gas jet escaped, probably as a result of frost, ignited at a guarded heater, always kept alight near the prompter's box, and caught nearby scenery. Fortunately there were no customers in the building at that early time. Staff raised the alarm, but the flames escaped under the iron safety curtain into the auditorium. The horse tramcars with their homeward traffic were diverted and the fire brigade with four steam engines took five hours to extinguish the blaze.

The scene dock, the carpenter's shop and the principal dressing rooms escaped serious damage. Likewise the manager's office behind the dress circle, the saloon bar and main staircase also escaped damage. However all the scenery of the special productions of *Lady of the Lake*, *Rob Roy*, and *Marmion* was destroyed.

Following the fire Howard & Wyndham Ltd arranged with the Grand Theatre for some of the shows booked for the Royal and the Royalty to appear at the Grand until the Royal could reopen in September. For example Carl Rosa Opera, booked for the Royal, would go to the Royalty and the Royalty

LEFT
Programme of Events, *one week in November, 1893*

productions for these weeks went to the Grand. Before that they had tried to secure the use of St Andrew's Halls and Bostock's Circus in New City Road without success – one reason being the difficulty in insuring scenery and props to be moved there.

The builders Morrison & Mason Ltd were called upon to rebuild the theatre under the eye of Charles Phipps. They were the builders of the new Municipal Chambers in George Square, completed in 1888, and of many other prominent buildings including the General Post Office in George Square and the Stock Exchange in Buchanan Street. Small changes to Phipps' original design included the removal of the boxes at the back of the dress-circle, and removal of the boxes flanking the proscenium at the upper circle. The top tier now had the same seating throughout, the split between amphitheatre and gallery was

PROSPECTUS FOR HOWARD & WYNDHAM LTD

This Company is formed to carry out an arrangement for the amalgamation
under the same management of

The Royal Lyceum, Edinburgh
The Theatre Royal, Edinburgh
The Theatre Royal, Glasgow, and
The Royalty Theatre, Glasgow.

The Royal Lyceum, Edinburgh, and the Theatre Royal and Royalty Theatre, Glasgow, are
at present managed by Messrs Howard and Wyndham, who have made arrangements for
taking over the management of the Theatre Royal, Edinburgh, at Whitsunday 1895.

Messrs Howard and Wyndham have agreed to make over their interests in the four Theatres to the Company. These Theatres are well designed and substantially built. For comfort
and safety they are perhaps unrivalled, and in the elegance of their appointments they rank
amongst the best in the provinces.

A combination of four Theatres of the standing and importance of those to be managed
by the Company will possess great and obvious advantages. The Company will be able to
arrange with the best Touring Companies on favourable terms, and to effect economies in
various directions. The Company through the close relations established by the Managing
Directors with some of the largest Provincial Theatres in England will have the further
advantage of co-operation with these theatres in arranging tours.

Messrs Howard and Wyndham, who have proved themselves popular and successful theatrical managers in Edinburgh, Glasgow and elsewhere, have agreed to act as Managing
Directors for not less than seven years. It is intended to make arrangements to retain the
services of the acting managers and other officials. Messrs Howard and Wyndham have
undertaken not to sell the £20,000 of ordinary shares they are to take for seven years, and
not to connect themselves with any theatre in Scotland other than the Company's during
that time. These and the other arrangements they have made show their confidence in the
success of the Company.

OPPOSITE
Cutaway drawing *of
the theatre building
by John Hepburn, as
of 1895*

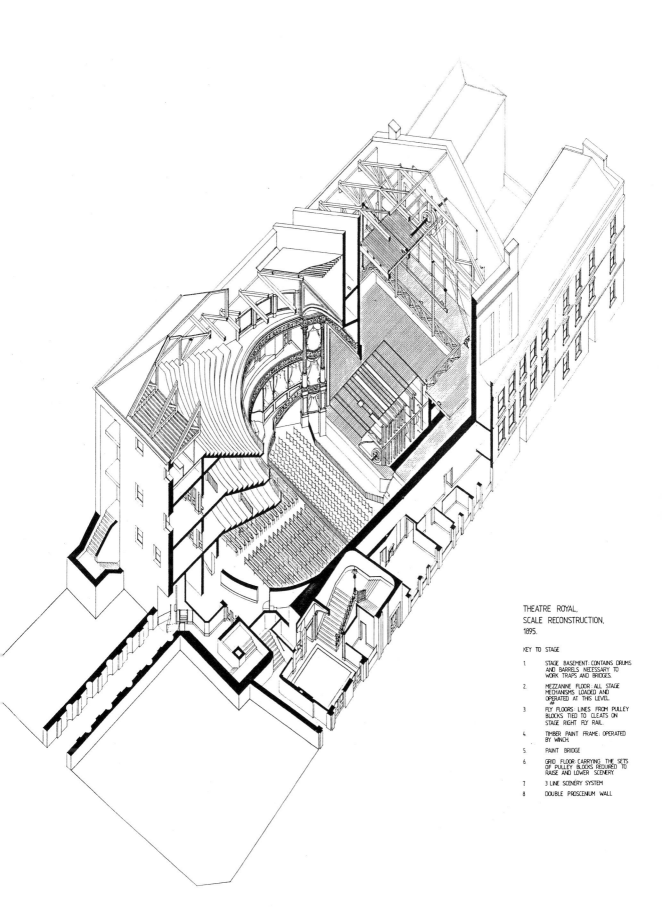

THEATRE ROYAL,
SCALE RECONSTRUCTION,
1895.

KEY TO STAGE

1   STAGE BASEMENT: CONTAINS DRUMS
     AND BARRELS NECESSARY TO
     WORK TRAPS AND BRIDGES.

2   MEZZANINE FLOOR: ALL STAGE
     MECHANISMS LOADED AND
     OPERATED AT THIS LEVEL.

3   FLY FLOORS: LINES FROM PULLEY
     BLOCKS TIED TO CLEATS ON
     STAGE RIGHT FLY RAIL.

4   TIMBER PAINT FRAME: OPERATED
     BY WINCH.

5   PAINT BRIDGE.

6   GRID FLOOR: CARRYING THE SETS
     OF PULLEY BLOCKS REQUIRED TO
     RAISE AND LOWER SCENERY.

7   3 LINE SCENERY SYSTEM.

8   DOUBLE PROSCENIUM WALL.

Michael Simons and the International Exhibitions

Michael Simons' committee for Entertainments and Refreshments was very much responsible for the pulse each day of the 1888 International Exhibition at Kelvingrove with a range of musical events, catering venues, amusement kiosks, the Switchback Railway, Ballini's anchored hot air balloon for viewing from 1000 feet, launches, gondolas and Venetian gondoliers on the river Kelvin, sporting contests in its Exhibition stadium, illuminations and firework displays in the late evenings.

The Grand Hall - complete with its mighty organ - held an audience of 3000; its platform accommodating over 400 performers, where military bands from the Armed Services and public bands from Britain and overseas joined with the Glasgow Choral Union and other choirs. The resident Exhibition Military Band made its debut in May under Edward de Banzie of the Royal and Royalty theatres. His orchestra of 50 players was paid £150 per week, in

ABOVE
International Exhibition
1888

BELOW
International Exhibition
1901

total, for their four months' contract of afternoon and evening playing. De Banzie invited guest soloist players from around the country to join for a few days at a time. When playing outside the Hall the Exhibition Band could attract about 10,000 around the North Kiosk, where Lord Kelvin's statue now stands. He conducted popular as well as demanding pieces. On playing Kappey's Military Fantasia in July complete with pyrotechnics "some strong-minded women and weak-minded men in Park Circus made complaints of the noise of the bursting rockets and maroons." A veto was put on the fireworks – for a while.

J Lyons & Co had one of the many catering establishments – the Bishops Palace Temperance Café where the waitresses wore Mary Queen of Scots costumes – which did so well that the firm decided to copy Glasgow with all its special tearooms and open tearooms in London, fully established there ten years later as Lyons Corner Houses. The founders of Lyons, which became the country's largest food empire, were the Salmon and Gluckstein families with whom the Simons were connected. During the Exhibition they gave free hospitality to the mem-

removed. For increased safety the auditorium walls were reconstructed in solid masonry. The theatre magazine stressed the new features for safety:

> One very important part of the construction of this Theatre which has never before been accomplished is that there are two Proscenium Walls 10 feet apart, and following somewhat the lines of the Pillars in the Proscenium Boxes. These walls are carried right up, and the Stage Roof and Auditorium Roof are thus entirely distinct, and separated with a clear space of 10 feet between them, there being also a Fireproof Roof formed immediately above the Proscenium Arch. The Stage Opening is filled with a Fire Resisting Curtain worked by hydraulica.

Once again the Royal opened, more accurately re-opened, to a full house on 9th September 1895, with George Alexander and his actors from the St James Theatre, London, to be followed the next week by Beerbohm Tree and his company. The Scotsman wrote:

> The new Glasgow Theatre-Royal was opened last night and there was a brilliant audience and a brilliant performance. So faithfully has the architect followed the model of the former theatre that but for the knowledge that it was destroyed six months ago those present might have imagined themselves in the old building, refurbished, redecorated and in some respects structurally improved.

ABOVE
Marie Tempest
popular actress

F W Wyndham introduced Mr Phipps the architect and thanked him and Messrs Morrison & Mason the contractors for their untiring efforts in so short a space of time. He spoke of the role of caterers (the word used most often as caterers of entertainment) and ended by saying "And now, ladies and gentlemen,

△

bers of all the bands. Perhaps it was a source there that the Baillie magazine reported in July 1888:

> "They say" that it is quite possible that Messrs Lyons may become lessees of a theatre in this city. They are already identified with the London Pavilion.

This was close to the mark. Before the month was out Simons had encouraged Mr Howard and Mr Wyndham to take up the lease of the Theatre Royal.

The 1901 International Exhibition also took place in Kelvingrove attracting even more visitors, this time over 11 million people, almost double 1888's record, and making it the most successful exhibition staged in Britain to that year. By personal interviews Michael Simons enlisted the co-operation of America's President McKinlay and other leaders to support the event. He was again convener in charge of music and recreation, with a similar range of amusements including the gondoliers affectionately known as Signor McHokey and Signor McCokey. The mighty Lewis organ in its Concert Hall is today's organ inside Kelvingrove Art Gallery.

BAILLIE MICHAEL SIMONS AND CIVIC DUTY

In Glasgow Corporation Michael Simons was one of a small number of the elected councillors who had started from very little. He was elected in 1883, and became a founder of the Glasgow Radical Association in 1885 encouraging working men into politics. He soon became a Baillie, and is understood to have been offered the Lord Provostship in 1888 but declined it due to his many other commitments. He retired from the Corporation in 1892 and became a deputy Lord Lieutenant of the city in 1905. Reviewing his career the Glasgow Herald proudly reported:

> He was the first Jewish person to be elected to a position of public trust in Scotland. He was a close student of social questions and on most subjects which moved him he was a powerful and passionate speaker.

In the aftermath of the crash of the City of Glasgow Bank in the winter of 1878 he was an active member of the Relief Committee to aid the beleaguered shareholders, chaired by Lord Provost Sir William Collins, especially in the feeding of thousands of needy families. He was an originator in 1886 of the International Exhibition to be held at Kelvingrove in 1888, and was prominent again in the International Exhibition of 1901. Inside the Corporation he was responsible for a major investigation into the finances of the city and the running of the City Chamberlain's office. In the 1890s a public committee, with Simons as sub-convener, "introduced bright entertainments at a cost within the reach of all." These were evening concerts on Mondays in the wintertime; the parks already had bands playing

▼

that we have successfully launched the good ship Theatre-Royal, I trust, manned by a good crew, she will sail prosperously on; and all the owners wish for and hope is, provided they give you a good bill of fare, that you will supply us with a large complement of passengers."

A special guest of honour was Mrs Howard, whose husband James had suddenly died a few months before. The management was well paid and because they earned over £160 a year their details were notified to the Inland Revenue so that a tax inspector could visit them. The Royal's manager was Thomas Aynsley Cooke, age 34, an actor and opera performer, living in Dalhousie Street. His annual salary was £208. The managing director, now only Fred Wyndham, was paid £1000 a year with a bonus on top of that of 5 per cent of the profits. Chairman Michael Simons received a fee of £157, and David Heilbron and Robert Crawford each £78. The dividends from their shareholdings more than compensated. Other staff at the Royal were:

E T de Banzie, Orchestra Conductor
(£218 a year)
R Beith, Bill Poster, one year only
(£260)
T F Dunn, Scenic Artist
(£234)
William Morgan, Stage Manager
(£260)

Each theatre employed a permanent

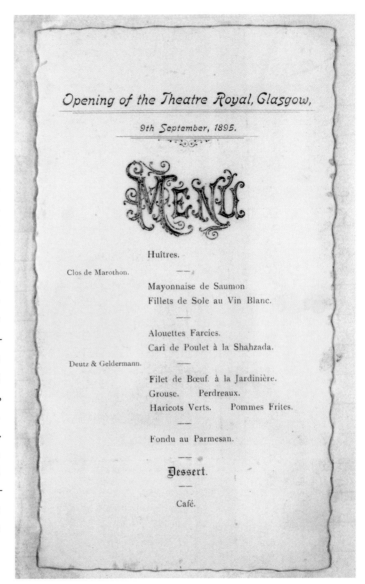

Opening of the Theatre Royal, Glasgow,

9th September, 1895.

MENU

Huîtres.

Clos de Marothon.   ———

Mayonnaise de Saumon
Fillets de Sole au Vin Blanc.

Alouettes Farcies.
Cari de Poulet à la Shahzada.

Deutz & Geldermann.   ———

Filet de Bœuf. à la Jardinière.
Grouse.   Perdreaux.
Haricots Verts.   Pommes Frites.

Fondu au Parmesan.

———

Dessert.

———

Café.

staff and stage crew of 15-20 people.

The manager's responsibilities were recorded to allay the fears of the insurance company:

DUTIES OF MANAGER
To receive drawings from the Theatre and deposit same in Bank and generally superintend the Management of the

ABOVE
Celebration Menu
for directors and guests, September 1895

△

in summer evenings.

This came about when an **Association for Improving the Social Condition of the People** was formed at a public meeting in St Andrew's Halls in 1892, comprising the Corporation, employers and church organisations. Initial studies were presented to the meeting recommending actions to be taken along the lines of "Labour Centres"; "Housing of the Poor" and "Recreation for the People". Simons' sub-committee on Recreation reported:

That while during summer the performance of music by military bands in the public parks forms an important part in the social life of the people, yet the cessation of this in winter is especially to be deplored, when, in consequence of the inclemency of the weather, there is the greater need, for supplying places to which crowds may resort, who at present scarcely have any resource except the public house if they leave what are frequently the one-roomed and crowded tenements in which they dwell.

It will be necessary to erect on a large scale and within each of the most densely populated districts, a covered place, which shall be as free as possible to the people, and where music or other attractions may be carried on.

ABOVE
Municipal Buildings
1890

One such centre at least, should be placed in each of the North, South, East and West of the city, Kelvingrove being a place which can accommodate the one for the West.

In all great blocks of workmen's houses accommodation should be kept for recreation-rooms, under the charge of the commission, and where a caretaker is resident....

It is not clear whether all of this came about. Increasingly from the 1850s the Abstainers Union, the Band of Hope, and the Good Templars all organised popular soirees, concerts and festivals combining serious music, music hall acts and choirs. The city's population was growing towards 1 million and more was required. The Corporation started its Penny Concerts in the afternoons at the City Hall. In 1892 during the long running East End Industrial Exhibition, held in Dennistoun, Simons and his Recreation Committee were applauded for creating its "bright surroundings, high class music, and attractions of a pure and elevating character."

▼

Theatre. He is responsible to the directors for the acts of the whole staff of the Theatre. Weekly returns are made to the company secretaries, audited monthly by auditors. Books balanced monthly. *"Every farthing must be paid into Bank the next day"*

Responsible for the value of stock in the theatre. *"Theatrical Properties, Dresses, etc £1,500, regular inventory book kept."*

Takings on average would be £200-£300 each day.

The value of the *"Carpets, seats, curtains and furnishings"* at the end of the first year for the four theatres was £9,500, of which the largest amount was £3,500 in the Royal.

A typical year 1895/96

The Howard & Wyndham company would remain at the top quality end of theatre in Britain throughout its lifetime, with the Royal its flagship. For the re-opening week, Beerbohm Tree and his fellow actors and actresses presented *Hamlet* on the first night, and for most of the week presented *Trilby*, being the rise to musical stardom in Paris of Trilby the beautiful artists model and laundress, and her sinister mentor Svengali. This was the dramatised version of George du Maurier's new novel of the same name, and which had been serialised in Harper's Magazine in the USA. The Trilby craze was sweeping America. Trilby – hats, hosiery, blouses, jackets, neckties, corsets, scarfs, gloves and shoes. Trilby - waltzes and marches, cocktails and punches, perfumery

and cigars, and even hotels. The craze touched the shores of Britain.

Sinbad the Sailor was Howard & Wyndham Ltd's pantomime for the winter with Marie Loftus and comedian Mark Sheridan, who took up residence in Glasgow. He appeared in many of the company's pantomimes across the country. Of his popular songs, the most remembered nationally are "I Do Like to be Beside the Seaside" which he premiered in 1909 at the Empire in Sauchiehall Street, and "Here We Are Again" in 1914. The seasons got into their stride with the Carl Rosa Opera performing *The Flying Dutchman*, *Mignon*, *The Meistersingers* (the first time ever sung in Scotland), *Tannhauser*, *Maritana*, *La Vivandiere*, *Pagliacci*, *Il Trovatore*, and *The Bohemian Girl*.

Musical plays and a farce *The Gay Parisienne* were followed by Sir Henry Irving and Ellen Terry treading the boards in *King Arthur*, and *The Merchant of Venice*.

Lady of the Lake was presented with "an increased orchestra and an augmented chorus," and very correctly advertised itself with "entirely new scenery by William Glover" because everything previous had been burned! The invention of the telephone was proving even more useful with towns now being linked by new national trunk services. Ada Blanche appeared in *The Telephone Girl* along with The Tiller Troupe of Dancers and a thirty member Chorus of Telephone Girls. It came back the next year by public demand. George Alexander took the

TOP
Mark Sheridan

MIDDLE
Telephone Girl *poster*

BOTTOM
George Robey

△

The People's Palace and Winter Gardens opening a few years later in Glasgow Green was one outcome of the expressed need to have buildings for recreation and music, to reach more people. New model lodging houses for working men, complete with a recreation room, opened under the Corporation, and were copied a year later by London City Council.

Another organisation, the Glasgow United YMCA, built a geographic network on the lines suggested, with the Southern Institute at Eglinton Toll, the Western Institute at Peel Street, Partick, and the Eastern Institute in Bridgeton. Each had large halls, committee and recreation rooms, library, and cafeteria. The Central Institute with these facilities and with a concert hall, hotel, lounges and restaurant was built as the YMCA headquarters in Bothwell Street, linked next door to the huge Christian Institute designed by Simons' architect John McLeod.

The winter of the same year as the Association's recommendations, 1892, saw unemployment affecting a number of trades in Britain. In Glasgow the shipyards, cotton and textile mills were hard hit. The Corporation paid unemployed men 1/- a day to work on special public projects, but some other cities paid 2/-. The Trades Council agitated for a better wage at such times of travail, for enough to feed a family. It would be twenty years before a national public safety net was introduced for the unemployed. To help families, charitable organisations provided breakfasts and soup dinners in halls, and some music halls, across the city.

Ex-Baillie Simons and two others headed the Glasgow Unemployment Relief Committee, which uniquely had the confidence of the Trades Council. Reporting on 150,000 meals already provided, and a butcher firm who provided 3/4lbs of meat to each of the unemployed households for their New Year dinner, Michael Simons appealed again in January 1893 "for the relief to continue for another two months at least, such is the extent of the prevailing distress." At each regular appeal his firm Simons, Jacobs & Co was often the largest donor. The same month at a demonstration in Glasgow Green, with speakers looking for more than temporary help, Keir Hardie MP advised the unemployed men to turn out of their lairs and hovels and parade their misery in the street, "demand not bread, but demand work that you might earn bread."

MICHAEL SIMONS AND GARNETHILL SYNAGOGUE

In the worship of God and in matters temporal the Simons family took a keen interest in the welfare of their fellow citizens. In the 1850s Benjamin Simons became treasurer of his congregation around the Candleriggs and arranged for a flat to be purchased at 240 George Street, at the corner of John Street, and converted to a synagogue. He was joined later by his son Michael and by David Heilbron in 1871. From 1872 to 1896 Michael Simons was secretary to the Glasgow Hebrew Congregation.

The two Simons were founders of the new Garnethill Synagogue, the first purpose built

Opposite
At The Stage by J.M.
Hamilton
1895

▼

lead in the swashbuckler *The Prisoner of Zenda*, the first dramatisation of the new novel based in a fictional Ruritania. The Trilby craze was still continuing, and the *Trilby* play returned. AF Reid & Sons, bakers with branches in Scotland and Johannesburg, sold Trilby Pies for 1d each, made at their Crossmyloof Cakery which claimed to be "The Largest Cakery in The World" producing 30,000 cakes per day. The annual staff dances of firms in the city were now known as the Trilby Dance.

In the depths of winter the military melodrama of *Tommy Atkins* made its mark – a second Boer War was getting nearer. For his next pantomime Fred Wyndham directed, and his stage manager William Morgan (who was the first husband of Mrs JB Howard) wrote *Robin Hood and The Babes in the Wood* starring music hall's favourite male impersonator Vesta Tilley as Robin Hood. The theatre's scenic manager T F Dunn oversaw the design of all eleven scenes, two of which were by Ernest Glover. In those days the designer of each scene was credited in the programmes. Vesta Tilley's husband successfully created a chain of variety theatres including the future Alhambra.

Rolling through and rolling in

The Glasgow Subway started its services in December 1896, adding to the city's good transport and bringing more business, although in a quiet moment in the theatre basement you can feel the trains travelling through the tunnels under a corner of the site. The theatre's

ABOVE
Garnethill Synagogue
(left)
Interior
(right)
Exterior

synagogue in Scotland, which opened in 1878 at 29 Garnet Street (later called Hill Street), where Benjamin laid the foundation stone the year before. The architect was John McLeod who had been chosen by Michael Simons to design their fruit auction hall and warehouses. McLeod's assistant was Edward Hay who went on to design the Scottish Co-operatve Wholesale Society's buildings in Morrison Street.

Michael Simons was also the first member and founder of **Lodge Montefiore, Glasgow** in 1888. Like all masonic lodges it is open to men regardless of race or creed. Its annual divine service is held in Garnethill Synagogue, most of the members being Jewish. Simons provided hospitality at his house in Bath Street. On occasion the Lodge members would adjourn to Charles Rupprecht's restaurant at 183 Hope Street, which became the Strand Restaurant, where "after a light and excellent supper, entertainment was provided by artiste Brothers Frank Knight, J B Bowie, W F Frame, G C H McNaught and A P Cubie." Owning theatres had its benefits!

advertising agents Wilson & Co of Jamaica Street introduced an outsize glossy brochure called The Glasgow Weekly Programme - advertising the coming entertainments in theatres, music halls, concert halls, zoos, rinks, and exhibitions. It was distributed free to hotels, stores, reading rooms, clubs, bars, tea-rooms and restaurants, which now boasted about their French, German, Swiss, Italian as well as British cooks. The Theatre Royal and the Royalty Theatre were always printed at the top of the list. Picture houses were added, and it continued to the 1920s. The Royal and the Royalty each continued to have equal prominence in advertising and content. Shows in one theatre could later repeat in its own place or in the other. The only differences were that

Carl Rosa seasons were Royal occasions and D'Oyle Carte seasons were Royalty occasions. Pantomime was the preserve of the Theatre Royal.

During the Naughty Nineties musical plays multiplied, many of them starting in America. The vintage fare of the melodrama of *East Lynne* was made up for by the musical variety show *A Trip to Chinatown*. The Royal's *Jeannie Deans* packed the theatre. American comedies were followed by a song and dance play *The Bicycle Girl* and Little Tich headed up new songs and dances in *Lord Tom Noddy*. A musical play *The Geisha* by Greenbank and Jones opened in 1899 and returned the next year, continuing the country's fascination with Japan in art and trade. Japan was invited to study shipbuilding on the Clyde, where much of her new navy was being built.

Summertime shows ran for long seasons starting each June. Holidays from work were not yet universal and entertainments were sought close at hand. One centred on four weeks of a Howard & Wyndham special production of Shakespeare's fairy comedy *A Midsummer Night's Dream*, with the resident orchestra under a Carl Rosa conductor. *Rob Roy* was a summer favourite and in 1899 and 1900 Wyndham's money-maker *Kenilworth* attracted the crowds. Sarah Bernhardt made her annual visits in July complete with her French company and orchestra, one afternoon only, sometimes to play *La Tosca*. She had first come to Glasgow to Charles Bernard's Gaiety and then to the Royalty before entering the Royal. As ever, glossy souvenir programmes were printed for the occasion and the seat prices were astronomical.

For a summer season, John Tiller presented a terpsichorean burletta *High Jinks, or Fun on the Sand* including his Tiller Quartette, the Teutonic Trio, the Excelsior Troupe of 24 children dancers, and a Grand Ballet of Fifty, all suitable for warm evenings; and repeated in coming years. John Tiller came from Manchester where his cotton business had closed, and he turned to his interest in theatre seeing the opportunity to instil discipline and training to chorus lines. In a few years his Tiller Girls were dancing in Europe and America. One August *The Derby Winner* written by Augustus Harris had reporters describing it as an example

of "the machine-made spectacular play including its racing scene to the finishing tape." Audiences could catch their breath in *Pygmalion and Galatea* by WS Gilbert, or choose to watch Dan Leno as the comedian in the musical *Orlando Dando*.

Serious drama came from Beerbohm Tree and his wife in their chosen classics; Henry Irving and Ellen Terry; and George Alexander led in *The Ambassador*. The Wilson Barrett drama company came back from their tour in Australia. Carl Rosa Opera continued to pack the house each spring and autumn, while a new farce *Charley's Aunt* became a regular favourite, written by Brandon Thomas and first produced by a former D'Oyly Carte Opera actor. At the height of the Boer War the need for diversion continued with the Royal staging a premiere of Robert Louis Stevenson's action romance *Prince Otto*, which he had written just after *Treasure Island*. The setting was the imaginary state of Grunewald somewhere near Bohemia. Also new was the dramatisation of JM Barrie's novel *The Little Minister* with the Lord Provost Sir David Richmond present at its opening.

In sporting circles football had grown to be king. Glasgow had staged the first inter-national competition years before and even ladies now had their women's football teams. The pantomime, *Puss in Boots*, contained special scenes devised by Fred Wyndham; one was a grand procession of well-known famous plays, for which he bought the costumes in Paris; another was a football field introducing

MICHAEL SIMONS AND THE FINE ARTS

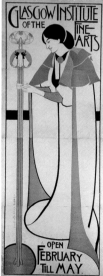

TOP
Institute Exhibition
poster

BOTTOM
McLellan Galleries
marble staircase

Members of the Glover family who had operated the new and old Royal theatres were also painters. Michael Simons, the new owner of the Royal and head of Howard & Wyndham Ltd, was equally interested in fine art. He was an early member of the Glasgow Art Club, and of the Royal Glasgow Institute of the Fine Arts which held exhibitions each year from 1861 in the Corporation's Archibald McLellan galleries on the north side of Sauchiehall Street. From 1880 the Institute changed to grand premises on the other side at number 175 designed by architect John Burnet, but the building itself was never very successful artistically and financially. It never changed to electric lighting; perhaps the budding Old Masters seemed more evocative in gas lighting.

Simons was a leading member of the association which campaigned for a city art gallery to be built in the West End Park in Kelvingrove. Once the city's municipal art collection had moved from the Corporation Galleries, on the north side of Sauchiehall Street, to the new Kelvingrove Art Galleries & Museum in 1901 – opening in time for that year's International Exhibition, and paid for out of the proceeds of the 1888 Exhibition - the Institute opened negotiations with the Corporation to return to their former home. Michael Simons was appointed Chairman of the Institute in 1902 and remained in office till 1919. The former Corporation building was upgraded and its interior extensively remodelled and made available to the Institute, with the shops at the front redesigned as *Les Magasins des Tuilleries* owned by Trerons with their advanced ideas about display technologies and where luncheons and teas were accompanied by the music of the Tuilleries Ladies Orchestra.

The last annual exhibition in the old Burnet galleries was 1911, the Jubilee year of the Fine Arts Institute and was regarded as a celebration of its increased standing in the United Kingdom. Simons arranged the sale of its premises to its neighbour Sir Andrew Pettigrew, of Pettigrew & Stephens, one of Glasgow's many distinctive departmental stores. The Institute's first exhibition in the new Galleries was in September 1913, with a record 53,000 visiting the Exhibition, and 6000 senior pupils attending from schools of the Glasgow School Board. The Institute Council purchased four paintings and donated them to Kelvingrove as a thank you to the Corporation in assisting the formation of the new Galleries in Sauchiehall Street. At the banquet inaugurating their new building Chairman Simons said:

> Much is being done in the city, and I hold the view that the duties which the Institute are performing ought to belong to the Corporation. I venture to suggest that we should have in Glasgow the municipalisation of Art.

"the likenesses of numerous followers of the leather." *Aladdin* in 1900 starred Scotland's Harry Tate, when top billing was moving to the Dame and not so much the Principal Boy. The comedian's best remembered phrases are "Goodbye-eeeeee" which inspired a wartime song and "I don't think so!" A year before the panto he made his own short silent films, and moved afterwards into talkies.

Michael Simons addressed the well attended public Annual General Meetings of Howard & Wyndham Ltd in the registered offices in St Andrew's Square, Edinburgh (held every year in March and only once delayed when Britain went on a three-day week in the mid 1970s due to trade union strikes.) He reported steady progress. Annual profits doubled in the first five years, and continued to climb. Simons did not believe in bank overdrafts, cash held at the bank was usually greater than the profits each year. He would borrow only using a small mortgage when any new theatre was built or bought.

Glasgow in 1901

In 1900 the Alexandra Music Hall lease to a tenant ended and the company took occupation of it "to utilise it in conjunction with improvements to the theatre." Simons engaged James Miller, architect of the International Exhibition 1901, to extend the social areas, toilets and circulation areas for patrons, and add to the rear of the stage a new large scene dock and entranceways from Rutherford Lane.

In the Music Hall, which started at the first floor, a full-height dividing wall was constructed behind its stage. A new Lounge Buffet for the theatre was created in this space above the public house, completed with parquet flooring, and light flooding in from the Hall's very tall windows overlooking Hope Street and Cowcaddens Street. This became the place to be and to be seen. To enter, the patrons climbed the Grand Staircase to the Crush Room foyer then took a few steps down and turned left in to the new lounge complete with its bar counter and gauntress backing on to the Music Hall stage wall. Today it contains the Charter Room, Gibson Room and

LEFT
Kelvingrove Museum & Art Galleries, *official opening. Michael Simons is back left.*

ABOVE
1901 International Exhibition *on opening day*

ABOVE
Phoenix Park
Garscube Road,
Cowcaddens

RIGHT
Maitland Street
Cowcaddens
1911

Boyd Room.

JH Muir in "Glasgow in 1901" describes the city's entertainment district of Sauchiehall Street:

"Sotherns will understand what manner of street this is if we tell them that Piccadilly (although their Charing Cross is wrongly placed) is the Sauchiehall Street of London. At the west end of both are the parks and terraces, at the east end the theatres. Our street has picture galleries like the other – the Royal Institute, the Corporation Galleries, and the rooms of the Royal Water Colour Society; the shops too, of the fashionable milliners, haberdashers, Court photographers, booksellers, universal providers, dealers in old furniture, and the necessary luncheon rooms at Assafrey's and Skinner's.

"It is the brightest and gayest street in Glasgow, the only street of pleasure.

It has more painted buildings and gilded signs than any other, and its sky-line is more irregular, piquant, and full of contrasts. The corner of Wellington Street is a halting place for the tramways, and a great centre for shopping. The English flower-girls that cry their wares in a foreign tongue stand here, and here towards five o'clock the first newsboys with the evening papers arrive panting from the town. On the other side of the street is the Wellington Arcade (where now is Marks & Spencer)…..with the German sausage shop, third-class businesses and faded toy shops. Across Renfrew Street it is continued by the Queen's Arcade, a place of trumpets (in brass), foreign stamps, scraps, transfers, drawing slates, socialistic pamphlets, and old books. At the other end it emerges on Cowcaddens, which is a kind of Old Kent Road, and at night is full of lights, and soldiers, and coster-barrows, and working folk a-shopping. Through the Wellington Arcade come the actors and actresses from Garnethill (where the theatrical birds of passage lodge) on their way to the theatres or to the Hope Street Post Office, whence, in a season of pantomime, principal boys in rustling skirts send off their remittances to their husbands in Queer Street.

"There is another arcade in the neighbourhood – the old, squat, red, ornamented one with the roof gone (taken, perhaps by a creditor doing diligence) that blocks the head of Hope Street opposite to the Theatre Royal. A little shop in it belongs to a bagpipe maker, and here o' nights lonely Celts assemble to hear the wailing of the pipes. Between this roofless little court and Sauchiehall Street is a district inhabited by queer fellows – herbalists, Italian barbers (with the "Apotheosis of Victor Emmanuel" hanging on their walls), vendors of daring photographs and sporting papers, horse dealers, theatrical costumiers, and bookmakers from Flushing who here "meet their old and new friends as per advertisement." From the little squalid lanes round the theatres down to the bright pubs and shady supper-rooms of Sauchiehall Street it is the Soho of Glasgow."

As the new century got to its feet twelve cinemas would add themselves to Sauchiehall Street.

The theatre directors were very busy. In February 1901 they placed the following advertisement in the Glasgow Herald:

SITES for THEATRES

The Directors of Howard & Wyndham Ltd having resolved to build TWO ADDITIONAL THEATRES in GLASGOW, one in the WEST END

between North and Buchanan Street, and one in the SOUTH SIDE between Eglinton and Main Streets, invite Offers of Suitable Sites.

The sites selected had theatres built to the designs of Frank Matcham, with exteriors finished in red sandstone. The first site, again constructed by Morrison & Mason Ltd, opened in 1904 on Bath Street at the corner of Elmbank Street and is the **Kings Theatre**. The second site was in Eglinton Street and opened in 1905 as the **Coliseum Theatre** but under the wing of Moss Empires Ltd. The two companies shared the same firm of secretaries at this time, and the directors ensured that competition would not be too close. The Coliseum staged variety performances and had visits from the Carl Rosa Opera company until 1925 when it became a cinema, the building remaining today. During the 1920s the Coliseum also staged a full production of Wagner's *Ring Cycle*, the acoustics being judged particularly favourable for opera.

Changes through the 1900s

A normal year had some changes in the

TOP
Harry Lauder *in*
Aladdin
1905

BOTTOM
La Loie Fuller *poster*

decade. *Kenilworth* was repeated but the stage versions of Scott were starting to lose their appeal and were being gradually phased out at the Royal – *Rob Roy* in 1908, and *Lady of the Lake* in 1917. The Moody-Manners Opera Company started up under Charles Manners and replaced the two seasons each year of Carl Rosa Opera who were suffering through the loss of their founder. If you wanted Carl Rosa you went to the Grand Theatre. Manners had sung with D'Oyly Carte before starting his own company with his wife Fanny Moody. In 1934 he donated his Moody-Manners music collection to the Mitchell Library in recognition of Glasgow's long involvement with opera.

New plays included *Sherlock Holmes* followed by *The Belle of New York* - a favourite which was the first long running American musical in Britain; and the curiously named *A Cigarette Maker's Romance*.

Theatres took a very short summer vacation. The largest exception was 1901 when the Royal closed for four months starting in May; this allowed the orchestra, stage and front of house staff to assist their chairman Michael Simons at the International Exhibition in Kelvingrove Park. Simons was again the convener of the Entertainments Committee and had a £20,000 budget for musical events, equal to many £millions today. The theatre reopened in September with a company of Japanese players from Tokyo, possibly linking with the Japanese Pavilion at the Exhibition, and the American La Loie Fuller in her "sensational dances" involving red, blue and white lights being projected onto her white silk costume – marrying light and dance.

The annual week's show of the newly formed Orpheus Club was in aid of charities, in 1903 the *Mikado* was performed in aid of the Glasgow Samaritan Hospital for Women, and the following year *Princess Ida* for the Victoria Infirmary.

Animated pictures and a new sister
Animated pictures were attracting audiences to something different, although most were in converted buildings or travelling booths. If anything confirmed the value of a large variety of film and a better venue it was the arrival of the Royal Canadian Animated Photo Company who hired St Andrew's Halls for two months in 1903, with a return visit in the autumn, where a huge and changing array of films of Canada, Britain, Glasgow and the Clyde was shown twice daily. Film of the Scotland v England football match at Sheffield was shown, and the Royal Visit to Glasgow was filmed in the day, and screened that night. Military bands provided concerts in the Halls. Simons was already building a new theatre and now gave thought to showing films.

The Royal and Royalty advertising took a back seat to the unveiling in September 1904 of their new sister - The King's along in Bath Street. The Royalty started to have pantomime, different of course to the Royal's, and the King's offered newer plays and major ballet companies. In the summers the King's remained open and the Royal and Royalty took a break.

The growth of Michael Simons' group of theatres as with Moss Empires and others in Britain brought a reaction. In America there was also now the privately owned Theatrical Syndicate which quickly grew to monopolise 700 theatres and looked to expand its activities on this side of the Atlantic. Some people thought that the demise of individually owned theatres would end artistic innovation. In March 1904 the main speaker, a lawyer, at a meeting in the Trades Hall discussing the old Glasgow Playhouses ended with these words:

At the present day the tendency of the big syndicates to secure a monopoly of places of entertainment is to be viewed with suspicion

and alarm. If the capitalists who cared little for art and much for money captured our theatres, then "good-bye" to the best we have. If that should happen the educated and artistic population will have to demand a municipalised or national theatre, which, while not entirely ignoring the lighter and more artificial sides of the drama, should cater principally for sensible and cultured people.

Sir Harry Lauder makes the world sing
When he was eighteen Harry Lauder appeared in small revues in Lanarkshire where he was a miner, and even tried the go-as-you-please evening in Mrs Baylis's Scotia. He toured the small halls round Scotland as a comedian and ventured into the north of England and then London, where one of his songs "Calligan, Call Again" made a name for him. While there he was approached to be in the next Royal pantomime as Roderick McSwankey, the apprentice to the Wicked Magician, not at the £7 or £8 a turn he was getting but at £200 a week. This was *Aladdin* in 1905, which ran for thirteen weeks to packed houses.

The theatre's music director Alfred Carpenter also composed light music including the popular interlude gavotte "Glasgow Belles." Just as most theatre conductors searched for a tune of their composition to repeat each night and see the music sales multiply over the season so did the pantomime stars for their songs. Lauder's showstopper at the Royal in 1905 was a new one "Ma

ABOVE
Book of Words
Little Red Riding Hood
1910

LEFT
I Love a Lassie
songsheet published in New York

CAIRNS' MARMALADE

THEATRE ROYAL

GLASGOW

HOWARD & WYNDHAM, Ltd.

Managing Directors { F. W. WYNDHAM
{ G. T. MINSHULL

Acting Manager PERCY O. HUMPHRYS

Thursday, 8th December, 1910,

And Every Evening until further notice at 7 o'clock.
Early Doors open at 6 o'clock.

Mr ROBERT ARTHUR

BY ARRANGEMENT WITH

HOWARD & WYNDHAM, LTD.,

WILL PRESENT THE INIMITABLE

HARRY LAUDER

And **ALL-STAR** Company, in the

Twenty-third **"ROYAL"** Pantomime,

RED RIDING HOOD

Written by **FRANK DIX.**
Composed by JULLIEN H. WILSON.

Boxes, £2 2s and £1 11s 6d
Orch. Stalls, 5s Dress Circle, 4s
Family Circle (which can be Booked), 3s
Upper Circle, - - 1s 6d
Pit, - 1s Gallery, - 6d
Doors open 6-45, commence 7. Early Doors (6d extra to Upper Circle, Pit, and Gallery), open at 6 o'clock.

STALLS AND CIRCLE
PROGRAMME
2D

Box Plans at MURDOCH, M'KILLOP & CO., Ltd., Music Saloon, 101 Hope Street. Booking Hours—10 till 4 (Saturday, 10 till 1).

Children in arms not admitted. No money returned.

OPERA GLASSES, 6d. EACH.

To be had from Attendants and Programme Boys.
To be returned Five Minutes before fall of Curtain.

Deposit, 2/6.

Scotch Bluebell" equally known as "I Love a Lassie" which became an international hit, with its chorus:

I love a lassie - a bonnie, bonnie lassie -
She's as pure as the lily in the dell,
She's as sweet as the heather,
The bonnie purple heather,
Mary, ma Scotch Bluebell.

The lassie he sang to onstage was 16 year-old Jose Collins who went on to her own singing fame in *Maid of the Mountains*. In 1910 Harry Lauder was the star of *Red Riding Hood* and premiered his song for that season "Roamin in the Gloamin." His songs travelled round the world. Artistes as diverse as Charlie Chaplin and the Russian opera star Chaliapin said that if you wanted to hear a good singer in diction and craft listen to Lauder. He became the first Knight of variety.

Forty years after its opening the admission prices in 1907 were:

Private Box	£2.2/-
Orchestra Stalls	5/-
Dress Circle	4/-
Family Circle (which can be rented)	3/-
Upper Circle	1/6d
Pit	1/-
Gallery	6d

The cheapest ticket was unchanged at 6d, just as it had been at the beginning. Structural improvements took place during the 1907 vacation, including re-seating.

A new comedy *The Stronger Sex* ran, which was noted for having been attended twice in London by Her Majesty the Queen and the Empress of Russia. The 1907 pantomime *Babes in the Wood* starring Mark Sheridan also featured Gladys Cooper, age 19, who was moving from being a chorus girl to light comedy. She was a popular pin-up girl during the 1914-18 War, changing

ABOVE
Gladys Cooper
Pin-up Girl

OPPOSITE
Programme Cover
1910

THE ALEXANDRA MUSIC HALL

Built in 1867, as part of the Theatre Royal buildings of James Baylis, the Hall's name remained unchanged for most of its life. Most likely it was named after Alexandra of Denmark who

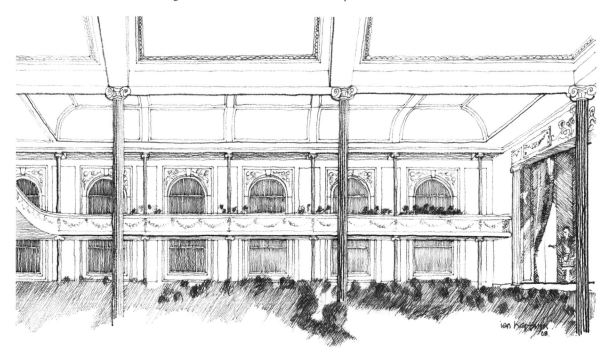

ABOVE
Alexandra Music Hall
Sketch by Ian Hepburn from surviving plans

married Edward Prince of Wales a few years previously. From 1880, after the theatre fire, to 1883 it was known as the Colosseum Hall – and was a base for the Glasgow Amateur Dramatic Society. The Society's stage manager, the painter Forrest Niven, started an acting family including his daughter Margaret (of *Bunty Pulls the Strings*) followed by her own son Sir Dirk Bogarde. The Society's Patron was the actor Walter Bentley, prominent in Britain, America and then Australia, where he founded the Australasian Actors Association. He was born in Edinburgh as William Begg, son of a Moderator of the Free Church of Scotland.

In 1884 it resumed its Alexandra name, and by the 1890s an internal stair had been added from the public house underneath into the Music Hall. In 1897 the hall was advertising as the Oxford Café Concert, admittance 6d, for New Songs, New Dances, New Costumes in a Star Company – open 6pm to 11.30pm. From July the advertising dubiously became

To Visitors and Strangers!
For a Jolly Night visit Oxford Café Concert….
Open till 12 pm. Concert from 8pm. Free.

In 1898 a restaurateur who had started a property business, Gray Edmiston, transformed

▼

over to drama in the 1920s and eventual Damehood.

Silent pictures had started in Glasgow in the late 1890s, attracting new custom and new habits. They could be shown over and over, and at less cost than paying wages to theatre casts. Music halls and some theatres experimented by adding short films into their entertainment of the day, "cine-variety" was the new craze. The Royal would join in, projecting films to a screen on the stage from the upper circles.

The Alexandra Music Hall had been lying unused for a while until Simons leased it in 1908 to the Scottish Cinematographe Ltd run by Ralph Pringle, the showman and cinema pioneer who opened in several places across Britain. This provided a rent to the theatre company but in some ways it may have been a test of the water to see what moving pictures were all about. Films were not going to go away. Simons's son Ernest became a founder director and shareholder in the small Majestic picture house, newly built in 1911 in Govanhill. Howard & Wyndham's consultant architect William Baillie Brown converted the Alexandra for film, and later improved its entrance from Cowcaddens Street.

Pantomime performances for good causes featured at the Theatre Royal, A charity matinee in aid of Glasgow Jewish Charities also had artistes from other city theatres. In 1909, 800 children were entertained at a pantomime matinee, appropriately *Cinderella*, and had their tea at the interval served by members of

the cast. This was through the Theatre Royal Cinderella Fund, which also arranged visits to the Zoo Circus nearby run by Mr Bostock. The Fund started in 1903, by members of staff subscribing one penny weekly and the manager's wife acting as Fund President. Over the years it helped thousands of poor children. The 1910 Orpheus Club's

ABOVE
Wagner Ring
programme
1911

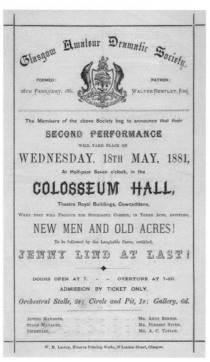

LEFT
Hall programme *of the Glasgow Amateur Dramatic Society, which included actresses Amy Glover, Julia Sleaman, 14 artistes and an orchestra*
1881

RIGHT
Hall programme
1898

it in October as the Alexandra Music Hall again - this time with a variety company managed by himself and a Mr Lees. This also had a short life but Edmiston's property deals flourished and he went on to become the Provost of Prestwick. The Theatre Royal Vaults also changed hands in 1898 becoming the Camel's Head Vaults, operated for some years by Alexander Walker the son of a hotel owner.

In 1899 showman Arthur Hubner from South Africa was advertising the Hall as the Royal Music Hall with prices similar to his Britannia Music Hall in the Trongate, but reserved seats could be had only at the Royal. He introduced Cinematographe, adding it to the variety acts. By April he was advertising two performances nightly 6.30pm and 9 pm, finishing at 10.45pm. "*The doors are quite distinct, the first house leaves by separate exits.*" Prices were cut almost in half to Gallery 2d, Pit 3d, Balcony 4d, Stalls 6d, and Chairs 1/-, with higher prices on Saturdays and Holidays in the winter.

The same artistes moved around his three halls, Britannia, Paisley Empire Music Hall and the Royal. The Royal Music Hall closed for a long summer and opened again in the winter. By 1900 it was empty. In 1904 it became Alexandra Assembly Rooms (much more refined!) before becoming the Bijou Picture Hall.

Ralph Pringle and the Bijou Picture Hall
Ralph Pringle had worked as a manager for the Thomas-Edison Animated Picture Company in Newcastle. However, by 1901 he linked up with Moss, Stoll and Thornton, the music hall proprietors and exhibited as the North American Animated Photo Company in Glasgow,

production of *The Rose of Persia* was in aid of The Glasgow Dental Hospital and The Glasgow Newsboys' League and Home. The theatre held a charity performance the next year of *Little Red Riding Hood* for the East Park Home for Cripple Children.

On the other side of the social spectrum cartoonists had a field day on the habit of ladies wearing their very large and stylish Edwardian hats to theatre matinees bringing difficulties to those behind. One cartoon drew an audience of fashionable women and large hats with men trying their best to see past them, and a notice on stage reading "This is a Theatre – not a Milliner's Showroom."

All theatres had cloakrooms with attendants looking after coats but the fashion of huge Edwardian hats flummoxed most managers. In this the Royal and others were outflanked by the modern and spacious West End Playhouse (Empress Theatre) designed by the architect of the Mitchell Library and newly opened at St George's Cross in 1913 where in view of its rule regarding the removal of Ladies Hats the management drew their patrons attention to the attachments provided on the back of the seats for their convenience and comfort:

> A Mirror for general use, an Ashtray, an Umbrella Stand, a small tube for Ladies Hat Pins, and a Cushion to which a Lady can attach her Hat, while under each seat is a Gentleman's Hat Rack.

Towards the end of the decade the Italian Grand Opera Company came, Carl Rosa Opera returned to the Hope Street lime-lights, Brandon Thomas players acted and JM Barrie's *Peter Pan* flew high. *The Real Napolean* was staged in which the leading actor and its part-author was Juan Buonapatre a great-grandson of the Emperor Napoleon.

Wagner's *Ring of the Nibelung* was being toured by Austrian ex-patriate Ernest Denhof, with the Scottish (National) Orchestra supplemented by the Covent Garden Orchestra, and in April 1911 at the Royal the complete Ring Cycle of operas was performed for the first time in Glasgow, and in English, on

Tuesday	*Rhinegold*
Wednesday	*Valkyrie*
Thursday	*Siegfried*
Saturday	*Twilight of the Gods*
(played at 3pm and finishing at 8.30pm)	

Some parts of the auditorium were re-seated for this, and the immense orchestra of 82 players necessitated a complete rearrangement of the stalls. The theatre sold translations of Wagner's work, photos, lithographs, and pictorial cards. The programme intimations advised:

> Evening Dress is optional, but Ladies are kindly requested to remove their hats.

Each opera is very long and the theatre declared:

ABOVE
Pauline Chase
as Peter Pan

△

Dundee and England. In the next seven years he constantly commissioned filmmakers such as Mitchell and Kenyon to make topical non-fiction films important to each town. On 19th March 1908 he opened Pringle's Picture Palace at the Alexandra Hall, charging 2d to 6d.

After the summer the Alexandra changed its name to the Bijou Picture Hall, which locals called the By Jove during its twenty year life. A performance comprised silent film, vaudeville acts, and the supporting Bijou band. Pringle started a Go-as-you-Please competition on Wednesdays, while on Thursdays *Every Lady will be admitted Free to all parts if*

ABOVE
Ralph Pringle

RIGHT
Hall advert
April 1899

BOTTOM LEFT
Hall advert
April 1908

BOTTOM RIGHT
Bijou *tickets*

ROYAL MUSIC HALL,
COWCADDENS, GLASGOW.

Lessee and Manager, ... Mr. A. HUBNER.

Open at 7, commence at 7-30; Saturdays, Half-Hour earlier.

HUBNER'S CINEMATOGRAPH

BOB GARDNER.   SISTERS LORRAINE.   J. P. DOONAN.

GEORGINA LEONARD.

DAVE HALLIE.   CHAS. GREY.

THE TWO WEIMARS.
Amateur Night every Friday.

PRICES—Gallery, 3d.; Pit, 4d.; Balcony, 6d.; Stalls, 1s.; Reserved Seats, 1s. 6d.   Saturdays—Gallery, 4d.; Pit, 6d.; Balcony, 1s.; Stalls and Reserved Seats, 1s. 6d.

PRINGLE'S PICTURE PALACE
Late Queen's Theatre, Glasgow Cross.

7   TWICE NIGHTLY   **9**

An Up-to-the-Minute Programme.

Animated Pictures
AND
HIGH-TONED VAUDEVILLES
Pringle's for Preference.
Also at Alexandra Hall, Cowcaddens

accompanied by a Gentleman." Some Thursdays had a Hair-dressing Competition.

Refreshments will be available during all the intervals. Arrangements will also be made for Light Dinners being served at their rooms, at 3/6d each, by Messrs J & W McKillop, Grosvenor Restaurant, Gordon Street. These dinners will be served in 20 minutes, and finish 10 minutes before the next Act.

Business across the company was good, apart from the loss-making Tyne Theatre in Newcastle which would be disposed of as soon as possible. 1902 saw Fred Wyndham's salary arrangement changed and doubled to an annual £2,000, but no bonus share of profits. In 1906 Simons emphasised:

> The endeavour of the Directors is to uphold the business as a solid one and to accomplish this it is essential to maintain the Theatres in an up to date condition.

Their new theatre, the King's, was opened in Glasgow, the Royalty was redecorated in July 1905 and its lease was extended.

The start of electric trams and the work of the City Improvement Trust brought about the demolition of the old Royal Arcade in 1905. This opened Hope Street up fully, with the new red sandstone tenement and shops of McConnell's Building being opened the following year to the designs of Honeyman, Keppie and Mackintosh. In 1907 the company took occupation of the tenement to the south of the theatre

at Rutherford Lane. Honeyman, Keppie and Mackintosh altered it to provide more dressing rooms and a shop fitted out as the main ticket sales office (always as close to Sauchiehall Street as possible.) The large windows of the sales office were styled by Keppie the same as the windows of McConnell's across the road. The main-door canopy was extended down Hope Street, stopping short of the sales office.

Robert Arthur Theatres and the other Robert

The success of the Theatre Royal and Michael Simons' chairmanship encouraged others including a **Robert C. Buchanan** who became managing director for local syndicates building or opening theatres (some quickly became picture houses.) He had been in charge of the neighbouring Grand Theatre for a few years, and then chaired a firm called Edinburgh Construction Co Ltd to build a King's Theatre there, which it did in 1906. He made himself managing director and arranged its variety bill of fare. Buchanan and the shareholders continued to have difficulty raising the second half of the money to pay the builders WS Cruikshank & Sons. The builder's son, A.Stewart Cruikshank, was interested in theatre business and became manager to Buchanan, no doubt keeping an eye on the building! In 1907 Cruikshank joined the Northern Theatres Investment Co Ltd, which was another Buchanan invention involving also Ernest Stevens once of the Grand Theatre, Glasgow and Robert Stevens

Robert Arthur

Robert Arthur, theatre impresario, was born in Govan in 1856. He served his apprenticeship as an engraver to his father who rapidly established a substantial business as "Lithographer, Colour Printer, Draughtsman and Engraver in Wood" based in Kyle Street, Townhead. By the 1880s the printing and design customers of Robert Arthur & Sons include a long list of showbusiness clients in Scotland, England and Ireland including music halls, theatres, circuses, waxworks, actors, and operators of dioramas, marionettes, and picture houses. The Glasgow theatres included those of James Howard and Fred Wyndham, and Charles Bernard at the Gaiety. He printed for the new business of his son.

Robert Arthur junior, as he was known in Glasgow, entered the theatre business becoming a stage manager at the Royal and the Royalty. He branched out under his own name to manage companies visiting Scotland including Turner's English Opera Company in 1886, and staging *Guy Mannering* in Dundee for the Christmas season 1888. His first long lease in England was the Theatre Royal Wolverhampton, and he soon leased Her Majesty's Theatre, Dundee, followed by Her Majesty's at Aberdeen (where he would move it to its current site of Rosemount in 1906, naming it His Majesty's). More theatres would follow in England, including Newcastle and London where he also started the Robert Arthur London Repertory Company in the 1900s providing actors for the production of plays in his theatres. The number of theatres he operated would exceed those of the new Howard & Wyndham Ltd. His sister Emily Arthur was a silver and pewter metal artist and another sister Anne Arthur taught embroidery at Glasgow School of Art, both were members of the pioneering Glasgow Society of Lady Artists which was also the first residential club for women in Britain.

Robert Arthur Theatres Co Ltd was formed by Arthur, then living at The Limes, Broughty Ferry, and his bankers in England in 1897, "To acquire and takeover as a going concern the business of a Theatrical Proprietor now carried on at Liverpool, Aberdeen, Dundee, Newcastle, Nottingham and elsewhere, by Mr Robert Arthur.
The company is to pay £155,000 to Mr Arthur for the goodwill, performing rights, and assets …………to be paid £40,000 in shares and £115,000 in cash." The theatres were:

Her Majesty's Dundee
Her Majesty's Aberdeen
Royal Court Theatre Liverpool
Theatre Royal Newcastle
Theatre Royal Nottingham

Most of the shareholders were in Dundee, Newcastle, Gateshead and London.
Of the four theatres he operated in London, the Kennington Princess of Wales had a weekly change of expensive West End productions, besides occasional visits from opera

▼

of the Marlborough Theatre, London, whose purposes were "to take over the King's, Edinburgh, The Grand, Glasgow, Howard & Wyndham theatres and other properties." Buchanan and his colleagues tabled a takeover bid for all of Howard & Wyndham Ltd for £160,000 but did not have the money to back it up.

RC Buchanan was not his real name. He was Robert Colburn, born in Glasgow in 1870, the son of a boilermaker. He added "Buchanan" and became a comedian in Lancashire and Scotland, before deciding to teach elocution which he did from his new home in Berkeley Terrace and at the Athenaeum. He then added theatre management to his portfolio.

In February 1908 the Edinburgh Construction Company made its last attempt to find money. It offered their Edinburgh King's Theatre to Howard & Wyndham Ltd for £35,000. Michael Simons declined the offer, he already had two theatres in Edinburgh. The next month the Edinburgh firm was re-organised with the Cruikshank family taking majority ownership of it in June and running it by themselves.

Elsewhere a former employee at the Royal and the Royalty was mightily prospering. This was stage manager **Robert Arthur** who had branched out on his own in the 1880s, and was buying and leasing a number of theatres in Scotland and England, including four in London. Mr Howard and Mr Wyndham's lease of Newcastle Theatre Royal expired in 1895 and Robert Arthur took it over

MR. ROBERT ARTHUR,
Managing Director of Robert Arthur's Theatres, Ltd.

with great success. By contrast Simons company took over the less fortunate Tyne Theatre, which had been started by Joseph Cowen junior, who became the radical Liberal MP for Newcastle.

For almost three years from 1909, Arthur's company and Simons' company had an agreement for the joint management of the Newcastle theatres, and the booking by Robert Arthur Theatres Ltd. of Howard & Wyndham theatres

ABOVE
Robert Arthur

△

companies.

Robert Arthur was outdoing Michael Simons' venture in Glasgow. He owned and operated more theatres than Simons, and the profits of the Robert Arthur company were 50 per cent greater, in the early years. However the amount of money going to him and the payments on theatre mortgages kept increasing. By 1902 the new company repealed the right given to him of being Managing Director for 10 years. At the same time his power over "the substantial direction of theatrical arrangements" was taken away; as was his right to have at least 2 months vacation each year.

When Robert Arthur was ousted from his company, The Robert Arthur Theatres Co Ltd, he was declared bankrupt for debts in the theatre business, losses from Stock Exchange trading and gambling in Monte Carlo. He found himself at ground level, but he did return to stage management. A few years before his death in 1929 he was manager of the Croydon Grand Theatre, London.

when touring in Scotland. In May 1909 George T Minshull was promoted to joint managing director of Simons' company, to share the load carried by Fred Wyndham, and pantomimes at the Theatre Royal for each of the next three winters were Robert Arthur productions.

With a number of new theatres, and its large mortgages increasing, Robert Arthur Theatres Ltd. saw its profits shrink by the year 1908 and become losses by 1910. Arthur's shareholders invited Michael Simons and David Heilbron to become directors, with Simons confirmed as chairman in 1912. Robert Arthur resigned and was replaced as managing director by Fred Wyndham. Arthur had remained the largest shareholder in his company but because of his debts he now sold all his shares, mainly taken up by Miss Jane Cowen of Gateshead, daughter of the late Joseph Cowen MP, from whom Arthur had borrowed to stay afloat.

Simons changed the head office from London to the Theatre Royal Newcastle and appointed his secretaries Greig, Carter & Co as secretaries to Robert Arthur Theatres Ltd. In September 1912 Howard & Wyndham Ltd took over the management of all Robert Arthur theatres in Britain.

The Royalty and Repertory

Simons was now chairman of three theatres in Glasgow, the Royal, Royalty and King's. Busy as they were, there was some duplication in the type of offerings. New works were always sought, especially as the public was getting a strong taste for the novelty of moving pictures. A young tour manager and director appeared on the scene, who had been apprenticed to the actor Beerbohm Tree, and had ideas for a repertory company to move away from older drama. With the help of playwrights and theatregoers in Glasgow Alfred Wareing formed the **Scottish Playgoers Ltd** in

1909 – the first Citizens' theatre in the English-speaking world, just pre-dating the Abbey Theatre in Dublin. Wareing coined the phrase "Citizens' Theatre" in its Prospectus:

> The Repertory Theatre is Glasgow's own theatre. It is a citizens' theatre in the fullest sense of the term. Established to make Glasgow independent from London for its dramatic supplies, it produces plays which the Glasgow playgoers would otherwise not have the opportunity of seeing.

He opened in April at the Royalty with a George Bernard Shaw comedy. Simons agreed to make it their home for their seasons each year, starting just a few weeks later, at the rate of £80 per week which included the full use of Howard & Wyndham's stock of scenery and properties. The veteran Willie Glover, their invaluable property master, became a member of Wareing's staff, and William's son became stage manager. Howard & Wyndham Ltd still held the lease and managed the Royalty. It was now advertised as The Royalty – Scottish Playgoers Co - The Repertory Theatre.

The Royalty, and its Repertory, stayed open in the summer, while the Royal shut to enjoy the weather; and the resident Scottish Playgoers toured to Simons' Royal Lyceum in Edinburgh. Numerous British and Continental playwrights visited the Royalty and had their work shown by the Scottish

Playgoers for the first time in Britain, from Gorky to JJ Bell and Neil Munro. The first English translation of Anton Tchekov's *The Seagull* was premiered in April 1909. Outwith these seasons The D'Oyly Carte Opera and others continued to play. Following one film showing at the King's in 1912, Simons introduced Charles Urban's series of Kinemacolour films to the Royalty in November that year including the *Delhi Durbar series*, and *Constructing the Panama Canal*, while over the festive season the films were *Jack and the Beanstalk*, and *Santa Claus*. Other short films followed to February.

In April 1913 the repertory season ended, in what was also the last year of Simons' long lease. It was succeeded from 28th April by a Picture Season, *Continuous performance from 2 to 10.30pm. Smoking permitted. Popular Prices.* Film continued to be shown by the proprietors – with *The Battle of Gettysburg* raging for hours in September.

The public now enjoyed huge choice during the Edwardian years. Theatres vied with each other, pictures took root (even some purpose-built cinemas appeared), music halls, concert halls, zoos, and skating rinks were thronged. The Royal had two major competitors opening within a year of each other. The Alhambra designed by (Sir) John Burnet opened in Wellington Street at Waterloo Street in December 1910. It was headed by Alfred Butt, of the Palace Theatre in London, who was a nephew of Michael Garcia a partner in the Simons fruit

LADIES OF THE GLOVER FAMILY

The Glover family influence continued in theatre in Britain and overseas. The ladies were as active as the men.

Elizabeth Glover, actress, and mother of nine children to Edmund, appeared on her husband's Theatre Royal stage from 1852 onwards. Her contemporary actresses included Mrs Howard and Mrs Wyndham. Against the chequered history of the family she married into in London she proved to be a good businesswoman. After her husband's death she was in charge of three theatres, the Prince's West Nile Street, the Theatre Royal Dunlop Street, and for over thirty years owner of the Greenock Theatre Royal until she died at her home in Hillhead in 1895. She loaned some money to her son William Glover but wisely did not give him access to the Glover Trust funds. Two of her friends who wound up her affairs were James Woodburn (who helped buy the Theatre Royal Hope Street in the 1880s), and the other was the secretary of the Institute of Fine Arts.

Phillis Glover, daughter of Edmund, acted on her father's stage in Dunlop Street and on her brother William's at Hope Street and Newcastle Theatre Royal, with a spell in London. In the 1870s she also worked on stage in New York, where her uncle Howard Glover had gone. Her mother's brother-in-law John Brougham was an actor there, then theatre manager before and after the American Civil War. He was one of the founders of the literary and bohemian Lotos Club of Manhattan. Novelist Florence Marryat described Phillis Glover "as a woman who led a very eventful life, chiefly in America, and was a versatile genius in conversation, as in everything else. She was peculiar also, and had a half Yankee way of talking….." She married twice, with her third partner being a poet from the North of England. Her late father may not have approved of all this, but would have liked the poetry.

Phillis Glover.

MORA, 707 BROADWAY.

ABOVE
Phillis Glover

Amy Glover, actress and sister of Phillis, married a photographer Henry Egerton, who was stage-manager at Dunlop Street. In the 1870s they moved to Newcastle's Theatre Royal where he became theatre manager to her brother William, and moved later to the Dublin Theatre Royal. Unfortunately her husband was burnt to a cinder when that went on fire. The Egerton family were pioneering photographers in Fleet Street, London, similar to Annan in Glasgow, and Amy devoted some of her time in colour tinting the photographs.

Younger sister **Fanny Glover** was regarded as the only one who married well, in 1874, and away from theatres – to the Anderson family, who owned the huge Atlantic Mills in Bridgeton. Her husband was a cotton merchant and they moved to India.

In the antipodes was **Julia Glover** daughter of actor Robert Glover, a younger son of Edmund, who had emigrated to New Zealand at the time of its gold rush, and with his new family toured extensively with travelling theatre companies. In the 1900s she was the principal actress in the Savieri Dramatic Company headed by her Italian husband. In turn their children worked in theatre and film in Australia, with daughter **Grace Savieri**, also known as Grace Glover, gaining most prominence as a silent movie star in the 1920s, and afterwards working on the London stage in the 1930s.

Jessie Glover was a sister of Julia and travelled throughout New Zealand with "moving picture" exhibitions in the mid 1890s. A baritone would sing and also give the descriptive lecture to accompany the featured items, supported by recitations delivered by Jessie. In 1899 she toured in Canada billed as "New Zealand's gifted young elocutionist and Scottish vocalist."

Rita Glover was born in Glasgow in 1902. Her mother was a chorus dancer in Edinburgh and Glasgow (dancing troupes were known as "the ballet") and her father Ernest Glover was a scenic designer in the Port Dundas studios of his father William Glover. The family emigrated to North America working in scenic design and theatre production, settling eventually in Los Angeles. She finished her education at the University of California and continued the family tradition of theatre and scenic art, setting and lighting. By 1937 she had been responsible for over 250 Pacific Coast productions. She also designed modern homes in 1936 and then became Art Director of the Pasadena Playhouse 1937-1947, and of the Hollywood Bowl. Rita Glover became Art Director of the Greek Theatre where she designed for James A Doolittle who kept legitimate theatre going in Los Angeles. She lectured at the School of Theatre and became Professor of Theatrical Art & Design at the University of California until her death in 1959.

ABOVE
Rita Glover
Looking at a Theatre Royal Rob Roy playbill in her Los Angeles office

WHAT HAPPENED TO THE ROYALTY?

In December 1913 the Regent Hotel and Picture House Co. Ltd was formed with public shareholders - and the ever present David Rattray - to buy over the Central Halls Co and reconstruct its office buildings into a 110 room commercial and tourist hotel to be known as The Regent Hotel; at the same time converting the theatre auditorium into an opulent 900 seat Picture House complete with lounge, tearooms and connecting balconies. This would be in the style of the marble-halled La Scala further along Sauchiehall Street. One of La Scala's directors was a promoter of the new company. However the war grounded the scheme.

ABOVE
The Royalty
Sauchiehall Street

The auditorium changed its name to the **Lyric Picture Palace** until the YMCA bought the whole complex at the end of 1916, making it their Hostel for Soldiers and Sailors at "the Lyric Buildings." Eventually after the war the **Lyric Theatre** opened for business and was continued by the YMCA into the 1950s. The Scottish Playgoers moved on to the King's for one season directed by Mrs Wareing in the absence of her husband who was exhausted and away recuperating on a cruise, and early in 1914 it was announced that the Repertory was to resume fully. The directors of Scottish Playgoers Ltd planned a season with their new producer Lewis Casson, which made a significant £700 profit, again at the King's. A year later they gave up the search for a suitable theatre, and recognised that many of their office-bearers were now away on active service in France and Turkey. Intriguingly the architect James Salmon junior, affectionately known as Wee Troot, sketched drawings for a new repertory theatre seating 2,000 – The Lantern – for the corner of Bothwell Street and Pitt Street, but it was not to be. In fact no major theatres were built in the city for the next 80 years until the Clyde Auditorium opened beside the new Scottish Exhibition Centre on the site of Queen's Dock.

With no further activities the pioneering Playgoers were wound up after the war, with the funds remaining being gifted to the St Andrews Society in Glasgow, to help their aims of creating a Scottish Theatre movement. This was the birth of the (second) Scottish National Players in 1921, working from offices in St Vincent Street, and having their productions in a number of theatres including the Royal on special occasions.

empire. And the Savoy Theatre designed by James Miller opened across Hope Street next to Renfrew Street in 1911. Both were large and luxurious theatres.

As it happened 1911 had a further attraction, the next of the great exhibitions opened in Kelvingrove Park. The Scottish Exhibition of National History, Art and Industry attracted 9 million visitors from May to November. The directors of the new Glasgow Alhambra Ltd reported to their shareholders "In view of the counter attraction of the Scottish Exhibition of National History held this summer in Glasgow and of the abnormally fine weather, the Directors resolved to close the theatre on 28th May 1911 for three months, but the company was fortunate in being able through Mr Alfred Butt Managing Director to have the contracts with artistes during the closed period transferred or postponed without practically any further loss. The theatre was again reopened on 4th September on the two houses a night principle, and since that date has been continuously successful."

Michael Simons reported to his shareholders:

Notwithstanding the keen competition which exists the company has held its own. ……. In spite of all the competition of picture houses and music halls, there is something inherent in the drama which will always attract to it a full measure of support as long as there are a sufficient number of talented playwrights who are able to give to the public that which will be of interest and which will touch a note of humanity, which, after all, is the dominant one in connection with the visits of the public to our theatres.

The Town Clerk's annual reports to the public show the numbers of places licensed for entertainments. Glasgow worked hard and knew how to play:

	1911/12	1912/13	1913/14
Theatres	18	23	19
Music and dancing halls	70	81	97
Billiard rooms	88	94	105
Permissions for shows etc	98	131	130
Cinematograph licenses	71	92	97

In the next two decades the number of cinemas would almost double, theatres stay much as they were, and dance halls and ballrooms more than double, earning the city the title of the "Dancing Capital" of Britain.

The Great War
Pictures, Plays, Opera and Pantomime

Towards the Great War

Pantomimes and patriotism were flourishing in the years leading to 1914, arts and the armaments race expanded all at the one time. Philip Simons, the chairman's brother, was the West of Scotland treasurer of the Navy League whose primary object was securing the national policy of "The Command of The Sea." Open seas were required for trade and peace.

Adding to the shows was a new opera company which sang in English. This was the creation of Thomas Quinlan who earlier had initiated, developed and financed the Beecham Opera Company. The Quinlan Opera Company staged 12 operas in each of their annual visits including the first Scottish performance of Puccini's *Girl of the Golden West*. The Quinlan orchestra was larger than that of Carl Rosa or Moody-Manners, and had a chorus of 50 singers. Costumes were designed and made by the firm of D.Carleton Smyth and Gertrude Wareing & Halley of 206 Bath Street, Glasgow, headed by Dorothy Carleton Smyth who taught at the Glasgow School of Art. She specialised in portraiture of theatre personalities as well as costume design in Britain and on the Continent, and designed the sets and costumes for the Quinlan Opera's world tour to South Africa and Australia. She was destined to become the first lady Director of the School of Art but died suddenly in 1933 before the post was vacated.

The newly formed Lyric Club staged the operetta *Ma Mie Rosette*. By public demand *Ben-Hur* was retained ...."complete with horses, camels and a company of 120 artistes. Twelve horses are required for the four chariots

ABOVE
The White Hunter
promotion outside the theatre
1910

OPPOSITE
Auditorium
showing seat numbers
1930

and Russian Red Crosses. On a return to Glasgow in 1915 Lillie Langtry, one of the long-serving mistresses of the expired King Edward VII, took the lead in a play by Sydney Grundy. The subject matter meant little and the newspapers focused on the real interest:

> It may be of special interest to ladies to know that the dresses worn by Mrs Langtry are by Madam Paquin of Paris, and the hats by Maison Lewis, London and Paris.

in the great race scene which is run on rollers or tread mills and moves across the stage by electric motors and takes one minute twenty seconds to run." A musical revue *Hullo, Ragtime!* opened with "a beauty chorus of 60."

In 1912 *Bunty Pulls the Strings* opened and returned the following years. Written by Graham Moffat of Glasgow it had taken London by storm, and became a Broadway show. More of his plays were staged. Moffat had formed his touring company the Scottish National Players in 1908 at the Athenaeum; and he founded the Glasgow Men's League for Women's Suffrage after his wife was jailed for being a suffragette. After the war he campaigned for Glasgow to run its own municipal theatre.

Early in the war months of 1914 *Tommy Atkins* reappeared; and Tolstoy's military play *Anna Karenina* was led by Lydia Yavorska (in real life Princess Bariatinsky). She was donating half the proceeds of the tour to the British

Members of the former Scottish Playgoers joined Esme Percy and Kirsteen Graeme's company in a four week repertory of plays by Shaw, Arnold Bennet, Lewis Spence, Galsworthy, Oscar Wilde and others. This included a new play, *Birds of Passage*, by Alexander Yuill of Glasgow who was a founder director of the former Repertory Theatre at the Royalty. The queues for it almost blocked Hope Street.

Moody-Manners Opera, renowned for their first class singing and sound orchestral playing, made a return after a gap of three years. With the exception of large productions and operas the Royal put its weeks of plays and revues on to twice nightly at 6.45 and 9pm. At this juncture, from September 1915, the Royal was the first modern theatre in Britain to permit smoking in the auditorium, possible now by public demand and the better fire safety regulations.

The Babes in the Wood panto featured Charles Naughton and Jimmy Gold both from Glasgow who later created the

Crazy Gang in London with Flannagan & Allen. Even the pantomime was now twice nightly, and a second pantomime *Little Boy Blue* came from Edinburgh in January 1916 and it ran twice nightly. The variety theatres and picture houses ran twice a night: the Royal's experiment had been tried but ended during 1916.

Plays by Ibsen had been staged years before but his philandering play *Ghosts* staged in 1917 was...... *for Adults Only*. Performances for war charities and hospitals increased. For example, the whole week of the play *Raffles* about a gentleman amateur cracksman was in aid of Jock's Boxes for the Armed Forces, run by the Glasgow Evening News Fund. Sir Thomas Beecham's Opera Company came in 1918, before it closed and resurrected itself as the British National Opera Company.

With the outbreak of the Great War the profits of the company fell by a third and stayed that way into the early twenties. The Government introduced Entertainments Tax in 1916 to help pay for the war – a terrible irony – it was soon increased and it stayed for decades. The continuing strength of Simons' company was such that the Theatre Royal gave a £10,000 guarantee to the mortgage lenders to Robert Arthur Theatres Ltd when it bought the Shakespeare Theatre in Liverpool, to be managed of course by Howard & Wyndham Ltd.

Silent films and busy orchestras

Film months started in 1916. Historian

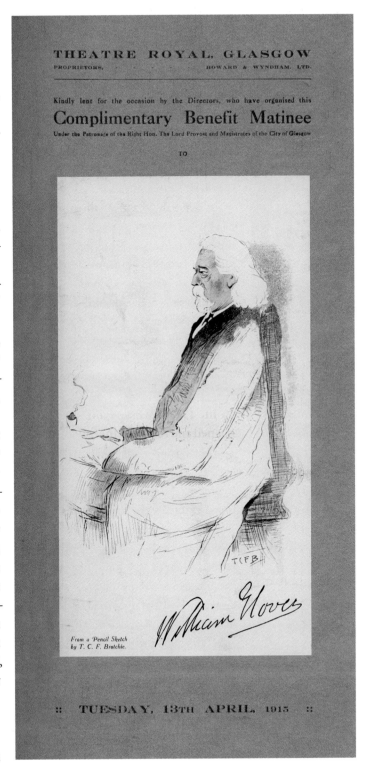

THEATRE ROYAL, GLASGOW

PROPRIETORS, · · · · · · HOWARD & WYNDHAM, LTD.

Kindly lent for the occasion by the Directors, who have organised this

Complimentary Benefit Matinee

Under the Patronage of the Right Hon. The Lord Provost and Magistrates of the City of Glasgow

TO

From a Pencil Sketch by T. C. F. Brotchie.

William Glover

:: TUESDAY, 13TH APRIL, 1915 ::

FILMS AT THE ROYAL

TOP
Britain Prepared

MIDDLE
D.W.Griffiths

BOTTOM
**Martin & Osa
Johnson**

In May 1916 films were introduced, silent of course. The patriotic film *Britain Prepared* by the American producer Charles Urban opened in the presence of the Lord Provost. Shown once nightly for a week, it was made for the Royal Navy the previous year by invitation from the Government`s covert War Propaganda Bureau and combined the Kinemacolour, Gaumont and Kineto companies. The first half showed the training of Britons as flying men, engineers, artillerymen, cavalrymen, and sturdy riflemen. The second half showed the manufacture of shells by Messrs. Vickers, and life aboard a submarine and the battle-ship HMS *Queen Elizabeth*.

At intervals of one or two months films of large scale were shown. The other months had plays, opera, or pantomime according to season. Simons may have been influenced in this pattern because it was known that the former Royalty Theatre planned to become a full time Lyric Picture House from June. The setting up for film took time and usually the theatre shut on the first Monday of each season to let the screen, projectors and film reels be set up and to give the orchestra time to rehearse the accompanying music. The Royal had three weeks in July 1916 of DW Griffiths` epic but racially controversial film *The Birth of the Nation* about the forming of the USA It lasted three hours, with an interval added, and all to Griffiths` full orchestral score played by the Royal`s augmented orchestra. It was shown again in 1917. Screenings were each afternoon and evening, and applauded at the end by the audiences. In August 1917 it had another Griffiths spectacular *Intolerance*, the first historical block-buster, which was scripted round four stories from Biblical times onwards, each cutting in and out of the others. It was also repeated next year.

The *Life Story of Lord Kitchener, or Awakening of the British Empire* was screened in April 1918 at 2.30 and 7.30pm. The following week – *Where are My Children*, was for adults, 16 years and over, and evenings only. "The Empire`s empty cradles need filling, and our Colonies need virile men and women." During May patrons watched Jules Verne`s story *Twenty Thousand Leagues under the Sea*, the first filming of the living worlds on the ocean floor, produced in Los Angeles by Stuart Paton from Glasgow.

For a month in the summer more film by DW Griffiths was shown, with his full or-chestral scores happily played by the orchestra - *Hearts of the World*, a romance set in a village in France during the Great War, complete with live footage from the Front, ending in liberation from Germany. And the fourth of Urban`s epics was in August *The Great Love*, about the role of women in the war. Another producer created lighter fare and adventure about lost treasure *The Submarine Eye* - it was slightly shorter at two hours and had been filmed in the West Indies for the Scottish Super Films Company Ltd.

Films appeared now and again in 1919, one being *Enlighten Thy Daughter*, a morality film, which was for adults only. *The Unborn* was a similar drama. Other morality films were *The Girl Who Doesn`t Know* – a plain-spoken message to parents - and *Fallen Woman*, both endorsed by the National Council on Public Morals. The German horror film *Dr. Mabuse*

▼

and film buff Charles Oakley reckons it was not until the American film, *Birth of a Nation*, had been shown in the Theatre Royal at *theatre prices* that the cinema was taken seriously in Glasgow. The prices were from 6d. to 4/-, tax extra. All silent films of course had captions at the important parts and, for long films, often a full score to be played by the orchestra. The film seasons concentrated on long films, leaving the "shorts" to others.

To comply with cinema licences, which many theatres had, the film projectors and rewinding equipment had to be in a fire-resistant enclosure surrounded by a barrier for the safety of the audience. For each film season the Royal constructed a projection enclosure, dismantling it at the end of the season. In 1916 and 1917 the Royal's enclosure was built at the back of the Pit, and the Pit's accommodation temporarily reduced by 120. From 1918 the "cinematographe enclosure" was erected on the stage, and in 1919 it was built of reinforced concrete and brickwork.

The post-war years of economic Depression and political uncertainties at home and abroad affected everybody. But the need for entertainment is always present.

Chu Chin Chow

Instead of a pantomime in 1919, one year after the Armistice, the Royal presented the Australian Oscar Asche's record breaking *Chu Chin Chow* musical in all its Oriental splendour. The daring costumes worn by the ladies

Howard & Wyndham's

HUMPTY DUMPTY

who came on to dazzle the audience in the Persian mannequin parade had already drawn the phrase – "More navel than millinery!"

As if to make up lost time, opera companies abounded during 1920. The pantomime *Humpty Dumpty* was produced by George Minshull the joint managing director, normally based in Edinburgh, and not as usual by Fred Wyndham. Minshull continued in charge of the

ABOVE
Programme cover
1920

△

made a return visit.

After a gap of four years with no film seasons, the early summer of 1923 saw new films appearing, each with the Royal's orchestra and a number of vocalists:

> songs appertaining to the Picture will be rendered at intervals during each exhibition by popular artistes.

The four films were *The Prisoner of Zenda* –"easily the greatest of all photoplays", *A Royal Divorce* – "the tragedy of Napoleon and Josephine", *The Loves of Pharoah* -"with a cast of 112,000 people in Egypt", and *A Sheik of Araby* –"a 20th century spectacle." In the autumn *Dr Mabuse* returned for two weeks, twice daily, and the theatre projected a film version of *The Marriage of Figaro*.

The film seasons had come to their end. However much later, when Stewart Cruikshank became managing director, there was another try at housing film. This was *Simba* in 1929. The explorers, husband and wife Osa and Martin Johnson from Kansas, ventured to Africa and made the first wildlife cinema documentary. Its advertisement read "4 Years to make, 2½ hours to show." The admission prices were only slightly cheaper than Carl Rosa Opera, and it ran for three weeks, twice nightly. The film can still be seen on videotape today.

Glasgow pantomimes for a few years. There were 12 scenes before the finale in "The Home of Twinkle Star in Mars." The "King of Humptyland" was the star Will Fyffe, now becoming a national favourite and a rival to Harry Lauder. For the 1921/22 pantomime *Robinson Crusoe*, again starring Will Fyffe, a

BELOW
Sothern Syncopated Orchestra

"cinematographe enclosure" made this time of sheet metal, and therefore fire-resisting, was created up in the Gallery, occupying part of the bar area. It was used for a few minutes during each performance.

Though times were getting hard there were plenty of entertainments in the city. But the public was shocked by the sinking of *SS Rowan* in October 1921 on her way from Glasgow to Dublin and the deaths of members of one of the original black jazz bands from America, the Sothern Syncopated Orchestra who were sailing to their next venue. Of 120 on board, 36 died including nine players (and Will Fyffe's wife). In dense fog late at night the *Rowan* was struck by an American freighter and then cut in two by the *Clan Malcolm*, outward bound for South Africa, which had come to the rescue at full speed. The survivors came back to Glasgow where the band had just completed three weeks at the Lyric in their Farewell Tour of Britain and the Continent following three successful years performing classical music, rag tunes, blues, slave songs and jazz. In 1920 there had been 328,000 paid admissions to hear them at the Kelvin Hall. The Royal staged a Relief Fund Matinee of variety and music in aid of the surviving members and to help replace their musical instruments, all of which had been lost. The Empire held a Grand Sacred Concert on the following Sunday for the fund. But the orchestra soon disbanded.

Amateur productions got back to normal after the war, indeed the Orpheus Club has never missed a year despite all wars. The Lyric Club's production was followed by the New Operatic Club, and the Orpheus Club. The Hutton Malcolm Amateur Operatic Club started at the Royal in 1920 until 1925, its production that year being the comic opera *Boccaccio* in aid of the Railway Benevolent Institution. In 1921 the actress Agnes Bartholomew presented the American comedy *Peg O' My Heart*, which included Hal Stewart (whose father was the founder chairman of the new Scottish National Players the following year.) It ran for a week under the auspices of the Trades House of Glasgow raising funds for the Royal, Western and Victoria Infirmaries. Its souvenir programme shows the young Prince of Wales becoming a member of the Incorporation of Hammermen, and

encouraging the audiences to support the appeal.

The full time Carl Rosa Opera came for long seasons, one in 1922 was for eight weeks and included Eva Turner among its principal singers. Allan Ramsay's Scots operatic play *The Gentle Shepherd* was staged in 1923 after a run in London. It was written and first produced in 1725, pre-dating The *Beggar's Opera*.

Radio arrives

Radio, better known as wireless, started up in 1923 with the BBC's 5SC station in 202 Bath Street. Two doors down at number 206 Simons' former house had become the North British Wireless College. Where it had been necessary to go out to hear a concert or play you could now be at home and listen with headphones on (loudspeakers came later) twiddling the cat's whiskers control for the best reception from the crystal set. New music came instantly from the wireless; jazz and new dance crazes came in from America. In its first month opera was broadcast live from the Coliseum Theatre in Eglinton

ABOVE
Carla Rosa Opera Company *arrive at the Royal 1922*

Street (claimed to be the first relayed in Britain) and later a broadcast of *Rob Roy*. From the Theatre Royal the BBC relayed Massenet's lively opera *Manon*. For the broadcasts they used the Star Room as their control unit, and the star for the evening was accommodated elsewhere. Unlike the other dressing rooms the No 1 dressing room was on the ground floor, near the stage door, and had a Star Room adjacent, complete with its own fireplace.

Speaking at the 1923 company meeting Michael Simons voiced his concern:

> at the extremely high wages of artistes in pantomime who previously were being paid in single £s per week and are now paid in double £s, with some reaching three figures. I wonder if pantomime is now a doubtful proposition – it may be that such an entertainment is beginning to get out of date.

Picture houses were clearly having an impact. Simons continued:

> The public is not satisfied with theatre as it is. In Glasgow there is a demand for a National Theatre. There has already been in Glasgow a Repertory Theatre, in which the company was interested. That theatre has come to grief, but the directors are nevertheless still open to consider suggestions for a theatre on similar lines.

Cinema kept growing. The huge Savoy Theatre a few yards away adapted itself, opening as the New Savoy cinema with its orchestral cafes, tea lounges and soda fountain. Their Roumanian Orchestra played every afternoon and the Ladies and Jazz Orchestras every evening. Tea Dances were held each afternoon in their Upper Café. At the Royal some film shown in the war was shown again in peacetime including the *Birth of a Nation*. To keep pace with the new picture houses new tip-up seats were installed in 1921 in the Upper Circle in place of the forms with dividing arms which previously existed, and three years later the form seating of the Pit was removed and tip-up chairs put in.

Advertising remained essential to theatre business. Professional billposting and "outdoors advertising" became a speciality of printers such as Andrew Cossar of Govan and, above all, the theatrical printers of David Allen & Sons of Ulster and Scots origin with presses in London and Glasgow. They also owned theatres in England and in Dublin, and were prominent shareholders in the Robert Arthur Theatres, and Moss Empires. During World War I, and again in World War II, many male billposters were called up for active service. The shortage was made good by recruiting women as billposters. Because of the huge sizes of the modern billboards and the weight of the poster paper it needed two women to do the work of one man. The show must go on!

Serious drama by Shakespeare and other classicists continued with Sir

Frank Benson, Henry Baynton and their touring companies. New kids on the block, going on to the 1930s, were the Macdona Players led by Charles Macdona who was a contemporary of Lewis Casson. They dedicated themselves to the works of George Bernard Shaw who often told them how to play each scene. Robert Fenemore's Masque Theatre company earned a reputation for being avant-garde with new plays including those of James Bridie, and had the happy knack of employing local amateurs to play small parts. In two consecutive years the new Scottish National Players staged *King James the First of Scotland* by Robert Bain. In 1924 they presented *Full Fathom Five* by John Brandane. One of the actresses was Bertha Waddell who went on in 1927 to found the Bertha Waddell Children's Theatre, the first professional theatre solely for children.

Touring musicals included *No, No, Nanette* several times; and in 1925 Charles B Cochrane's song and dance show *Little Nellie Kelly* starred Phyllis Harding. Musical fare was enhanced by the growth of societies who became mainstays of the theatre, their roll call now was the Glasgow Grand Opera Society, Lyric Club, Philharmonic Opera Society, St Mungo Opera Club (which changed its name to the Glasgow Light Opera Club after the South of Ireland became independent), Orpheus Club, and the Pantheon Club.

Opera for all

In opera the British National Opera company vied with the Royal Carl Rosa company, each with regular seasons at Hope Street. Carl Rosa had the longer seasons, usually between four and six weeks at any one time, each evening being a change of opera with some new work added. In 1924 the British National performed 16 operas in three weeks – *Magic Flute, Carmen, Mastersingers, Tales of Hoffmann, Golden Cockerel, Marriage of Figaro, La Boheme, Aida, Tannhauser, Faust, Madame Butterfly, Gianni Schicchi, Hugh the Drover*, a first performance in Glasgow of *Alkestis* and also for a first time Sir Alexander McKenzie's *The Eve of St John* (based on Sir Walter Scott's ballad), and *The Perfect Fool*. Both of these were conducted by Malcolm Sargent making his first appearance in the city as an opera conductor. The company gave talks, with music of course, to organisations in the area including the staffs of Beardmore's Shipyard and of John Brown's Shipyard in Clydebank. By arrangement with Glasgow Corporation a special performance of the *Golden Cockerel* was held at the Royal for school children, who were each given a copy of the story beforehand.

For good measure in 1925 Carl Rosa Opera added a triple bill on two days of their season, being scenes from *Lucia di Lammermoor*, a scene from the ballet *Cameos*, and Mozart's *The Impressario*. As another extra they staged for the first time in Glasgow Harold White's Irish opera *Shaun the Post*. In *La Boheme* staged by the British National the soprano Kathlyn Hilliard

TOP
G.S Melvin

BOTTOM
Nellie Wallace

was performing for the first time in her native city. She recorded popular and jazz records with her husband George Baker, before her early death. John Barbirolli was known through the wireless and not yet in the flesh in the city until he took up the baton of the British National. The Weekly Herald observed his energy:

> but Mr Barbirolli protracts the silences in a manner somewhat trying, while his insistence that conversation shall cease before the orchestra begins is ill-advised. He should have courage and begin...
> all extraneous noises would cease immediately.

By the end of 1926 the British National Opera was in financial trouble, from which it would not survive. High costs of "high" art were blamed. Mr Manners wrote to the Press:

> Moody-Manners Opera for 20 years rarely made more than bare expenses from "Tristan", "Siegfried" and others but repaired all losses out of "The Bohemian Girl" and "Maritana". Neither Sir Thomas Beecham nor the BNOC played these two. They were my profit. When the BBC broadcast "The Bohemian Girl" a few weeks ago they sold 70,000 librettos for the performance on that one night. The BNOC is a self-confessed derelict.

Beecham campaigned for an Imperial Opera company with himself as king and priority over all others, to which Carl Rosa with its longer roots from the 1860s and greater courtesy replied "no thanks." In 1929 when the Carl Rosa programme included the bicentenary of *The Beggar's Opera*, the Weekly Herald noted that it had been first seen in Glasgow in 1729, the year it was written, when the Provost gave his consent to an English acting company performing it in the Dancing Hall above the Weigh House, Candleriggs.

Pantomimes in the Twenties featured among others GS Melvin, Wee Georgie Wood, Naughton & Gold, Mark Lupino of the Lupino lineage of knockabout mimers and acrobatic dancers once described as The Royal Family of Greasepaint, Nellie Wallace (from Glasgow) whose signature tune was "Here's to the Red, White and Blue" and the successive pantomimes of Will Fyffe from 1920.

Will Fyffe, and I Belong to Glasgow
He was a character actor acclaimed in Britain and overseas with studies of being Dr McGregor, with the refrain of "Dr McGregor and his wee black bag," an Engineer, a Bridegroom at 94, and many more. His songs include "Sailing Up The Clyde" and the one probably best remembered when he is the representative of the British working man reflecting on the end of a busy week and looking with disdain at the "capu'talists who pass by in their big motor cars pointing their scinger of forn" as he celebrates his Saturday in "I Belong to

Glasgow." The chorus and verses went round the world at dances, concerts, and on records:

I've been with a few o' ma cronies, one or two pals o' ma ain
We went in a hotel, did very well
Then we came out once again
Then we went into another, and that is the reason I'm fu'
We had six deoch-an-doruses, then sang a chorus
Just listen...... I'll sing it to you:

I belong to Glasgow, dear old Glasgow town,
But there's something the matter with Glasgow
For it's going round and round.
I'm only a common old working chap as any one here can see
But when I get a couple of drinks on a Sa'urday.....
Glasgow... belongs to me!

Reported as being the Queen Mother's favourite comedian, he appeared in no less than seven Royal Variety Performances between 1922 and 1938.

Michael Simons, the architect of so much in business, art and entertainment, was now in his eighties and passed away peacefully at his home at 2 Kensington Gate in the West End in November 1925. The fruit businesses continued as Simons & Co Ltd., and the theatre businesses continued. David Heilbron, his old friend, succeeded him as theatre chairman. Robert Crawford, the other member of the original trio, had died in 1912. Heilbron gave way to Simons' son, Ernest Simons, then living in Kelvinside, who remained as the chairman of Howard & Wyndham Ltd and of Robert Arthur Theatres Ltd until his own death in 1944.

BELOW
Theatre perspective *1925*

Stewart Cruikshank continues The Royal Tradition

The Royal's managing directors Fred Wyndham and George Minshull carried on but Ernest Simons knew his production team were of retiral age, he also realised the Edinburgh Theatre Royal would never be up to the mark. In August 1928 the company bought the Edinburgh King's Theatre and hired its managing director A. Stewart Cruikshank.

Wyndham retired but remained a director of Howard & Wyndham Ltd., and Minshull resigned. At the annual company meeting in 1929 the new managing director Stewart Cruikshank confirmed what was now evident:

> All Companies providing entertainment for the public are at this moment passing through a rather difficult stage.
> While we still have with us the ever increasing counter attraction of the silent pictures, where cheap prices prevail, along with comfortable seating and environment, we are now being faced with the additional novelty counter attraction of the Talking Film.

Frederick William Phoenix Wyndham who developed as an actor, producer and manager in the 1880s took his final curtain call in April 1930. As a mark of respect the silversmiths Samson, Mordan & Co of London, who specialised in pens, produced a solid gold pen and chain inscribed "Souvenir of FW Wyndham who died April 30 1930." His seat on the board was filled by Ernest Simons appointing a new director Charles B Cochran, showman supreme, who was well vouched for by the Simons' business colleagues, the Salmon and Gluckstein families of J. Lyons & Co. The Salmon family, noted for their interest in the social welfare of fellow citizens as well as their food catering expertise, continued to work closely with members of the Simons fruit businesses. Nigella Lawson, television cook and food writer today, is a member of the Salmon family.

Cruikshank outlined the Theatre Fare of the company and its range, emphasising "the educative and artistic side of Theatre." Distinctions were being sought from cinema. Glasgow in particular was

OPPOSITE
Side Circle *view*
1920s

A. STEWART CRUIKSHANK

Alexander Stewart Cruikshank was a master builder who at age 30 in 1906 became the manager of the Edinburgh King's Theatre, constructed by his father's firm. It was operating as a variety theatre under RC Buchanan until June 1908 when Cruikshank took over its programming. He introduced larger scale pantomimes and plays, musicals and opera.

In the 1920s Cruikshank also presented pantomime for other theatres including the Coliseum in Eglinton Street, Glasgow, and the Pavilion, Renfield Street, Glasgow with *Dick Whittington*, starring Lily Morris and Jack Edge. These runs were not long, but there were longer runs for Moss Empires at the Theatre Royal, Nottingham. He was establishing a name for himself in a wider circle. His theatre continued to operate in its own name until 1928 when Howard & Wyndham Ltd's chairman, now Ernest Simons, decided to buy it over.

SIR CHARLES B COCHRANE

"The British Zeigfield"

CB Cochrane was the consummate showman in the first half of the 20th century. He promoted shows of all types in Britain, New York, and occasionally on the Continent, which had huge popular appeal, giving him financial success mixed with grief on two occasions when he was bankrupted but bounced back. He promoted wrestling matches (including one at Ibrox Park), boxing matches, roller skating, ice skating in Berlin and Paris, and circuses at London's Olympia. He produced plays and revues in a number of London theatres. In 1916 one was called *Half Past Eight*, at the Comedy Theatre. This title would be revived twenty years later in Scotland, and still talked about today.

For ten years he was the manager and promoter of the Royal Albert Hall. After a visit to Paris to see the chorus line introduced by John Tiller he decided to start his own chorus of dancers for the *Cochrane Reviews*. These were his Young Ladies, and in the 1920s their costumes he insisted would be ahead of fashion. At the invitation of Major Montague Gluckstein of Lyons & Company (who was a colleague of Michael Simons) Cochrane put on the *Trocabaret* for three years at the Trocadero Grill Rooms. This was the first restaurant of style in London where people other than the super rich could afford to go. After their evening shows the Cochrane Young Ladies would go on to the Trocadero, and a second salary, as the chorus line in the midnight cabarets.

In the 1930s he could engage the best of lyricists including Vivien Ellis, Rodgers & Hart, and Noel Coward who appeared as the principal in many of them. Cochrane went on to sell the film rights of his shows to Hollywood. He was knighted in 1948, around the time of his final major show *Bless the Bride*.

ABOVE
C.B. Cochrane *and Wendy Toye review a script*

LEFT
A.Stewart Cruikshank

opening luxurious cinemas in the city centre (many with full stage facilities for stars of radio and film, top bands and vocalists) and in the expanding suburbs. British and American films, newsreels, cartoons, and advertising reels brought new fashions, new music, excitement and glamour. The city had more cinemas per head of population than any other city outside the United States, and at Green's Playhouse had the largest cinema in Europe seating 4400. Large cinema groups, most notably ABC, expanded from their origins in Glasgow. Expansion of the theatre circuit took place bravely when the Manchester Opera House was bought in 1931 with a loan guarantee again provided by the Theatre Royal.

The Thirties were difficult Depression years and the risk was very

real of theatres trying to undercut each other, while cinemas kept on expanding. 1933 saw Howard & Wyndham Ltd and Moss Empires Ltd form a jointly owned booking company "to secure attractions for touring the Theatres. In order to eliminate unnecessary competition in Edinburgh, Glasgow and elsewhere the parties have made additional arrangements, specific to each city." In Glasgow this arrangement covered the Royal, King's and Alhambra. The joint company would be the booking managers for the Alhambra, managed by Moss Empires, and all would share attractions by rotation. The King's and Alhambra agreed not to compete with each other for amateur lets. The pooled revenue would be shared 50:50 between the two companies. Three years later the agreement was ended, glorious competition ruled!

In the mid-twenties improvements had been made to the frontage on Hope Street, when the large square tower, complete with cupola, was added to the

skyline above the main door. A floodlit rotating beacon was installed on it in 1931. All saying – this is the place to be. For the added comfort of the patrons in the Stalls and Dress Circle new seating was introduced with automatic tip-up.

The Macdona Players and the Masque Theatre Company continued strongly and were joined by the Brandon-Thomas Seasons of Plays for seven weeks each year from 1933, when they performed dozens of plays in repertory. One of their actors was a young Wilson Barrett who combined with Esmond Knight in 1939 to form the Wilson Barrett Players basing themselves at the Alhambra from 1940. Frequent changes of plays were one way of combating the changes and choices of films at the picture houses.

The Sir Walter Scott Centenary celebration year of 1932, a hundred years after the novelist's death, was specially marked at the Theatre Royal with four weeks of his greatest works being performed including *Jeannie Deans, Rob Roy,* and *Guy Mannering.* In 1837

Glasgow had been the first city to erect a statue to Scott, the centre spot in George Square, for his inspired writing and his defence of the right of Scotland's banks to issue their own banknotes.

Community drama in church and other clubs was vibrant, and often the starting point of many professional careers. For the Empire Exhibition 1938 a drama festival was proposed, with James Bridie also campaigning for "a company of professional, mostly Scottish, actors under a Scottish director to be engaged for the duration of the season." However the Bellahouston organisers went deaf. Instead the Royal hosted the Scottish Community Drama Association's May Festival of full-length plays.

Cruikshank started the Howard & Wyndham Repertory under the direction of Ronald Adam, signing the top drama stars to tour the theatres, usually covering spring and summer at the Royal. Their second year at Hope Street was 1939 for a record 24 weeks, ending on the fateful day of 3rd September 1939.

For music and musical plays the Thirties had many high points. Physically the highest was *Peter Pan,* now with Jean Forbes-Robertson flying through the air. And the lowest point had already been reached for 15,000 musicians across Britain who were left without work because silent pictures were no more. Benefit variety concerts were held in Glasgow and elsewhere in aid of "Musicians Disemployed through Talkies" with musicians and artistes

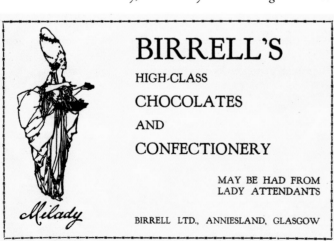

taking part including Tommy Lorne and the Carl Rosa Opera both then at the Royal. The organisers described the hardship being experienced and looked "to the day when the American import will no longer be, and of audiences being able to enjoy the dignity of live music." A forlorn hope.

Musical colour

The Orpheus Club, the Lyric, and the Glasgow Grand Opera Society played to busy houses, and Jack Buchanan's musical comedies were all the rage. In 1935 "*That's A Good Girl*" was presented with musical director Louis Freeman and his Band. Still much remembered he was a gold medal pianist who established orchestras and bands for decades playing at dances, functions, and on Atlantic liners. His father was the Royal's orchestra leader for a time in the 19th century. Another Buchanan show was "*Stand Up and Sing*" in 1936. The following year Glasgow Light Opera Club presented "*The Vagabond King*."

The Boy Scouts produced the "*All Glasgow Scout Revue*" and came again in 1937 with the confident title "*The Gang Comes Back*." Not to be outdone the Boys Brigade advertised their first "*BB Fanfare*" in September 1939 but the war stopped it until the first show in 1944 and every second year thereafter.

Erik Chisholm

In opera the houses were full for the seasons of Carl Rosa, and for the new Covent Garden Opera company, although its prices were the highest.

THEATRE ROYAL GLASGOW

Proprietors, HOWARD & WYNDHAM, Ltd.
Managing Director - A. STEWART CRUIKSHANK
Manager - - - - J. C. HUMPHRYS

Programme

THEATRE BARS
Open during
Performances.

Charges reasonable—no higher
than outside prices.

BOX OFFICE AT THEATRE
Hours—10 to 9   Telephone: 1930 Douglas

Tea, Coffee, Ices, Chocolates and Light Refreshments
may be had from the Attendants

*The Management does not accept responsibility for the non-
appearance of any artiste mentioned on this programme,
and reserves the right to change as circumstances demand.*

TOP
Idomeneo
programme
1934

RIGHT
Erik Chisholm

The greatest highlight was the continuing achievement of the pianist and composer Erik Chisholm, born in Glasgow where, in 1928 at the age of 24, he formed the Scottish Ballet Society and the next year founded the Active Society for the Propogation of Contemporary Music, in association with fellow musician and composer Francis George Scott. Over the next ten years the greatest composers in Europe, including William Walton and Bela Bartok, came to perform their works usually for the first time in public – a total of around 200 new compositions. The Glasgow Grand Opera Society engaged professional and amateur singers for its annual productions at the Theatre Royal. Erik Chisholm was the Society's musical director and conductor for all of the Thirties, during which they also gave premieres of operas.

In the Royal in 1934 he gave the British premiere of Mozart's *Idomeneo*, for which the scenery and costumes were designed and made by the Art School (who also provided the ballet), and in 1935 Berlioz's huge opera *The Trojans* was premiered for the first time outside France. Special trains known as the Berlioz Express came from London and Oxford with opera lovers keen to see the triumph. The opera is so long that it was performed in two halves in consecutive evenings with different casts. Another premiere the next year was *Beatrice and Benedict* also by Berlioz and translated by the novelist Guy McCrone. Chisholm formed the Glasgow Cine Club, was the musical director of Margaret Morris's pioneering Celtic Ballet, and during the war he conducted the Carl Rosa Opera company and was music director of the Anglo-Polish Ballet which toured Britain and later Italy. He became Director of Music, East Asiatic Command, with ENSA and brought music to the troops in India and Malaya. Settling in South Africa he revitalised the University of Cape Town's South African College of Music and developed its Opera School and Cape Opera which toured Southern Africa, disregarding racial barriers. He composed over one hundred concertos and songs, twelve operas and nine ballets.

Heights of pantomime

The Royal's giants of pantomime played well, some especially well. Growing up in Cowcaddens, Tommy Lorne served his comedy apprenticeship at the Grand and the Princess's, and became pantomime Dame at the Pavilion. He was signed up by Stewart Cruikshank for pantomime in Edinburgh in 1927, and then for four (out of five) years from 1929 at the Theatre Royal. In what ever guise he was in, the tall gaunt frame of Tommy Lorne had audiences rolling in the aisles. Two of his phrases were "In the name of the wee man" and "Ah'll get ye, and if Ah don't get you the coos'll get ye." The total cast, sixty in number, cost £850 a week which included Lorne's wage of £225. In his first two pantomimes at Hope Street, which were *Sleeping Beauty* followed by *Goldilocks*, a young lady Alice Simons got a part as "Sweetie", and was paid the going rate of £5 a week (a good wage). She was a granddaughter of the late founder Michael Simons, and allowed on stage now that the next generation was in charge.

After the Royal, Lorne toured successfully in England in a new company which he jointly owned with a member of the Simons family. For these tours they engaged their own cast including Dave Willis. Lorne died suddenly in 1935. It was a loss to all his fans and to the Royal – when he was on stage the theatre made a profit from each pantomime of about £14,000 which in today's money is around £3m each year. His record stood for over twenty years until the appearance of a young man from Hillhead, Stanley Baxter.

The leading star of *Dick Whittington* in 1930 was Fay Compton, the same year as her nationalist brother Compton McKenzie was elected by the students to be the Rector of Glasgow University. She was paid £250 per week, two and a half times that of the show's Dame,

ABOVE
The Courier. *The Royal and King's Theatre magazine, 1935*

LEFT
Erik Chisholm *conducting The Trojans*

LEFT
Tommy Lorne

BELOW
Fay Compton

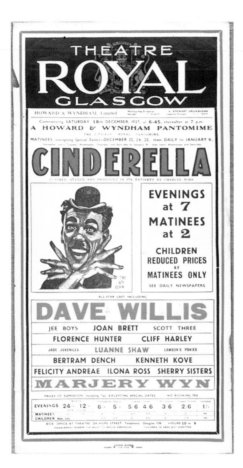

top. His was a genial 'little' man style of comedy, the master of comic mime and movement, almost balletic - " peopling an empty stage in such classic sketches as *The Lonesome Lancers* where he danced a whole set and conjured up all his partners." Many of his songs related to his size including *I'm a Tyrolean, No' a Big Yin, Jist a Wee Yin.*

With his wee black moustache and bowler hat he parodied the Fuhrer Hitler, complete with his song *I'm Getting More Like Hitler Everyday* to the extent that Nazi Germany lodged their complaint with the British Foreign Secretary to stop him – this was before the war. At the Royal he headed five consecutive pantomimes until 1942. CB Cochrane went backstage one night and said to him "you're the only person I know who can go onstage, show your face, do nothing and get roars of laughter from an audience."

For the Summertime

In 1933 Stewart Cruikshank launched the annual summer shows which started as *Half Past Eight* in the King's and later in the Edinburgh King's. These successfully rivalled and outclassed the seaside revues which normally took business

Harry Gordon, and slightly more than Tommy Lorne the year before.

Dave Willis came on the Royal scene in 1937 with *Cinderella* one year after the Royal's winning series staggered sadly with a pantomime put on by Prince Littler. Similar in build and looks as Charles Chaplin he was described by Chaplin as the best comic in Britain. Growing up as a lad in Cowcaddens he helped his brothers' conjuring act in the music halls and joined the children's chorus in the Theatre Royal pantomimes by 1909. Cine-variety work in the city followed by theatre shows here and in London brought him to the

away from the cities in these months. The Royal's main turn came in the early 1950s. What had been an experiment proved to be the best quality entertainment of song, dance and laughter, changing weekly or fortnightly, at a ticket price two thirds the normal rate with all the comforts and benefit of first-class theatres. The shows usually ran for over three months with Dave Willis holding the record runs in both cities, the highest of many being thirty-one weeks in Glasgow.

Going to the Theatre

Reverend Stanley Pritchard, the BBC's broadcasting minister, writes in his memoirs that of all the art forms, opera was the one that claimed him from an early age.

"I was about eight, when I was taken to my first opera, at the end of the First World War. The choice was *Il Travotore* – not a particularly moral story, but it had enough blood and thunder about it to please any child who loved theatre, and the tunes were jingly enough to remain in the memory. This was followed in quick succession by visits to *Faust*, *Carmen*, *La Traviata*, and of course what came to be known as "the English Ring": *The Lily of Killarney*, *The Bohemian Girl*, and *Maritana*.

"Three opera companies came to Glasgow in those days. Moody Manners Company, Britain's largest touring company before 1914, and the O'Mara Grand Opera Company of primitive staging but who had a faithful following. And the Carl Rosa who were at the height of their fame; in an annual six week season they could stage up to thirty operas, ranging from Puccini, Gounod and Verdi to the much more adventurous claims of Wagner and Myerbeer. They had singers like Eva Turner, Gladys Parr, Norman Allin, Walter Widdop and Doris Woodall; and they had a chorus which sketched in the background sounds with enthusiasm if not always accuracy.

"The Theatre Royal will always be linked

LEFT
Entrance foyer *and fireplace, 1930s*

RIGHT
Foyer *and staircase, 1930s*

in my mind with these early visits to a magical world of sound. The Gallery, hard wooden tiers without backs, cost one shilling, but it was worth paying an extra sixpence for the "early doors". Once past the pay desk, where you got a metal disc for your money, the orderly queue disintegrated and there was a free-for-all up the endless stone stairs to ensure a front row seat. Two massive black iron rails prevented the more enthusiastic from plunging over the front barrier, and accidentally obtaining a seat in the stalls below. These rails always remained ice-cold, and it was a secret delight to lean your brow against them, amid the heat and sweat of a gallery crowd. That crowd knew their operas well and had an Italian enthusiasm in recognition of a good top note.

"It was not easy to sing demanding roles night after night, and the fog of a Glasgow winter produced many problems. (Dame) Eva Turner remembers her landlady providing a cure for a sore throat. It consisted of hot flannel with sliced onions wrapped inside. It certainly strengthened the voice and she was able to sing Isolde the following night. It was acceptable to the audience but not, evidently, to Tristan (Walter Widdop) who in the clinch of the Love Duet exclaimed in a loud whisper "You've been at the pickled onions again!"

In the queue eating your sandwich
The thoughts of two women, in Anna Blair's "Miss Cranston's Omnibus," are

of the attraction of theatre compared to cinema. They would go to the cinema for Spencer Tracey. <u>Anything</u> with Spencer Tracy.
"But mostly it was theatre. My friend and I thought we were a bit superior going to the Brandon Thomas rep and the opera. Mind you it was just the gods. We would be earning about 18 shillings a week at the time. You knew everybody in the gods......not their names right-enough, but you spoke to them week by week.

"When it was the opera you'd be standing in the queue eating your sandwich. Then the doors opened and you went belting up the stair, because it was 1/6d "early doors" and 2/3d "ordinary doors". "Early doors" you got your choice of seats. When they played the National Anthem at the beginning you could always tell the regulars because they sat down at the beginning of the last line to get their bottoms on the bench first...... the rest had to wiggle theirs in between as best they could. It was hot too. You sat fair steamin' up there in the gods.

"Later we got permanent weekly seats for the Wilson Barrett drama company. And you went dressed with your best coat and hat, and your handbag under your arm. You wouldn't have *insulted* Wilson Barrett or Richard Mathews by going casual. You'd your tea at the interval too. Oh we werenae-half ladies by then! The company had Kitty de Legh, and Phyllis Barker, George Larchet and Simon Lack (when he was still just Alex

McAlpine from Tollcross). I had a real crush on Wilson Barrett. Oh my they were terr-ific, wonderful!"

Lavinia Derwent discovers

In her memoirs the story-teller and writer Lavinia Derwent tells of starting work in the city in the 1930s, the picture palaces, music halls and dance halls "But I soon abandoned the music hall when I discovered the real theatre. At first I patronized the little theatres where actors and actresses were trying out their wings ….. their acting was excellent. When I ventured to the "real" theatre the names were bigger but the acting no better. Here I could see beautiful people in the flesh, the ladies attired in lovely Parisian gowns with never a crease or a safety-pin to be seen. They moved gracefully about the stage after coming down some stairs from a sunlit garden to ring their parlourmaid who brought in afternoon tea complete with sugar tongs. The ladies deftly manipulated the sugar tongs, sipped their tea without slopping a drop into the saucer, and nibbled little sandwiches without a visible chew.

"The actors were not the only ones drinking tea. During the interval, while the male members of the audience sloped off to the bars, their ladies were handed little teatrays ordered in advance from the Tea Service Room, containing all the appurtenances, apart from tongs, for a refreshing interlude. We sat primly in our places trying to eat the biscuits as daintily as the beautiful

ABOVE
Lounge Buffet
at the Dress Circle level
1930s

people on the stage, and not to rattle the teaspoons if the attendants had not collected the empty trays before the curtain went up. What with the men returning late to their seats and the teatrays jangling, the beginning of the next act was always a dead loss. There were whispered "hushes" from all sides while the performers tried not to look annoyed."

Managing the Theatre

Cruikshank introduced a large, printed and bound Management Book in 1933, revised in the 1940s, for the six core theatres owned by the company. Each manager and his staff knew it inside out, and it was shared with visiting companies. Altogether 190 pages, it had theatre layouts, pricing tables, technical information and staff routines as well as colour pages for use as business forms, and reporting schedules. It was an operating manual which has its resonance today. Even the revenues

NOTES COVERING THE ROUTINE DUTIES OF MANAGERS

Staff discussion

The Manager will discuss the staffing each Monday forenoon of the Stage, Property, and Electrical Departments with the Heads of these departments.

Evening Duties

The Manager and Assistant should be in attendance during the assembling and dissembling of each audience. The Manager should walk round the auditorium at least once during each performance spending a few minutes in each part of the house to satisfy himself that the conduct of the staff is beyond reproach. (It is recommended that the time and route of this "inspection tour" be varied as much as possible.)

Dress Clothes

It is understood that full Dress Suit is worn at Evening Performances, and Morning Clothes during Matinees.

Courtesy to Patrons

As it is the company's business to please the public, the Manager must pay particular attention to see that every member of the staff is polite, and check at once any semblance of abruptness or insolence from employee to patron.

Female Staff

It is essential to engage girls, smart, intelligent, and of good appearance. Middle-aged women cannot be engaged.

Male Staff

Only men of good appearance, young and intelligent to be engaged.

Complimentary Tickets

Managers please remember that our seats are our only goods for sale, and the issue of complimentary permits must be carefully controlled. This permit system is much abused, and while it is necessary upon occasion to dress the house, the greatest care must be taken in doing so.

(Dressing the House means issuing free tickets to help make a quiet night look busy.)

BOX OFFICE ROUTINE and STAFF REGULATIONS

During the busy season the average number of box office girls employed is 4.

Hours, in shifts, are 10am to 9pm.

Change over to an Evening Pay Box in the foyer is 45 minutes before rise of curtain.

It is most necessary that the Manager studies the plans a few days ahead so that he can alter the dividing line for each part of the House according to demand, this will obviate rows of empty seats between different priced parts of the House.

Politeness

It is most important that the staff should realise that patrons should always receive the greatest courtesy. Men attendants should always stand to attention when spoken to by patrons. They must, when addressing patrons, salute and stand to attention. All attendants must always address patrons as "Sir" or "Madam".

Uniform

Uniforms must be kept scrupulously clean. On no account should polish be used on buttons. They should only be rubbed with a clean cloth. Jewellery of any description is expressly forbidden. All attendants must wear black shoes.

Ushers must wear black stockings.

General

All members of staff will stand upright at their posts.

All attendants must be at their posts a quarter of an hour before the House opens. They must not leave until the whistle is blown.

---

from cloakroom charges, sales of programmes, bar refreshments, teas, ices and chocolates, and hire of opera glasses, were meticulously accounted for.

Advertising was crucial to success, 80 per cent on newspapers and 20 per cent on billposting and boardmen. Each week, orders were placed for giant hand-painted posters at the city's main approach roads, printed billboard posters, 150 shop and public house posters, 2,000 circulars and throwaways. For newspapers Press copy each week had to be at least 12 paragraphs about the next show, with a plentiful supply of photographs. "Ladies preferred."

Nightly and weekly returns of attendance, sales and costs were prepared and posted off to the managing director A.Stewart Cruikshank in Edinburgh and the chairman Ernest Simons, now based at the London Fruit Exchange, Spitalfields, with weekly abstracts to Granville Heilbron in Glasgow and Charles B Cochran in London. The weekly reports required the manager to add notes about the weather; the opposition shows in neighbouring theatres; and any other remarks. When it was a show by a visiting company the manager gave his response to a number of questions:-

State type of Entertainment ------ Musical, Dramatic, Farce, Tragedy, or Comedy.

Starting time, length of interval, First, Second, Finishing time?

How is it accepted by the audience?

Is the Company satisfactory; and is the Production mounted, staged and dressed adequate to our Theatres?

Would you recommend a Return Visit?

All seats were bookable in advance except for the Gallery. Much later the benches were changed to chairs, making pre-booking possible in the gods. The queue for going heaven-ward started 40 minutes before the start and stretched

GLOVER AND GIBSON GO TO HOLLYWOOD

In 1907 **Ernest K Glover**, scenic artist in his father's studios in Glasgow, decided to emigrate to pastures new. Canada wanted people for its new country; theatres needed designers. With his young family he arrived in Calgary, a growing town because of its oil discoveries, and set up business. Moving on to Vancouver as a set designer for nine years there, including productions for the Empress Theatre, he turned south over the border to Seattle working with producer Tom Wilkes. After six years they finally settled in Los Angeles, with commissions from Wilkes and others. He was a producer and designer for over ten years with the Henry Duffy chain of theatres in California, including the El Capitan theatre, known today as the Hollywood Palace.

In 1934 he produced a favourite of his family, a historical drama with music, Sir Walter Scott's *Rob Roy* at the open-air Hollywood Music Box. The LA Times wrote *"it held the audience, the music found pleasing."* In the 1940s he also designed a number of plays on Broadway, including his final major design *School for Brides* which enjoyed 375 performances to June 1945. Some of his family entered showbusiness, most notably daughter **Rita Glover** who became a stage designer and producer in her own name, becoming Professor of Theatrical Art & Design at the University of California.

George Gibson served his apprenticeship to William E. Glover. After learning the skills and secrets of stagecraft, illusion and design in the Glover studios and the Theatre Royal he joined the thousands emigrating from Scotland, many times more than the Highland Clearances a century before. With a letter of introduction from Glover he sailed to New York in 1929 but on arrival found the theatres were dark as the extent of the Great Depression became clear. It was easier to find employment in the burgeoning Los Angeles film industry and he travelled on west to stay with Ernest K Glover and family. The Glover home at Crescent Heights was an open-house, in good times and hard. He worked as a scenic artist in film studios including 20th Century Fox where his first Hollywood film was *Cavalcade*, and in 1934 became an illustrator with Metro Goldwyn Mayer Studios.

In 1936 art director Cedric Gibbons approached Gibson and asked him to create and head MGM's first department of scenic art. Gibson had carte-blanche and brought together young artists *"to form the Cadillac of the industry, a world-renown department of scenic design."* From 1936 to 1966 he was responsible for the art of hundreds of films including spectaculars such as *Wizard of Oz*, *Showboat*, *Singing in the Rain*, *Brigadoon*, *American in Paris*, *Oklahoma*, and *Shoes of the Fisherman*. He had a unique management style cultivated from his Glasgow days, emphasising the importance of artistic teamwork. To hone their skills he conducted weekly sketching trips with his artists around Southern California. During World War II he was attached to the US Marine Corps, as a map-maker and model builder for proposed landing sites on Japanese-held islands in the Pacific. He was appointed President of the California Water Color Society, painting on into his nineties.

round into Cowcaddens Street; once up the stairs to the roof a packer made certain that everybody moved up close on the benches, and more people could get in. The Royal's capacity in the Thirties was now 2,294:

Stalls and Pit Stalls	636
Standing	32
Grand Circle	326
Upper Circle	332
Standing	12
Gallery/Balcony	708
Standing	176
Box Seats	72

The Stalls had 24 rows and 2 boxes, the Grand Circle had 11 rows and 8 boxes, and the Upper Circle had 11 rows and 2 boxes. The theatre capacity became 2013 later, mainly when the Balcony standing was ended. Initially the Theatre Royal with a capacity of 2294 persons was the largest, followed by Manchester Opera House with 2266. Changes by local city councils because of safety concerns reduced all capacities over time. To help those fortunate enough to have a car the programmes declared that:

> Car Parking accommodation for at least 300 Cars can be found in Hope Street opposite the Theatre in Messrs John Paterson (Motors) Ltd magnificent New Garage.

At the Dress Circle level the Lounge Buffet was modernised complete with Lloyd-loom chairs:

> Ladies, may we remind you that our New Buffet (Fully Licensed) is now open for Tea, Coffee, Ices.

The company drew up plans at the end of 1937 for a new, large L-shaped Stalls Buffet as suggested by the city authorities. This would replace the Pit Bar at the end of the Cowcaddens arched entrance corridor and use some of the space underneath the Bijou Hall, but the approach of war changed the Corporation's priorities.

ABOVE
Before and After
programme covers before 1939, and in the 1950s

OPPOSITE
(top to bottom)

Ernest Glover

George Gibson

"The Pier" *drawing by George Gibson*

George Gibson *and Deborah Kerr look at the Student Prince set, 1954*

War and Peace

From 1939 hundreds of thousands of people were on the move to the armed services, and key workers to the shipyards, aircraft factories, engineering works, armaments factories, steel works, coal mines and hospitals in and around Glasgow. Vast numbers came in from Canada and the Caribbean, from Poland then France, and eventually from the United States. For people at home and in transit going to the pictures, dance halls or theatres was a way of putting the fears to one side.

Cruikshank switched the *Half Past Eight* show into the Royal from the King's with George West and Jack Raymond waving the flag at Hope Street from 23rd September 1939 to the end of October. Life would try to be as normal as it could be. Young artistes and staff were being called up for active service and others would go off to entertain the troops in due course. Theatre life reflected public life, morale fell in 1940 as did theatre takings. In that year the Royal made a loss for the first and only time in its history under Howard & Wyndham. By 1942 confidence was rising.

In his wartime pantomimes and many shows to follow Dave Willis added another bashful character, this time in the Air Raid Precautions, because he was "the nicest lookin' warden in the A.R.P." Wearing his steel helmet and with his gas mask over his shoulder he would tell the audience about his new job. *In My Wee Gas Mask* was sung everywhere.

Oh my head is up among the clouds,
Ah made it on the brain,
I've joined the ARP.
And when I see an aeroplane –
I've got my mask
I've got my task
I'm up to ninety nine!
Wait till I tell you all about
This fair wee job of mine:

Wi' my wee gas mask, I'm working out a plan
Tho' all the kids imagine that I'm just a bogey man
The girls all smile and bring their friends to see
The nicest lookin' warden in the A.R.P.

Whenever there's a raid on, listen to my cry
An airy-plane, an airy-plane away-way up-a-kye
Then I run helter-skelter but don't run after me
You'll no get in my shelter for it's far too wee.

OPPOSITE
Sketch
*showing outside walls
painted in bands
1933*

AIR RAID PRECAUTIONS

You will be notified by the Management if a warning is given. Do not be alarmed because the warning does not mean that an air raid will take place and it is not likely to occur for at least five minutes. If you wish to leave for home or the nearest shelter you are at liberty to do so. If not just remain in the building, which is much safer than on the streets.

KEEP CALM, KEEP SMILING, IT MAY NOT HAPPEN

We recommend that patrons should carry gas masks with them when outside their homes. If you wish to leave the auditorium there is accommodation for a number of people in the different parts of the theatre.

A list then followed, for each level, of lavatories, corridors and stairs to accommodate people. The first bombing air raid on Glasgow was in July 1940, and the last in March 1943. As time went on the ARP notice became:

AIR RAID WARNINGS

Indicators have been fitted each side of the Stage in full view of the Audience. In the event of an "Alert" being sounded then indicators will be lit, with the word "Alert" (Red Light.) In the sounding of the "All Clear" the indicators will change to "All Clear" (Green Light.)

At the start of the war the programmes had a large notice about air raid precautions, which changed its wording after a year or two, as shown above.

Other regulars in pantomime included Cliff Harley, Jewel & Warriss, Elizabeth French, Florence Hunter and a speciality dance act with the wonderful name of Arnaud, Peggy & Ready.

Actors and actresses in repertory, usually with the new HM Tennent Players – part of the Howard & Wyndham stable - included Lewis Casson, Robert Donat, Alastair Sim, Diana Churchill, Yvonne Arnaud, Edith Evans, John Gielgud and Robert Morley. Most continued into the 1950s when they were joined by Ian Fleming, Edith McArthur and Eric Portman.

Shakespeare, Shaw, and plays relating to Nazi Germany were presented, as were Agatha Christie thrillers and plays by JB Priestley. Ernest Hemingway's *The Fifth Column* about the Spanish Civil War had its premiere. Of an earlier period, Anna Neagle starred in *Emma* by Jane Austen, James Bridie's *Mr Bolfry* was directed by Alastair Sim. Peter Ustinov's *Princess Ida*, was in aid of the British Sailors Society. And *Flare Path* by Terence Rattigan was based on the experiences of Royal Air Force families.

Considered to be the most significant of wartime's contribution to drama was *There Shall be No More Night*, about the Russian invasion of Finland, written in 1940 by Robert Sherwood, a Pullitzer Prizewinner and confidante of President Roosevelt.

Music and dance

More ballet started to be seen at the Royal, with Ballet Rambert in 1940 followed over the years by the Carl Rosa Ballet, the Anglo Polish Ballet directed by Erik Chisholm; Lydia Kyasht's Ballet de la Jeunnesse Anglaise; and Ballets Joos in its 11th season in 1943 led by Kurt Joos who had fled Germany in 1935. The Anglo-Russian *Merry Go Round* was a show of ballet, song and mime.

The Scottish (National) Orchestra played for the Sadlers Wells Opera who were new to the Royal. The Orpheus Club and the Glasgow Grand Opera Society also took the stage. D'Oyly Carte Opera maintained their visits and the London Philharmonic Orchestra presented concerts. Musicals included *No No Nanette*, *The Gypsy Princess*, *Desert Song*, and the *Maid of the Mountains* - presented by Emile Littler starring Sonnie Hale, and produced three years in a row. *Old Chelsea* starred Richard Tauber, who wrote and directed it. Comedy plays as ever were popular. The Glasgow Herald wrote in August 1944:

Arsenic and Old Lace is not a Lease-Lend commodity but as

a prevention of war weariness it might be listed among the vitally necessary things America has sent to Britain in wartime.

In early 1945 some of the plays were presented by companies who had come from stage tours in France and Belgium. With the ending of war there was hope for a better world, a wish to enjoy peace. Celebration and exhaustion were mixed together. In September a variety show

ABOVE
Dave Willis

ABOVE
Glasgow Theatre Charity Gala,
1943. Manager Jake Stewart, Sir Harry Lauder shaking hands with King Peter of Yugoslavia. Beside Lauder is Harry Gordon (left) *and Will Fyffe* (right).

Back Home was by aircrew ex-prisoners of war from Stalag Luft III in sketches originally played by them in their prison camp in Germany. This was in aid of the International Red Cross. Franz Lehar's *The Merry Widow* was also presented in September to packed houses, its third season in twelve months. The Evening Citizen wrote:

> After about 40 years of the lilt and laughter of *The Merry Widow*, the only criticism to be made of it is that it was a favourite of Hitler.

Royal Majestic Circuses
Circuses replaced the annual panto-mimes in two consecutive years, the last

one in December 1944 being the return of Harry Benet's *Royal Majestic Circus* whose human performers included the Australian Aces' motor cycling Wall of Death, Koringa with her crocodiles and reptiles (one time not reappearing after a quick curtain drop when a crocodile bit too hard), and Mlle. Garcis "spectacular on the tight rope". Every night the trapeze artiste walked along a high wire from the Circle to the stage, holding only a balancing pole. Of equal appeal were the elephants, lions, horses, and dogs. In both years the stage contained a large cage with seven young lions, under the care of their owner Mr Chipperfield. The cage, linked to dens backstage, was the same one used by the Empire Theatre in its 1939/40 circus. The circus was very profitable even after the cost of strengthening the stage. The following year the theatre reverted to pantomime. One reviewer wrote:

> If *Cinderella* is less spectacular than Howard & Wyndham's pantomimes of the past, one has to remember that austerity is still a reality.

For 1945 to 1947 the three pantomimes of *Cinderella*, *Mother Goose* and then *Sleeping Beauty* starred George West and his feed Jack Raymond who packed the houses and helped create the highest annual theatre profits so far in the Royal. They were firm favourites also in the Royal Princess's pantomimes in the Gorbals, where West held the national record of appearing in 21 successive pantomimes. He came from Cowcaddens and had started in variety halls with Tommy Lorne. James Bridie described George West as a great clown in the French tradition, wearing what was almost a clown's make-up, a "fright" wig, and elaborate funny clothes. He had three years of top billing in the *Half Past Eight Shows* in the King's before the war.

In *Sleeping Beauty* the 32 girls of the Ballet dancing troupe were each paid £4 a week; one of the members was Kathleen Garscadden who went on to become Auntie Kathleen in the BBC Children's Hour broadcasts from Queen Margaret Drive. The cast included the Airdrie Ladies Pipe Band which Cruikshank also employed the

year before in Edinburgh. For their performances the 8 girl pipers, 4 girl drummers and a Drum Major got £75 a week in total. The famous sand dance speciality act of Wilson, Keppel and Betty was paid £175 a week. For its pantomimes and opera seasons the Royal advertised:

> To give all our Patrons an equal chance in advance booking Postal Bookings, only, will be accepted and require a stamped addressed envelope for reply.

Nearer the time the box office sold the tickets at the window. Prices for most shows ranged from 1/6d. to 9/-.

Because the King's housed the *Half Past Eight Shows* with Dave Willis, Harry Gordon, Jack Holden, Helen Crerar, Beryl Reid and others which ran for five to six months each year, many

LEFT
George West *and feed Jack Raymond*

shows normally at the King's now came to the Royal instead - including the Sadlers Wells Ballet (one of whose repertoire was *Miracle in the Gorbals*) and the D'Oyly Carte Opera performing the favourites of Gilbert & Sullivan.

Peter Pan returned in peacetime as did the amateur societies and the *Scout Gang Shows*, as quickly as they could. Plays included *All This is Ended* with an all ex-Active Service cast in 1946, and *There Shall be No More Night* made another return. Carl Rosa Operas resumed in 1947, other musicals included *The Wizard of Oz*, and the *Song of Norway*; while revues ran across the summer of 1948 including Joyce Grenfell and Elizabeth Welch in *Tuppence Coloured*. The opera societies often presented different operas on alternate evenings of their week – in 1948 the Glasgow Grand Opera presented *The Bartered Bride* and *Eugene Onegin*, which was then only rarely performed in Britain. In a few years time their guest producers would include Peter Ebert and Anthony Besch.

Unity theatre

The Theatre Royal staged some of the pioneering performances of the Glasgow Unity Theatre which was started in 1941 when some of the amateur clubs in Glasgow, notably the Clarion Players, the Workers' Theatre Group, the Transport Players and the Glasgow Jewish Institute Players, came together to promote work of a socialist viewpoint and to attract a working class audience. Normally they were based in

the Athenaeum, and also travelled with their work to London. For three weeks in 1948 the Royal housed the world premiere of Bendict Scott's *The Lambs of God*, and for the first of a number of visits there was Ena Lamont Stewart's *Men Should Weep*, and Robert Mcleish's *The Gorbals Story*.

During the Second World War Simons and Cruikshank joined the board of Stoll Theatres in London, chaired by Prince Littler, and supported Littler's plan for Stoll Theatres to take control of Moss Empires theatres headed by Val Parnell. This was achieved in 1943 and Cruikshank, the gentleman and professional, also joined the board of Moss Empires. He found Parnell difficult – perhaps a clash of giants. In 1945 he objected to Parnell wasting the time of Howard & Wyndham managers by contacting them about theatre sizes and facilities. He wrote to Parnell drawing his attention again to the Management Book with all the details; and wrote to Prince Littler:

> This man Parnell is a nasty piece of work.......I would be much better pleased if we can manage to dispense with his services.

With the passing of Ernest Simons at the end of 1944, Stewart Cruikshank became the company chairman. The board was joined by Granville Simons, grandson of the founder, by Stewart Cruikshank junior and by Prince Littler. The war was nearing an end but nobody knew when. The summer of 1945 approached. One day across the pages of the Royal's weekly ledgers, kept so steadily in black ink, were written in the brightest red ink:

£65 V-Day wages extra to staff
Peace signed 7 May. Officially over 8 May

At each annual meeting Cruikshank spoke of things to come. In 1946 he said:

> With the end of the war there has been a steady decrease in the floating population in the various towns where our theatres are situated, and the effect of this will be felt....

And reported in 1947 that the company:

> Purchased land at Rutherford Lane adjoining the Royal for the purpose of forming a car park, a very necessary benefit to patrons of a theatre situated in such a busy area with little or no facilities for car parking, and for future extension if necessary.

Business tried to return to normal but found 1946/47 even more difficult when:

> We have had electricity cuts, black out conditions, shortage of fuel for heating and exceptionally severe weather to contend with....... all have tended to keep patrons away from the theatre.

In December 1949 Alexander Stewart Cruikshank died in Edinburgh as a result of a road accident. He was 72. Prince Littler said of him "He was the most respected figure in British theatre business." As well as his pantomimes and *Half Past Eight* shows he was especially proud of bringing the musical *Rose Marie* from America, for which he held the British rights. The company started by Michael Simons in 1895 now owned or managed over 20 theatres in Britain, and would reach 25. Prince Littler became chairman and Stewart Cruikshank junior followed his father as managing director.

WILLIAM F GLOVER AND BILL GLOVER JUNIOR

Around the turn of the century **William F Glover** was a busy man in theatres. He had joined his father William Glover in the studios at Port Dundas, and was a property manager for Howard & Wyndham Ltd. He also trod the boards. In the Britannia Panoptican, at the Trongate, he was the feed to a young Stanley Jefferson who would become Stan Laurel, the slim half of Laurel & Hardy. While expanding the work of the studios during the day he became the manager in the 1920s of the Gaiety cinema, in Anderston, which had been the handsome Tivoli theatre.

Sets were always the dearest single item of production for theatre companies and it was important to provide the best at the best cost, and on time. Artists he employed usually started as apprentice scenic designers. One such artist was George Gibson who had studied in Edinburgh and at Glasgow School of Art. During the Depression he moved to America, spreading the gospel of Glover art to the highest levels of the new film industry in Los Angeles.

Bill Glover junior joined the artists in the studios and was largely self-taught in painting and design. Brought up in Garnethill, Glover was a friend and contemporary of Tom Honeyman. At the outbreak of the Great War, and just out of school, he joined the Royal Flying Corps in 1914 to 1917, and was an aero engineer and fitter at Rossleigh Motors off Otago Street. During the war more than half of Britain's aircraft engines were made in Glasgow. In civilian life he won the Glasgow School of Art Medal for Fine Art 1917-18.

Telegraph address "Stagecraft, Glasgow"

In 1930 the Glovers decided to move the studios from Port Dundas, to new purpose-built premises. A steel-framed building complete with corrugated roof was built in Garscube Road, with ceilings 30 feet high for the sets. It contained preparation and paint areas, store areas for flats and backdrops, and costume storage. Other costumiers in the 1930s were Josephine Smith, and James Bamber, theatrical wigmakers. Bamber the Barber supplied most wigs, and had started business in Buchanan Street in the 1860s.

Sets were designed and prepared for theatres in many parts of Britain and many companies, including from 1934 the new Glyndebourne Opera company. Pantomime design was lucrative and for long seasons. Likewise, sets were made for seaside theatres with their busy summer seasons for all holidaymakers. Visiting companies to Glasgow would seek out scene makers and, whatever a theatre manager may say, would always ask for Bill Glover by name.

The new medium of cinema required attention. Sets were designed and supplied to early filmmakers. One client was Scottish Films Ltd. of St Vincent Street, run by Maurice Sandground. That company was wound up in 1929 with the liquidator selling the rights of two silent films, containing Glover work, to Wardour Films, a company created by John Maxwell of Glasgow, founder of the ABC chain of cinemas.

Bill Glover's studios worked as scenic artists for Kelvingrove Museum &Art Galleries designing backcloths for displays including the animal room and elephant setting. The huge backcloths for the Ibrox Tattoo were created to obscure the shipyard cranes and factory chimneys and to create entrance ways for the troops to enter through the "mediaeval castle" gates. For the Empire Exhibition 1938 the firm designed and produced the backcloths for the Clachan, displays for the Canadian Pavilion, and other sites in Bellahouston Park. They designed and constructed all the sets for Sir Charles Cochran's show *Me and My Girl* premiered in London in 1937. The sets were sent off by train to Cochran's depot in Redruth, Cornwall. The star Lupino Lane was a cousin of the Glover family through the original Julia Glover. Its chorus and dance "The Lambeth Walk" became famous, --even becoming the daily anthem of the Empire Exhibition. "Leaning on a Lamppost", and "The Sun has got its Hat On" completed the show's trio of hits.

ABOVE
In the studio
Bill Glover preparing for the Empire Exhibition

The Glovers and Howard & Wyndham chief Stewart Cruikshank were business colleagues and good friends until his death in 1949 after which they found his son a different type, who wanted to bring production much more in-house to his company. After Scottish Television bought Theatre Royal the new owners let Glover Studios use the full width and height of the stage (outwith television hours) to paint and finish extra-large cloths too big for their own building. William Glover the First would have approved of the generosity! When Bill Glover died in the 1960s the curtain finally stayed down.

WHAT HAPPENED TO SIMONS & COMPANY?

The Simons fruit businesses met the growth of supermarkets in the 1960s, extended their distribution services, and continued to trade nationally. In 1979 the group became a part of the Geest Group, famed for bananas and horticulture. When Geest reorganised in 1986 the Simons Group name finally disappeared.

A great-grandson David Simons, who runs a language college in North London, wrote a stage play "Women of a Certain Age" which had a major theatre tour in 1998 with Vicki Michelle (of Allo Allo fame). It must be in the family genes!

ABOVE
Simons Fruit Lorries

THEATRE ROYAL

Howard and Wyndham's

"half-past eight"

Fun in the Fifties
...and Farewell?

Rationing of food and necessities became stricter after the war than during it. The Labour government introduced the much needed National Health Service but also decided it would nationalise and centralise whole industries and utilities. An exhausted country had had more than enough of scarcities, restrictions and now a Korean War, and a new government took its place in 1951. Theatres were holding their own against competition from films, as people wanted to resume normal life.

Competition kept everyone on their toes. AE Pickard, the wizard of advertising stunts and eccentric millionaire owner of picture houses, got into his car one evening and was driven up Hope Street to the Royal. Telling his chauffeur to wait in the car at the front door, Pickard walked in, bought a ticket for the front stalls and took his seat just as the curtain rose. After the first scene he got up – for all to see -- and walked back down the centre aisle saying loudly "There are better shows at Pickard's picture houses!" and left the building. Everyone knew what was coming to the theatre, by advertisements in newspapers and cinemas, handbills and roadside posters and through news releases in the press, much of it co-ordinated by George Stewart's firm Rex Publicity, based in Glasgow, who had the contract for many theatres and for the ABC cinema chain.

Four months of pantomime, four and more weeks of amateur societies added to the Royal Carl Rosa Opera company weeks, took up half a year. Societies included the Pantheon Club, the Gang Show, BB Fanfare, the Orpheus Club, Glasgow Grand Opera Society with *Carmen*, and the *Pearl Fishers* in their Bizet Festival 1951 (this was the first time in Britain that the *Pearl Fishers* had been performed in English), and joining in the fun the Hamilton Academy Choir boldly presented Edward German's comic opera *Merrie England*. The summer and autumn featured plays and revues including Joyce Grenfell and Elizabeth Welch in a sequel to *Tuppence Coloured*, this time *Penny Plain*. In drama the audiences flocked to Flora Robson, Sybil Thorndike, Lewis Casson, and listened to new plays such as *A*

OPPOSITE
Half-Past Eight
cover
1952

Festival Circus poster, 1951

ABOVE
Ram Gopal

RIGHT
Festival Circus
poster, 1951

Street Car Named Desire and the Unity Theatre's *The Gorbals Story*.

Dance included the arrival at the Theatre Royal of *NY Norsk Ballet* which started life in Oslo in 1948, and Ram Gopal took the stage in 1951 with his *Indian Ballet* and Orchestra. The same year the theatre had a season of the Celtic Ballet of Scotland directed by Margaret Morris, who led her modern dance company on major tours over the next few years to America, Europe and Russia.

Along at the King's Theatre in 1950 Dave Willis headed the *Half Past Eight Show* throughout its run until it ended in September – only because other shows waited to come in; at that point the Royal took in Harry Gordon's version of the *Half Past Eight Show* from its Edinburgh run, until the end of October. The city was enjoying the best of fun. The well loved radio show *The McFlannels*, written by Helen S Pryde, ventured on stage in May 1951 with a tale of another city – this was *The McFlannels in Edinburgh* with John Morton, Ann Downie and Arthur

Shaw, produced by the BBC's Howard M Lockhart. The next month saw a Special Holiday attraction for children to coincide with the opening of the Festival of Britain in London, and associated Festivals in Glasgow and elsewhere. For two weeks the *Festival Circus* was alive with the sights and sounds of lions, baby elephants, zebras, llamas, baboons, horses, dogs, clowns and acrobats.

Dave Willis starred in *Cinderella* in 1951, having finished another long run at the King's with the *Half Past Eight Show*, after Harry Gordon again opened at the Royal in the autumn with *Half Past Eight* from Edinburgh. As part of the Festival of Britain the Glasgow Grand Opera Society presented *Jeanie Deans* and *Mefistofele* produced by Peter Ebert, with the Scottish National Orchestra in the pit. The designs for both were by Jefferson Barnes, head of the Glasgow School of Art.

Television spreads

There was one invention and the spread of it in peacetime that would totally change the balance of entertainment. It was television. John Logie Baird demonstrated his invention in many ways, firstly to an audience invited to his laboratory in London in 1926; then by transmitting moving pictures over 400 miles to his native city in May 1927, to the Central Hotel in Hope Street; and transmissions across the Atlantic to New York in February 1929. Theatre and cinema companies wanted to know more, and contracted Baird to transmit

ABOVE
John Logie Baird

television as part of their entertainments on offer. The world's first public performance of television being screened in a theatre was at the London Coliseum in July 1930 - "Living Celebrities and Artistes televised three times daily by this marvellous invention." He also invented colour television.

The BBC's regular television service, of a few hours a day to the London area, started in the 1930s but was suspended with the outbreak of war. After 1946 the service slowly extended its way up the map. BBC transmissions in Scotland began in March 1952 from Queen Margaret Drive opening with performances from the Royal Scottish Country Dance Society (which appropriately was started in Glasgow by ladies coming together in 1923 whose husbands, boyfriends or brothers had died in the First World War.)

Few people could afford to buy a receiver, but the interest in what could be seen steadily grew. Community centres even started television clubs where, for a small charge, families could watch for two hours a week. Public houses sought permission to instal television sets.

More of the best

The Royal's answer was more of its best, including The Italian Opera Company in each of the next five years, who sang always in Italian, with principal performers Margherita Carosia, Kyra Vane, Carlo Zampighi and Piero Ferraro. The Italian government gave the company a subsidy for overseas touring. Sometimes a winter's night could affect a performance. In October 1954 the Evening Citizen's review had the headline

BELOW
Half-Past Eight
poster, 1952

FOG DULLS an OPERA "SPARKLE":

Fog robbed last night's performance of Verdi's "La Traviata" by the Italian Opera Company of its sparkle. It marred top-register phrasing. Theatre Royal fans kept the auditorium clear, but the damage was done probably during pre-curtain strolls.

A Viennese Operetta Season the same year was performed by members of the Vienna State Opera (which was homeless at the end of the war) and included the chorus and ballet from Vienna, and the Italian tenor Gianni Raimondi. The opera company was based in Rome and had a female General Manager, one of the first in any opera company. She was Jean Grant, age 28, from Glasgow who was a piano accompanist originally and now lived in Italy. A young Alexander Gibson conducted the Scottish National Orchestra for the Glasgow Grand Opera Society's *Faust* with guest singer Ignatius McFadyen of the Covent Garden Opera. Carl Rosa Opera performed 11 operas in two weeks, starring Charles Craig, Jane Heddle Nash, and the principal soprano Khrystyna Granowska who was a Polish refugee received into Glasgow during the war.

Stanley Baxter storms the Royal

From 1952 to 1954/55 the Theatre Royal could have changed its name to The Stanley Baxter Theatre. 1952 was a Baxter *Half Past Eight* summer and

THEATRE ROYAL, GLASGOW
HOWARD & WYNDHAM LTD.

Managing Director   STEWART CRUIKSHANK
Manager   J. G. STEWART

FOR A SEASON   (CHANGE OF PROGRAMME EVERY THURSDAY)
First Performance THURSDAY, 29th MAY 1952

MONDAYS to FRIDAYS	SATURDAYS & HOLIDAYS
ONCE NIGHTLY AT **8.30 p.m.**	TWICE NIGHTLY AT **6 & 8.30**

STEWART CRUIKSHANK
PRESENTS

GEORGE LACY

GEORGE **LACY**	AND	STANLEY **BAXTER**

In HOWARD and WYNDHAM'S 1952 Edition of

'HALF-PAST EIGHT'
A COCKTAIL OF SONG, DANCE & LAUGHTER
with

ANDREW MACPHERSON
MARION WILSON   BOND ROWELL   CICELY HULLET
ANTON & YOLETTE
ANNETTE GIBSON   JAMES HEYS   PAMELA WARDEL
FOUR IN A CHORD
THE "HALF-PAST EIGHT" GIRLS

THE ENTIRE PRODUCTION DIRECTED BY **HEATH JOYCE**

Dances Staged by Cherry Willoughby. Orchestra under the Direction of Jack Bolsworth

PRICES OF ADMISSION (Including Tax)

Private Boxes (Seat 4)			Stalls	Grand Circle	Back Stalls	Upper Circle	Balcony
42/-	28/-	14/-	7/- 5/-	7/- 5/-	3/6	3/6	1/6

TELEPHONE SEATS MUST BE CLAIMED BY 12 NOON THE DAY BEFORE
THE DATE OF PERFORMANCE

BOX OFFICE AT THEATRE. Hours : 10 a.m. to 8.30 p.m. 'Phone DOU 6822
Seats may also be booked at Travel Trips Ltd, Cadzow Street Post Office, Hamilton ; Outdoor Shop & Agencies Ltd., 74 Causeyside Street, Paisley ; and Lewis's Royal Polytechnic Ltd., Argyle Street, Glasgow.

STANLEY BAXTER

MARION WILSON

PAMELA WARDEL

CICELY HULLET

ANDREW MACPHERSON

a Baxter *Cinderella* pantomime winter. The Royal's manager considered Stanley Baxter's *Cinderella* panto the best ever. There was no way they could ever accommodate all those who wanted to see the show. And he even saw ladies, complete with their expensive fur coats, pay 1/6d for a seat in the gods because that was all that was available.

1953 was a Baxter and Radcliffe *Half Past Eight* summer and 1954 was a Baxter and Alec Finlay *Aladdin* pantomime winter with Alec Finlay being Widow Twankey – the first time he had played Dame in his long career.

As events were to prove, this *Aladdin* was the last of the super-profitable pantos in Hope Street. The top stars Baxter and Finlay were joined by the singer Alistair McHarg, and by Lucille Graham as the Principal Boy. She was the first female singer to sing to the troops in Malaya during the Emergency. Baxter had also entertained the troops. The principal dancer was Bruce McClure who had trained with Margaret Morris's Celtic Ballet. The man behind the shows was the Australian born choreographer Freddie Carpenter who had danced his way to Britain, and was now producing three separate pantomimes across the country.

Stanley Baxter came to notice in the Citizen's Theatre, and in radio variety shows from 1949 alongside Jimmy Logan. His catch phrase became "If you waant me Thingmmy, Ringmy!" As a comic impersonator he became matchless. After the successes of the Howard & Wyndham revues and pantomimes he moved into film and television, especially the lavish national spectaculars of the *Stanley Baxter Shows* on ITV and BBC spanning over twenty years. These shows are sold today on DVDs. He mimicked

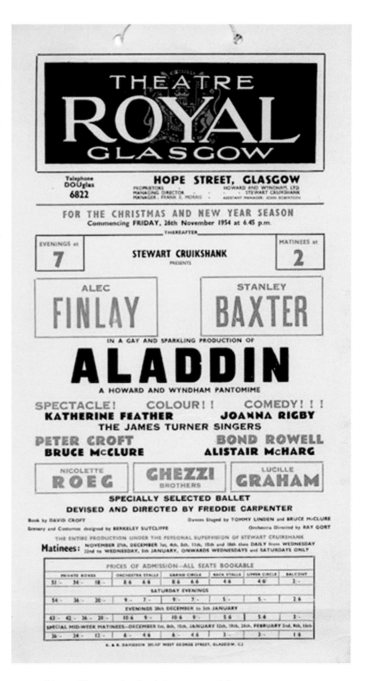

ABOVE
Aladdin *poster 1954*

STANLEY BAXTER REMEMBERS

ABOVE
Stanley Baxter

BELOW
Alec Finlay *and*
Baxter rehearse

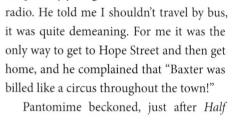

"When Jimmy Logan and I became household names on the radio series *It's All Yours!* I was approached by Howard & Wyndham to top the bill with George Lacey in *Half Past Eight* in 1952 at the Royal. And Jimmy went with Howard & Wyndham to Edinburgh. At this time I was keen on acting in plays in "legitimate" theatre and was at the Citizens for three and a half years. I became illegitimate when I turned 26!

Each show ran for three hours full and fast each night and changed weekly. This gave me Sunday off at home in Clouston Street to prepare in one day material for the next week's programme. Much of it came from the journalist and author Alex Mitchell and I surrounded myself with old joke books. So many people came to the shows, and trying to get in, that the company changed it next year to fortnightly changes, to let more people see it. George Lacey was a veteran from England and gave subtle performances on stage but backstage he was difficult to work with and rude to everyone, especially young ones who came from the radio. He told me I shouldn't travel by bus, it was quite demeaning. For me it was the only way to get to Hope Street and then get home, and he complained that "Baxter was billed like a circus throughout the town!"

Pantomime beckoned, just after *Half Past Eight*, and *Cinderella* was a huge success that winter and on to Easter. For years after, my family thought it was my best pantomime! I remember Bartlett & Ross in their perpetual role as the Ugly Sisters and Nicolette Roeg was a delightful Cinders. The company wondered who to invite to join me for the next summer 1953. I suggested Jack Radcliffe who was then working at lower level theatres such as the Empress and the Metropole. He rose to *Half Past Eight* and we had full houses for months.

I knew Howard & Wyndham were going to team me up with George Lacey again for pantomime in Edinburgh but I was changed back to Glasgow when the company bought the Alhambra Theatre. Stewart Cruikshank said "I'm launching you in our first pantomime at the Alhambra alongside Jimmy Logan." I thought that the shows would work better with a mix of young and old on stage, more than two young ones, and I told producer Freddie Carpenter my idea. He said it sounded OK but I would need the boss to agree. Brave young man, so I thought, until I got to Renfrew Airport and boarded the plane to the company's offices in London. After walking through yards of deep carpeting to his big desk I explained my idea to Stewart Cruikshank and said if he agreed then both the Alhambra and the Royal would be filled to capacity. He did, and the theatres were overflowing. Alec Finlay and I opened at the Royal in *Aladdin* and Duncan Macrae and Jimmy Logan

ABOVE
Cinderella
Baxter as "Buttons"
and Nicolette Roeg as
"Cinders"
1952

at the Alhambra in *Goldilocks and the Three Bears*. Alec Finlay was wonderful to work with, a gentleman of great kindness. I remain grateful to him sharing his stagecraft and his sketches.

I was keen to do plays and Cruikshank arranged a season of plays with me in Glasgow, and Duncan Macrae in Edinburgh. I still wanted to go off to London and try my hand there and when I finally told Stewart Cruikshank this in his offices he wished me well but said if I ever changed my mind I would not be welcomed back by Howard & Wyndham.

I remember the lovely audiences at the Royal and the big orchestra they had, complete with a harp (few theatres could afford a harp) which they always used for the transformation scene at the pantomimes. The theatre has very good acoustics, which can work both ways of course. In quiet moments in plays you can hear what members of the audience say to each other. At the Citizens I came across the script of *The Skin of Our Teeth* written in wartime by Thornton Wilder. It was a fascinating but strange play about the eternal family through the history of the world. I went to the Royal to see it, with Vivien Leigh in a leading role. Characters wandered at random and the audience was split about it. In one scene Vivien Leigh, the viper woman, was lying across the thrust apron into the audience – and could hear two ladies in conversation:

Miriam, would you like some tea at the interval?
"No!" said her friend, "no, they're not getting another penny out of me!"

And in plays such as *Julius Caesar*, all with togas and sandals, you could hear a friend saying to her pal "You can get these sandals at Dolcis."

the BBC's venture into language programmes which started with *Parliamo Italiano*. His *Parliamo Glasgow* by the fictitious scholar visiting the city began as sketches in the Alhambra *Five Past Eight* shows and transferred to radio and several TV series. The books of the series are still best sellers.

The Alhambra joins the family

During 1954 Howard & Wyndham Ltd bought the Alhambra Theatre from Glasgow Alhambra Ltd and started to transfer shows to it, especially the most popular large shows such as *Half Past Eight* which opened at the Alhambra as the fabulous *Five Past Eight Shows*. To make way for these the Wilson Barrett company was moved up Hope Street to the Royal, opening their season of plays with *The Love of Four Colonels* by Peter Ustinov, Edith McArthur in *Murder Mistaken*, a young Geoffrey Palmer in the *Seven Year Itch* and Terence Rattigan's *The Deep Blue Sea* which was produced by Nancy Poultney one of

the few woman producers in Britain. New actors who joined him included Lennox Milne and Walter Carr. Wilson Barrett also had a repertory company in Edinburgh and one in Aberdeen, but it was unprofitable.

In autumnal revues the Boys Brigade mounted the *Centenary Fanfare* to celebrate the birth of the movement's founder Sir William Smith; and *Pay the Piper* featured Elsie and Doris Waters (away from their Gert and Daisy routine), jazz singer and dancer Elisabeth Welch (whose mother was Scottish and father African American) and tenor Ian Wallace from Glyndebourne Opera. Music and lyrics were by Michael Flanders and Donald Swan.

Ballet fans enjoyed Ballet Rambert; and were able to watch and listen to Moira Shearer, the most talked of ballerina after her film *The Red Shoes*, when she turned to acting at the Royal in *I Am A Camera*, a comedy dramatisation of Christopher Isherwood's book about Berlin in the 1930s. The Sadler's

WORKING IN THE THEATRES

For the three Glasgow theatres owned in 1955 the number of staff and some of their pay rates are in the Howard & Wyndham archives at the Victoria & Albert Museum.

		ROYAL	KING'S	ALHAMBRA
Number of staff		17	18	24
Ushers and bar staff (they each got a £5 annual bonus)		9	9	not known
Manager	Salary per week	£14	£13	£15
	Annual bonus	£225	£300	£400
Stage Manager	Salary per week	£10	£8 5/-	£10
	Annual bonus	£30	£50	£100
Bar Manageress	Salary per week	£4	£4	£6 12/6d
	Annual bonus	£50	£50	£10
Head Box Office Clerk	Salary per week	£5	£5	£5 18/-
	Annual bonus	£25	£25	£50

Cruikshank always regarded the position of Head Box Office Clerk as the "Head Woman" in each theatre.

The salaries of the group management are not available:

Freddie Carpenter	Chief Producer
Charles Ross	Producer
Lionel Blair	Dance Producer
Daphne Willis	Ballet Mistress
Reg Allen	Scenic Artist and Production Manager
Geraldo	Musical Adviser

Wells Theatre Ballet visit in 1955 was directed by Ninette de Valois and choreographed by Kenneth MacMillan who was from Dunfermline – the same as Moira Shearer.

Showtalk interview and changes

As part of the newspaper features on the next round of pantomimes the Evening News "Showtalk" columns carried an interview with Stewart Cruikshank junior in November 1954:

"Pantomime is business, he said. The high jinks of dames and vernacular comics for 12, 14, even 16 weeks around the festive season can be said to subsidise drama, opera and ballet in some cases, from spring to late autumn. Howard & Wyndham pantomimes are big business on a very long-term scale.

The production cost of a brand new pantomime can be anything up to £30,000 for scenery, props, wardrobe, book, music and direction. That is not counting wages of permanent staff, who are for months engaged on building and painting, or cast salaries. The most fabulous season for a record run, could not reach anything like this enormous outlay.

"But because of the company's chain of theatres the same pantomime can travel round five main centres with changes of cast and comedy material, but the same essential structure requiring only upkeep costs. Even on a five-year plan it may be three years before full original costs have been met out of profits

The Evening News concluded:

> In this age of many rival
> entertainments Mr Cruikshank
> considers it only good business
> to offer people the best that can
> be found……. And if it is more
> business than art, remember how
> little Arts Council largesse comes
> to Glasgow, and how seldom. In
> Russia, Italy and Germany the state
> or municipalities subsidise art in
> the theatre. Here most of it is left to
> business enterprise.

By July 1955 the Wilson Barrett

LEFT
Moira Shearer *flyer,*
1955

repertory company was in financial crisis and folded. Audiences had dwindled and the summer was hot. One of his last plays was a successful comedy *Ghosts and Old Gold* written by "Reid Kennedy" who was a 27 year old Airdrie medical student Jean White. Barrett had staged 500 plays in 17 years. Speaking to the Press he said:

> The 10,000 people who used to flock
> to the Alhambra theatre financed all
> my other work in Scotland. For the
> past eight seasons the profits from
> the Glasgow season had carried
> the company during its periods
> in Edinburgh. The 2,500 evening
> crowd of the Alhambra did not
> switch to the Royal.
> Television is the real enemy. Not

TOP
Stewart Cruikshank

BOTTOM
Freddie Carpenter

New fairy—old stage-hand

ABOVE
Dress Rehearsal

BELOW
Duncan Macrae *flyer,*
1955

only does it keep people at home, but it doesn't allow those who are paying up their sets on hire purchase a theatre visit.

To fill the gap in plays Howard & Wyndham presented new productions starring Duncan Macrae and Roddy McMillan. To consider a new repertory venture Cruikshank met with Stanley Baxter and Duncan Macrae to discuss a possible 12 week season from

March 1956 of two companies. Baxter in Glasgow at the King's in place of the Royal, and Macrae in Edinburgh, and then they would switch over. The first and only season was successful, with Stanley Baxter's company attracting the largest audiences.

Each year at the start of students Charities Week the Glasgow Students Charities Organisation presented *Stardust* for one evening. In January 1956 the all star variety show was hosted by Rikki Fulton and Stanley Baxter, with Arthur Blake at the piano. The TV cabaret star Neville Taylor from Guiana was reported a huge favourite – having been a student at Glasgow University. Carl Rosa Opera, the Lyric Club, and the Pantheon Club played to full houses as did *Peter Pan*, and the Boy Scout *15th Gang Show* (with Louis Freeman still in charge of the musical arrangements). Musical plays included Leslie Caron in *Gigi*, with Tony Brittain as her leading man, and George Gershwin's *Lady be*

THEATRE ROYAL, GLASGOW
Proprietors—HOWARD & WYNDHAM LTD. Managing Director · STEWART CRUIKSHANK
Manager—F. E. MORRIS.   Phone—DOUglas 6822-3-4.
Commencing MONDAY, 17th OCTOBER, 1955
Nightly at 7.30 p.m.   Matinee—Wednesday and Saturday at 2.30 p.m.

FOURTH ANNUAL TOUR
SCOTTISHOWS
present
Scotland's Stage and Screen Star

DUNCAN MACRAE
in
Alexander Reid's Famous Comedy
'THE WORLD'S WONDER'
With Edinburgh Festival Cast

Good starring Sonnie Hale.

In May the next season's bookings would be publicised but there was only one week announced, and rumours spread that the theatre was to go over to ITV. The week was a private booking by the Moral Rearmament Mission, which had support in many areas. The movement had widespread national coverage, declaring that social and spiritual renewal was required between nations; there must be an awakening to the dangers posed by communist regimes, and "mankind must choose between atomic war or the world renaissance." 14,000 tickets were distributed for the week. Involving players from many countries, two plays were staged *We are Tomorrow* and *The Dictator's Slippers*, and a musical *The Vanishing Island*. This brought a protest from the Musicians Union who complained to the Mission and to the American Federation of Musicians that the evening used recorded music despite a solitary conductor; automation was not to be encouraged.

In May it was reported that Canadian newspaperman Roy Thomson agreed to buy the theatre for television purposes, and that he had formed an alliance with Howard & Wyndham Ltd giving him first call on artistes under contract to the company.

A number of shows opened after a long holiday recess including the Italian Opera Company, and the first appearance in Britain of the famed Jose Greco, his Spanish Dancers and Flamenco guitars, following five years of touring

LEFT
Jose Greco
Flamenco group

the USA and the Continent. The Royal's press conferences, and sometimes rehearsals, always took place in the first floor Buffet Bar, or Grand Circle Bar as it was better known. So too for Jose Greco and his dancers, already acclaimed for their *fire, vitality and colour*, who gave an impromptu full flamenco dance on the parquet flooring of the Bar – until Will Hay, publican of the corner bar ran all the way up the stairs – out of breath and full of adjectives – to "stop that xxxxxx din,….. the ceiling's shaking, and my bottles are dropping off the shelves all over the place."

BELOW
Radcliffe & Logan

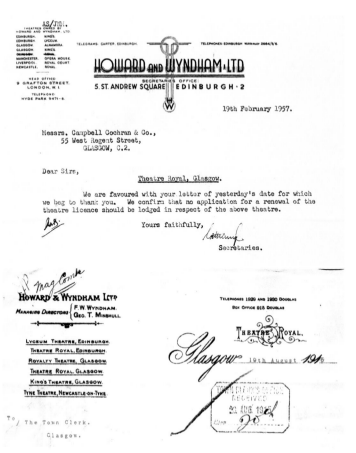

ABOVE

Letterheads

(Top)

No longer requiring the Royal, 1957

(Bottom)

Developing the Royal - 1915

OPPOSITE

Farewell, *February 1957*

Jack Radcliffe the dapper gent

As the dapper gent observing life, and equally at home in the hurly burley of pantomime, Jack Radcliffe topped the bill in many theatres, in film, and appeared in the Royal Variety performances in London, and in Scotland - which he also compered. He was a musician and baritone in the earlier days of touring revues before changing to character acting and comedy. His stage feed and business partner was Helen Norman, who was a leading light in her own name. He made popular the song "The Star o' Rabbie Burns" with its chorus:

Let kings and courtiers rise and fa',
This world has mony turns
But brightly beams aboon them a',
The Star o' Rabbie Burns.

And before that he had published a wartime song "My Shadow misses your Shadow" by Charles and Elton who also wrote for Vera Lynn and Donald Peers. Much of the Radcliffe style passed on to a young Jimmy Logan.

The Royal's last night as a theatre - much bemoaned and blamed on the growth of television - was reached on Saturday 16th February 1957 in the presence of a full house led by the Lord Provost. Jack Radcliffe and Aly Wilson completed the last pantomime *Robinson Crusoe*. Among speeches from the stage the producer Freddie Carpenter reflected that the Royal:

was not really closing down, but starting on a new career at the exciting age of 92.

Martin Brownlee, "The Man in the Stalls" for the Evening Citizen reported his Last Night thoughts of the Theatre Royal:

Our musical education was largely gained there from the Moody Manners…. to the Carl Rosa Company. Eva Turner's voice ringing gloriously above the orchestra, Beatrice Miranda growing all too ample for her "Butterfly", Frank Mullings pealing forth a tireless tenor.

FAREWELL PERFORMANCE

SATURDAY, 16th FEBRUARY, 1957

GLASGOW'S THEATRE ROYAL
" Rings Down the Curtain"
for the Last Time

THE ROYAL'S FINANCIAL HEALTH FROM 1929

Up until 1954 the Royal was always the most profitable of the Howard & Wyndham theatres in Scotland.

The Theatre Royal's annual profits

Year end, February	£	Comments
1929/30	16,802	Tommy Lorne in *Sleeping Beauty* £12,780
1930/31	18,808	Tommy Lorne in *Goldilocks* £15,062
1931/32	7,896	
1932/33	8,984	Tommy Lorne in *Cinderella* £11,560
1933/34	8,325	Tommy Lorne in *Babes in the Wood* £10,511
1934/35	2,256	*Goody Two Shoes* not a success
1935/36	6,176	
1936/37	8,872	
1937/38	12,063	Dave Willis in *Cinderalla* £5,213
1938/39	6,531	Dave Willis in *Robinson Crusoe* £7,613
1939/40	3,804	Dave Willis in *Goldilocks* £6,919
1940/41	*367 loss*	Dave Willis in *Babes in the Wood* £3,407
1941/42	6,097	Dave Willis in *Cinderella* £5,392
1942/43	14,487	normality returns
1943/44	20,903	all shows profitable including the Circus
1944/45	23,708	all shows profitable including the Circus
1945/46	24,850	George West in *Cinderella*
1946/47	27,589	George West in *Mother Goose*
1947/48	22,344	George West in *Sleeping Beauty*
1948/49	25,627	Douglas Byng in *Goody Two Shoes*
1949/50	19,727	Dave Willis in *Jack & The Beanstalk*
1950/51	15,181	
1951/52	17,045	Dave Willis in *Robinson Crusoe*
1952/53	36,907	Stanley Baxter in the *Half Past Eight Show* £14,000 and in *Cinderella* £17,500
1953/54	42,753	Stanley Baxter and Jack Radcliffe in the *Half Past Eight Show* £21,700 with Molly Urquhart. Jimmy Logan and Harry Gordon in *Puss in Boots* £16,300
1954/55	22,480	Stanley Baxter and Alec Finlay in *Aladdin* £19,800
1955/56	9,612	Shows move to the Alhambra. Wilson Barrett losses. Jack Radcliffe and Harry Gordon in *Dick Whittington*
1956/57	4,588	Jack Radcliffe in *Robinson Crusoe* Theatre becomes STV's television studios

For 1952/53 and 1953/54 the Howard & Wyndham archives show the Theatre Royal was the most profitable of their owned theatres in Britain, when it was running eight pantomimes across the land. It was surpassed only by the Alhambra from 1954/55 onwards.

A theatre so long a utility of the city
has been a part of our lives. Going
to it often, we were a congregation.
We shared an experience of pleasure
and mental stimulation. This was
a public meeting place of friends.
It was not mere rhetoric when the
habit was to call a theatre a temple
of drama. Frivolous or grave as it
might be, it enlivened existence.

The Glasgow Herald's Christopher
Small finished his retrospective the next
morning:

Everybody linked hands and sang
"Auld Lang Syne" with unmistakable
fervour, and the curtain came
down for the last time: unless
Independent Television has any
use for such an old-fashioned
mechanism.

ABOVE
Charcoal drawings
by Margaret Morris,
February 1957
(right)
**Last Night, Curtain
Call**
(left)
**Going to the Last
Night**

Roy Thomson
Creates Scottish Television

Summertime in 1957 was hectic in Hope Street. New things were happening and "that old fashioned mechanism called a curtain" rose again on the 31st August. After a luncheon hosted by the Independent Television Authority and speeches in the City Chambers the Lord Provost Andrew Hood, dignitaries and special guests joined the audience, all in evening dress, making their way into the theatre, to the sounds of a pipe band playing in the street.

A variety show with film inserts and interviews of international and national talent was taking place, including the ballerina Moira Shearer. Her husband Ludovic Kennedy, a newsreader for Independent Television News, was also there. Just before 6pm the audience was asked to stay totally quiet, no noise. Unknown to them, on stage - and behind the curtain - Ludovic Kennedy read out the ITN News from Glasgow instead of the usual London. The curtain rose at 6.30pm with Jimmy Nairn announcing to all viewers "**This is Scotland**". The show was "a sixty minutes tour of a country – its landscapes, its ordinary people, its celebrities, its heritage past and present" with a cast including Deborah Kerr, David Niven, Jack Buchanan, Alastair Sim, Moira Shearer, Jimmy Logan, Stanley Baxter, Kenneth McKellar, Fay Lenore, Glasgow Police Pipe Band, Clyde Valley

Stompers, Mitchell Singers, Five Past Eight dancers and Geraldo and his Orchestra. Scripted by Robert Kemp, it was introduced by James Robertson Justice. The show was produced and directed by Rai Purdy and watched in Scotland by 750,000 viewers and by millions more across the whole of the early ITV network in Britain, including the large areas served by the new Associated Rediffusion, Associated TV and Granada stations.

To reach that number of people in Scotland the Theatre Royal would need to play to a full house for about 15 months. The rest of the evening's programmes on television were *Scarlett Pimpernel*, *Wyatt Earp*, and the *Office of Strategic Services* films and the *64,000 Challenge Quiz*.

What had happened was the brainchild of Roy Thomson from Canada who was now the owner of the *Scotsman*

OPPOSITE
Scottish Television Theatre *at night*

ROY THOMSON

Lord Thomson of Fleet

At age 60 Roy Thomson settled in Britain in 1953, coming from Canada where he had sold radios, created radio stations and owned a chain of newspapers. With the wealth he had created and papers he owned he felt he would have been made a Press Baron if he had been here, as happened to Lords Beaverbrook, Rothermere and others. But the Canadian Premier had not put his name forward.

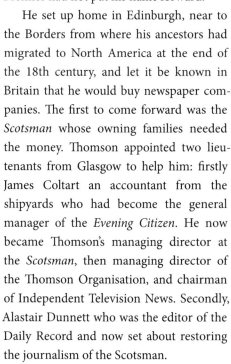

He set up home in Edinburgh, near to the Borders from where his ancestors had migrated to North America at the end of the 18th century, and let it be known in Britain that he would buy newspaper companies. The first to come forward was the *Scotsman* whose owning families needed the money. Thomson appointed two lieutenants from Glasgow to help him: firstly James Coltart an accountant from the shipyards who had become the general manager of the *Evening Citizen*. He now became Thomson's managing director at the *Scotsman*, then managing director of the Thomson Organisation, and chairman of Independent Television News. Secondly, Alastair Dunnett who was the editor of the Daily Record and now set about restoring the journalism of the Scotsman.

Thomson, and others of the first STV board, especially Coltart, supported the Moral Rearmament Movement, and would arrange functions for the staff during which MRA representatives would mingle. There was no hard sell involved but the positive social responsibility ethos was encouraged.

Thomson was always uncomplicated and open in the running of his companies, his democratic style was often at odds with Britain's older companies. However to stress his British and Scottish credentials he tried hard to become one of the "great and good."

This brought mixed responses in the early years, most people being wary of his motives.

Another pioneering step was in 1963 when he set up the **Thomson Foundation**, chaired by James Coltart, to improve the skills in mass communication media in order to support post-war democracy, especially in the new nations emerging in the Commonwealth and other developing areas. The Foundation would assist the setting up of newspapers and media services and educate and train journalists, producers and administrators from these countries. At Kirkhill House, Newton Mearns, television engineers and producers were educated and trained, while in Cardiff the Foundation's centre of journalism was started and continues today. No doubt Thomson's business interests were helped, including the growth of television services – one of the first Thomson television services overseas being for the Jamaican government.

In 1964 he was awarded his peerage Lord Thomson of Fleet, and continued through to the 1970s amassing a second personal fortune from television, publishing, holiday, and oil businesses. When he died in 1976 his remaining shares in STV were sold off.

ABOVE
James Coltart

newspaper in Edinburgh. He had experience of radio stations but none of television stations. From what he saw in North America he knew that television had potential and he expressed interest in commercial TV when its possibility was being discussed in the House of Commons.

For and Against ITV

Debate on whether there should be commercial television in Britain came to the surface in 1952. If in favour of ending the BBC's monopoly you were on the side of "*independent TV*" (Roy Thomson promoted it as *free* television) and you described the BBC as "*State TV*." Pressure groups for having ITV included individuals with experience of electrical retailing and television programming, and the younger MPs in the Government. If in favour of keeping the BBC monopoly you spoke in favour of continuing "*national TV*" and against "*commercial TV*" which would swamp the country with American advertising, American programmes, and loosening morality. Those against TV being paid by advertisements included the Labour Party and trade unions – who did not wish to support any private sector growth post-war – the Churches, advertising agencies (for fear of US domination), cinema and theatre companies. While theatre companies toed this line publicly a few privately prepared for new television, including Stoll Moss and Howard & Wyndham

OPPOSITE
(top)
STV Logo
(bottom)
Roy Thomson

TOM HONEYMAN

ABOVE
Tom Honeyman

From his medical student days Tom Honeyman was interested in amateur dramatics and art appreciation. He was a doctor for ten years at the same time as his colleague Osborne Mavor (playwright James Bridie). He became an art dealer with the firm of Reid & Lefevre of Glasgow and London. Honeyman became the popular, audacious and first professional Director of Glasgow Art Galleries & Museums in 1939 until 1954. To the already impressive lists of Old Masters in Kelvingrove he added paintings by the Glasgow Boys, the Scottish Colourists, Cezanne, Van Gogh, Matisse, Picasso, Renoir, Corot, Courbet, Seurat, Bonnard, Braque, Dali and others. One of his crowning glories was reaching agreement in 1944 with Sir William Burrell, by which the vast Burrell Collection was donated to the city.

Many of the Corporation councillors complained that Honeyman was more popular than they were. Which was true. In his biography Honeyman wrote, that for his shows and exhibitions, he wanted to copy the panache and success of the impresario Charles B Cochran – who was a director of Howard & Wyndham and a frequent visitor to Glasgow.

He became the chairman and founder of the Citizens Theatre with James Bridie and others, their plays being produced at the Athenaeum in Buchanan Street before the Royal Princess's Theatre in Gorbals was offered on a generous lease by its owner Harry MacKelvie. With the Secretary of State for Scotland Tom Johnston he was a founder member of the Scottish Tourist Board. He was elected Rector of Glasgow University in 1953.

At the reopening in 2006 of the refurbished Kelvingrove Art Galleries Lord Norman Macfarlane wrote:

> Tom Honeyman was hugely intellectual and bright. That may have sometimes made things difficult for those working with him, but he was Glasgow's greatest ever ambassador. The modern Kelvingrove was made by him.

Influencing television

Honeyman was appointed to the **Independent Television Authority** in 1954 which had the duty to oversee commercial TV as it thought fit. He was also the member with special responsibility for the interests of Scotland during his four-year term.

Under the Television Act each company was required to *educate, entertain and inform* – the same objectives as the BBC. The companies were required to broadcast nothing that offends against good taste, in programmes and in advertising. Under the Act each contractor was expected to be broadly representative of the area being served. Honeyman helped shape ITA's approach to the intended new services.

The Act required ITA advisory committees in each licence area to help guide the programme producers. A Religious Advisory Committee was formed and an Educational Advisory Committee soon followed.

After making a tour of television stations in North America he reported on television in

▼

Ltd. Prime Minister Churchill's cabinet was undecided. It was not even on their election agenda. It was the advice of Lord Woolton, the popular wartime Minister of Food and now chairman of the Conservative and Unionist Party, who convinced Churchill that the public could be trusted to decide which channels they chose to watch.

Nobody knew how to introduce commercial TV, which was permitted in July 1954 by the Television Act. Wisely the Government passed that responsibility to an Independent Television Authority under the chairmanship of Sir Kenneth Clark, whose members included Tom Honeyman.

Roy Thomson did not wait for ITA to finalise its plans. He said he would apply for a Scottish TV contract and by early summer 1954 he was in contact with the Secretary of State for Scotland James Stuart to impress on him that his Thomson Television company would include the wartime Secretary of State Tom Johnston, the Duke of Hamilton and others (most likely none had been approached). He suggested that advisory boards be created across Scotland advising on television content and reporting to Roy Thomson, without waiting for ITA to decide what style of accountability would start in England. Stuart noted "I see no harm in exploring some avenues."

In 1956 the Dean of Guild Court approved Thomson's plans for altering the Theatre Royal to become television

△

Canada and the USA (particularly New York) which had varying styles of content and operating. Honeyman's report was discussed by the Authority in 1957, with the chairman Sir Kenneth Clark adding the preface:

> the Authority will find in the report much of it to help it in discharging that most difficult of all obligations, the control of programme quality and balance.

At Tom Honeyman's suggestion the same year a Scottish Committee was created " to advise the Authority from time to time on the general conduct of independent television in Scotland."

At the end of 1958 the Scottish National Party, some local authorities, Dickson Mabon MP and others, campaigned and lobbied Parliament for a "Scottish Television Board" to operate commercial-advertising transmitters and to use the remaining TV channels. The surplus revenues would be used to promote the arts in Scotland. Greenock Town Council campaigned to become the television authority for their area. However the ITA declined a Scottish Television Board, citing uncertainties over when transmission would move from the current 405-line screen definition (to what would become 625 lines), colour possibilities, and the likely allocations of more channels to the BBC and to the existing independent companies.

studios and offices. A staff of 110 was predicted, compared to 53 employed by the theatre company. The actual number in the TV headquarters came nearer to 200 – with Thomson always aghast at the overstaffing in British firms and trade unions compared to North America.

The Independent Television Authority decided to own all transmitters and use the General Post Office lines for ITA to publish and transmit television programmes from each of the area contractors. In deciding the licence pattern they concluded that the BBC was strong competition but too London-oriented, and that any area which could sustain a broadsheet newspaper could sustain a TV area. As a result five large TV companies were formed

first, capable of networking to counterbalance the BBC national network, and then medium sized companies were formed including Scottish Television, Tyne-Tees, and Southern. Smaller ones would follow including Ulster, Border and Grampian. The number and final mapping of ITV contractors was then adjusted only to respect Britain's geography and the reach of TV transmitters. For central Scotland one licence was awarded covering Glasgow and the West (with its *Glasgow Herald*) and Edinburgh and the East (with its *Scotsman*). The television signal would be helped over high ground by ITA building a transmitter mast at Blackhill on the hills near the BBC's mast at Kirk o'Shotts. The Blackhill mast is over 750

feet high and is the highest of any ITA station.

Test transmissions started from Blackhill in March 1956, using Channel 10, to help dealers install household aerials and adjust the sets. The BBC's programmes were on Channel 3. To help the trade and customers, test transmissions each day from Blackhill the ITA showed a sunny photograph of Loch Lomond from Rowardennan, published in the books of photographer and author Douglas Bolton. A number of his other photos were also used from ITA masts down south.

It was estimated that 90 per cent of Scotland's population would be within range of the new service, and there would be 50 hours of TV weekly, of which 10 hours would be programmes made by the new contractor. Once it opened the actual hours were slightly different from that, and 80 per cent of the country's population was within reach – over 4 million people.

Winning the TV licence

During 1956 the ITA issued contract papers to the three applicants for the Scottish licence requiring that the shareholders were persons resident in Great Britain and that they could raise no less than £400,000 to fund the start up. Each contractor had to be independent of all other contractors. Roy Thomson could afford to fund this in total from his Canadian money but knew that a Scottish shareholder

ABOVE
Test Image
Loch Lomond at Rowardennan

RAI PURDY

ABOVE
Rai Purdy

Rai Purdy grew up in Toronto and became a pioneer of radio broadcasting in Canada, after training as an actor. He established the first coast-to-coast radio playhouse, Canadian Theatre of the Air, pioneered quiz programmes, weekly serials, and light entertainment shows in front of live audiences. During the war he was recruited by the Canadian Army into their broadcast unit and was in charge of the Canadian Army Shows broadcast from Montreal across the Dominion. From there he was made Commanding Officer of the Canadian Auxiliary Entertainment Unit based in Britain, and went with the forces in 1944-45 to Holland, France, Belgium and Germany.

His wife Verity Sweeney was a classical dancer and choreographer and joined her husband in Glasgow to help develop a number of the programmes of STV. On his return to Canada at the end of 1959, on loan from Roy Thomson, he produced for the Canadian TV Network and later created his own production company.

venture would be received best by ITA and the public. However the new ITV companies in England were losing millions of pounds and Scotland was still wary of Thomson's motives. Only a few individuals responded positively to his invitation to invest (even with the financial loan and guarantee he offered in his letters.) Howard & Wyndham Ltd had no qualms and invested in 10 per cent of the shares. The Thomson Organisation owned and controlled all the voting shares. In August 1956 the £400,000 of shares and loans was detailed by Thomson to the ITA:

> The £400,000 will be used for developing the business, for the purchase of fixed assets (£40,000 for a theatre property in Glasgow; £250,000 for television equipment from Marconi, Pye and others) and for the cost of entry to Independent Television News.

Once the pantomime finished in February 1957 work started on the alterations to the Royal. Scottish Television exhibition vans started to tour round central Scotland showing the type of things to come and listing all the towns and places that would be served. In May, Thomson got confirmation of the television contract award, fully signed on the 19th June - and transmissions had to start by 31st August. His licence was the first in Britain to be given for transmissions on 7 days a week, the others being for weekdays Monday to Friday, or weekends only.

Roy Thomson recruited fellow Canadian Rai Purdy from the CBS television studios in New York where he was a producer and director to become Director of Programmes at Hope Street. At a press conference Purdy said he had three aims :

1.   to give first class entertainment
2.   to give Scottish talent every

opportunity to develop

3.   to provide as many cultural programmes as possible

He announced plans for a weekly variety show, a weekly drama show with Scots actors, a cash quiz show, and Scottish News. Programmes he would show from the network would include *Sunday Night from the Palladium*, *I Love Lucy*, and *Dragnet*.

By comparison BBC radio and television in Scotland was often stolid and largely anglified; its news reporting was establishment-minded and its journalism compliant to politicians. As soon as

it started Scottish Television won over a majority of the audience. But much had to be done before any of this.

Royal changes

The entrance foyer became a reception and telephone switchboard area, and the fireplace was covered over. The raked stage was levelled, extended, and on one side was built out deep into the Stalls. The whole stage floor was screeded in concrete, with thick seamless linoleum laid over it allowing free camera movement. This left about 160 seats in the stalls. The back stalls

ABOVE
A New Life
*STV in Hope Street,
1957*

ABOVE
First Night
James Coltart welcomes Sir Kenneth Clark and wife Lady Clark to the Royal.

from America and Britain were also relayed. Videotape pre-recording was introduced some years later.

Studio A was the theatre's stage, with make-up rooms built along the left-hand wall, and was used for large audience shows. **Studio B** was the main working studio and was built on the right hand to the back of the stage, from which came the *News*, and *Advertising Magazine* programmes such as *Man about the House* with Bill Tennent. Current affairs programmes, including *Here and Now*, came from this studio. **Studio C** was added the following year by converting the cooperage next door where television scenery was made initially. Scenery production moved to a unit in one of the shipyards, and after some years three STV buildings were erected in Balmore Road for making scenery, storage, and the garaging of outside broadcasting vans. The stage door for the studios was from Cowcaddens.

TV scenery for shows and dramas was different in construction from theatre scenery. Flat painted sets had been used effectively when the audience was seated far out in the auditorium but cameras now gave very close close-ups and doors had to be solidly made, all furniture and fittings had to be real.

Studios lights were installed on numerous and smaller clamp bars knocked into walls and unlikely places or suspended from ceilings giving greater flexibility for all the required angles and positions, in contrast to the existing large bar lighting system of the theatre.

underneath the Grand Circle housed the Control Room and its equipment for sound, vision and lighting.

In the Circles new boxes were built, next to the theatre boxes, and glazed in to make small hospitality rooms for VIPs, including advertisers, to see the live programmes. Public seating also remained in the central parts of the Circles. Altogether 700 people could be seated in the theatre for shows. Before the Control Room was built an Outside Broadcasting van was parked in Hope Street and cables led out through a window to it, using it as the Control unit.

All television was of course **black and white and live**, no prerecordings were possible for either indoor or outdoor productions. Cinema films

In the bowels of the building, at a level below the orchestra pit, was the essential Central Control, from which a cable was laid to the back door, then went under the road surfaces to the Post Office Telephone Exchange in Pitt Street sending the signal to ITA's Blackhill transmission mast. At this subterranean level was a tiny, claustrophobic room known as **Studio D** used for continuity announcements and the News and weather at lunchtime. Centred upon the Royal there would be a total of five studios giving 9,100 square feet of floor space.

The new large mast towering above the theatre was for incoming signals from the Outside Broadcast vans at football matches, news-scenes, political venues, and concert halls elsewhere.

For offices and staff areas the theatre manager's office at the rear of the Grand Circle became the staff canteen and tea-ladies headquarters; the Grand Circle Bar at the top of the main stair was changed into two levels of offices parallel with Hope Street. More offices were to be built in the Bijou Hall area, which also gave extra storage space. The Upper Circle Bar area was converted into a Board Room and next to that was a room with a bed and chairs used overnight by either Roy Thomson or James Coltart.

The programme planners took a dressing room as their office, and publicity staff were based elsewhere further down Hope Street. The company also took a floor of the new Fleming House in Renfrew Street for the booking of artistes. The same building later contained the Scottish offices of ITA.

Thomson planning and recruitment

Roy Thomson was always astute in his deal making and financial control. From ITV companies in England he arranged a long term access to their networked programmes at a fraction of the going rate. They were in financial difficulty and welcomed any extra revenue. In return he offered them the series being planned of world-wide documentary programmes under John Grierson, whom Thomson had signed up and was the pioneer and recognised father of documentary film.

During the setting up period in 1957 construction and electrical firms were in and out the building and some of the joiners and electricians were offered jobs as lightingmen and trainee cameramen. Others came from the GPO and the BBC. The theatre manager and some of the crew and usherettes stayed on from Howard & Wyndham. Outside film cameramen, used at sports venues, news stories, and for inserts to drama productions, came from newspapers. Rai Purdy and Thomson held auditions every week in the theatre and sometimes in Maryhill Hall – Thomson recalling how he:

sat in the dark of Theatre Royal auditioning all sorts of singers, players and laughter-makers.

Very few had television experience, and everybody had to be versatile and learn on the job. Experienced directors and technicians were brought up from London, and they too had to lend a hand with the building work. Thomson added:

> Press photographers learned to work the big cameras, radio mechanics handled the cables, and repertory actors announced the news.

TOP
STV Logo, *1964*

BOTTOM
Geraldo

Journalists learned the ways of television production; Jack Hardy was appointed General Manager and head of publicity, and for many years made everything tick. The announcer team did the news, continuity, voice-overs for trailers and commercial slides – and there were no auto-cues then. Recruits who became regulars around the camera included station announcer Jimmy Nairn (who had just completed a season at the Citizens Theatre), chief announcer Michael O'Halloran, newsreaders Jack Webster, Gordon Roddick, Elaine Wells, Bill Simpson and Morag Hood (before both became distinguished actors) and Arthur Montford (who also became the sports presenter, assisted by Bob Crampsey), sports producer John Wilson who started the Scotsport programmes, and roving reporter Bill Tennent.

Logos, curtains, and music

While a curtain would rise for the theatre audience something else was needed to "unveil" the entertainment on the television sets in peoples' living rooms. Each station broadcast their own logo (known as an ident) before each of their own programmes. The first from Hope Street contained the letters STV and a lion; followed in 1964 by the words Scottish Television with the Lion Rampant in the centre. The lion logo would spin furiously and come to a halt just before the programmes. Unfortunately there were times when the lion ended upside down—much to the annoyance of the Lord Lyon King of Arms who let it be known that a birling Lion Rampant was not acceptable. The spinning stopped.

The theatre's Fire Curtain, weighing about 2 tons, was retained for the early years. The Royal and King's theatres and other theatres used the city's hydraulic power system to raise and lower them. Now and again if the system pressure in the city altered unexpectedly the heavy curtain could descend very slowly and out of control to the floor. Several times this happened, gradually separating the audience and some television cameras from the singers and high-kicking dancers on the other side.

The famous Geraldo was in charge of Scottish Television's music and provided orchestras for shows, as he did for Howard & Wyndham. He commissioned a full *Scotlandia Overture*, played and recorded for the start of each day's programmes at lunchtime, and again in the early evening. Every ITV station in Britain had their own signature music, played for many minutes each time when the signal was being made stable for the transmissions to follow. *Scotlandia* included segments of Loch Lomond, Comin'through the Rye, Wi'A Hundred Pipers, and other airs all played at a healthy speed. It lasted till 1985.

Everything was now ready. Music was pre-eminent in the new programmes from the Royal, from large orchestras and a range of bands to variety shows, song concerts and opera - the quality, glamour and professionalism of the music shows were to be hallmarks of STV for three decades. In the first four months to December 1957 the number of TV sets in central Scotland more than doubled to 436,000.

On one occasion the Scottish National Orchestra were rehearsing for an evening concert to be televised and Geraldo did the score reading for the producer Rai Purdy to make sure cameras were pointing to the right sections of players, but from the angle available it was impossible to catch the clarinet player in an important solo section. At a break in the rehearsal Geraldo approached and asked the conductor if the clarinettist could stand up at the crucial time. The conductor looked, snapped his baton in two, and said in his Germanic accent "If you want Glenn Miller, hire Glenn Miller!"

ABOVE
Stage for opening night
STV, 1957

BELOW
This is Scotland
rehearsal, 1957

Entertainment Direct to your Home

This is Scotland on the 31st August 1957 opened the Theatre Royal to its new public role. Initially a normal day of STV programmes and network programmes started at lunchtime and ended around 10.30pm with a closure mid afternoon. STV produced 9 hours of their own programmes each week, compared to BBC Scotland's 4 hours. Both these figures increased over the years.

September 1957 was the start of the *One O'Clock Gang* compered by Larry Marshall, a live show of comedy, music, interviews and information for viewers …....…."Sit back and relax, it's the One O'Clock Gang!" It was the first daytime variety show of any commercial station in Britain and proved to be highly popular, running for 1,760 daily programmes each weekday until 1966. *Scotsport* started, anchored by Arthur Montford, and would become the longest running sports programme in Britain. In the same month the first *Late Call* was transmitted near the close of each evening's programmes.

In October STV launched the first of 300 weekly programmes *This Wonderful World* by Dr John Grierson, founder of the *documentary* film movement, a word he coined himself. This was originally aimed at a minority audience but was watched by millions over the

UK network. He introduced his own film clips and those of many others around the world to show the splendour of nature and mankind's place in it, all from his desk in Studio A - with the windows behind opening into the subject matter of the week. He pursued the cause of film as an instrument of education and enlightenment.

ABOVE
Sports Desk
Arthur Montford (centre)

OPPOSITE
The One O'Clock Gang
Jimmy Nairn, Dorothy Paul, Charlie Sim, Moira Briody, Larry Marshall and three guests (centre).

GRAND OPENING OF THE SCOTTISH TELEVISION THEATRE

Reporting the grand opening the Glasgow Herald noted:

> As the live audience waited for the speeches and the variety show they became uncomfortably aware of the major difficulties facing entertainer and technician in television. The heat in the auditorium, aggravated by arc lamps and silencing screening, rapidly became more oppressive. Fur wraps were early removed and the souvenir programme brought into use as a fan.

In his speech Roy Thomson promised "an infinite variety of programmes and believed that Scottish Television would become part of the community life of Scotland." Tragically and unknown to the audience an electrician on duty collapsed and died 40 minutes before curtain-up.

At the luncheon the ITA chairman Sir Kenneth Clark declared his confidence in independent television. He expressed:

> My hope that the new service in Scotland will produce successors to dramatists like James Barrie and James Bridie. Only trial and error will show how many of the programmes will have a strongly Scottish flavour and how much the Scottish people want to be reminded of themselves. It will show too how much they wish to take flight to that wonderland across the Atlantic.
>
> Although the worst of the variety programmes which will reach you on the network will be rather foolish and rather vulgar, they will be no worse than those to which you have been accustomed by our august rival; and I can assure you that the best of them will be considerably better.
>
> Although television must be recognised as a popular medium it could not be allowed to drift on the tide of popular preference. They had to look for what was best in popular preference and build upon that, and from this experience they could try to create new fields of democratic interest.

After the opening there was a civic reception at the City Chambers for the artistes and guests. At the end of the first weekend of independent broadcasting the paper's journalist turned to the advertisements:

> The commercials are in their jingles and animation as witty as anything offered. At this stage they are positively looked forward to; especially such as "Rael-Brook Toplin, the shirt you don't need to iron"; "Omo adds brightness, Brightness, BRIGHTNESS!" and a delightful local one with four ghostly little cooks producing Duncan's chocolate.

Thomson launched a weekly TV Guide with programme news and interviews for the new station. It was written and edited in the theatre by Cliff Hanley, followed by Gordon Irving, and printed by the Scotsman presses in Edinburgh. It sold 300,000 copies a week and merged with The Viewer which had started with Tyne Tees Television.

Variety shows and light entertainment concerts featured strongly with music supplied by the George Keenan Orchestra of 10 players including a brass section with supporting vocals by the Kay Gordon Singers, and by the Arthur Blake Concert Orchestra which had a large string section. The Arthur Blake Singers were also formed, and Blake became Head of Music for the company in 1970. The John Currie Singers presented more serious music. The Tommy Maxwell Quartet played in the daily *One O'Clock Gang* and other shows. Archie McCulloch compered *Fanfare*, a weekly talent contest with prizes, and in the late evening his wife Kathy Kay sang in *Bedtime with Kathy*. In 1958 at the end of its first full year STV ran a pantomime *Cinderella* written by Eddie Boyd and starring Edith MacArthur, Larry Marshall and Louise Boyd. The following year singer Alistair McHarg started his musical series *The Pleasure of Your Company*, which reviewers thought merited national networking.

Lively Audiences and Large Advertising

A majority of viewers watched STV in preference to BBC, and advertisers flocked to have their products and services screened. In "live theatre" the Royal knew how successful a show was, or not, by adding up the numbers of

ABOVE
John Grierson

LEFT
Arthur Blake

patrons paying for a seat but that could not apply to television. Whereas the BBC measured audiences through street interviews, the commercial companies started a more scientific survey, its principles still used today, and known then as JICTAR ratings from the Joint Industry Committee for Television Audience Research. Several hundred houses in each area served were selected and a metering machine provided which recorded on a tape the channels watched and the length of viewing. The householder also kept a diary, and the companies paid the BBC annual licence fee. The tape was collected weekly and analysed.

In measuring their audiences companies wanted these measured high, and advertisers wanted them lower - to have lower advertising fees! The STV and advertisers were not allowed to know who the householders were, but stories grew of some ITV companies offering new free sets to some households. By 1959 STV could claim 2 million viewers.

The company's main advertising sales office was in London, with other offices throughout the country. Advertisements were measured in seconds and sold as a *cost per thousand viewers*. STV were permitted to transmit a maximum of 7 minutes of advertising in each hour. There was bidding for slots right up to the time of transmission; and there was also pricing for *guaranteed home impressions*, usually a cumulative series of showings. From the Blackhill transmitter came the networked programmes signal by GPO

wires to the Theatre Royal where the advertisements were inserted and sent off back to Blackhill.

TV companies were monitored by ITA to meet the requirements of the licence granted, and to ensure that programmes _and_ advertisements broadcast "nothing that offends against good taste." This was harder to do for advertisements; for example it was difficult to advertise beer _and_ show people drinking it in a pub. Whisky distillers took a self-denying ordinance not to buy advertising time. Control of advertising continued to be difficult until the ITA's first Head of Advertising, Archie Graham from Scotland, wrote a definitive book on it. The advertisers had to sell what they advertised. There was much testing of products, opening of beer bottles, and slicing of pies.

There was no product placement in programmes unlike more recent times. Products would have labels masked or turned away from the camera. It was important to be independent throughout. There was always a check to see if actors in the programmes were doing voice-overs in advertisements being run during it. If so the programme took precedence and the advert was retimed.

Serving a Nation

The first officer in Scotland for ITA was Lord Belhaven, a colourful character who had managed to shoot his own foot during the war. He and his successors gave benign support to STV and sometimes informal guidance at operational level when new programmes were being considered. Belhaven delighted in using Scots words in his messages to ITA London, sending them scurrying to their dictionaries. He described the Theatre Royal purchase as "an imaginative gesture which appealed to Scotland." Extracts from his report to the ITA board in June 1959 describe some of STV's activity:-

"The theatre auditorium can accommodate 700 for each performance, and by July 500,000 will have seen live transmissions from the old stage. Studio C was completed in August 1958, providing 4,200 sq ft of space.

"A new three storied block to be completed in July will accommodate in one building the following departments, Film, Engineering, Outside Broadcasts, Sales, Press and Publicity, Schools, Legal and Copyright, Administration and Accounts. The Wardrobe, Carpenter's Shop and Property Store already make all scenery and costumes and even the puppets used in the children's programme of "Mr Fixit."

"From the beginning the audience welcomed the company as a national institution and, as is the way in Scotland, were not slow to praise and criticise.
The growth of audience has been startling, from 1 million viewers in November 1957 to 2 million in May

1959. It has increased its audiences during the last two years, in the main through its own productions. Of the audience seven out of ten prefer STV's programmes to those of the BBC. STV serves a nation and thus enjoys advantages and incurs responsibilities such as do not fall upon other Companies.

He describes a number of the programmes from Cowcaddens including the

"Lunchtime programme ONE O'CLOCK GANG, the most successful show of its kind……….
The evening variety show THE RADCLIFFE - FINLAY programme is a marked success.
JIG TIME is a cheerful programme of Scottish dancing and music…
(involving the folk group The Reivers founded by Enoch Kent and Josh

BELOW
Jig Time
with Jimmy Nairn
1963

ABOVE
Here And Now
*Bill Tennent with
Alistair Cooke*

is grown, how steel is made, and highlighting all those industries which contribute to the national economy, while a weekly discussion programme over 13 weeks is also planned.

"Dr John Grierson's documentary programme THIS WONDERFUL WORLD has received the countrywide praise which it deserves and is perhaps the best television programme in Britain. Dr Grierson will shortly add a new programme of his own, a documentary for children.

Macrae)
The children's puppet show MR FIXIT has been sold to nine other countries…

"STV NEWS presented twice daily five days a week offers more regional information than any other Company. SCOTSPORT for a time had a monopoly of film rights from the Scottish Football Association……. SCOTSPORT gave Europe its first outside broadcast from Independent Television in Britain. JUNIOR SCOTSPORT is being introduced to cover the whole field of local sport for children.

"The current affairs programme, HERE and NOW, twice weekly, covers many aspects of Scottish life and controversy. (This was the first TV news magazine programme in the UK.)
The Outside Broadcasting team will be showing a series of information programmes showing how food

"A very thorough search for Scottish talent was conducted in a programme called STARS IN YOUR EYES, during which over 5,000 artistes, both professional and amateurs, were auditioned over a period of 26 weeks. This contest was won by Miss Joan Summers …winning her a prize tour of Canada and New York with an introduction to many people and institutions in music and entertainment. On her return, the New York Metropolitan Opera wrote to say they recommended a year's training in Italy as her first step in an opera career. Thomson paid for this from his own funds."

Part of her prize was a wardrobe of clothes from Sellyn's fashion store at St George's Cross. After her training in Rome she stayed on in America and became an opera singer, soprano soloist, and later voice coach, winning also the Concert Artists Guild award in New York in 1965. On return visits to Britain she sang with Glyndebourne Opera, STV, and Scottish Opera when it started. One of the judges in the Theatre Royal was (Sir) George Martin, songwriter and producer for artistes including the Beatles in later years. Her earliest records here are with the Kirkintilloch Junior Choir, often in duet with Moira Anderson. Today Sir George Martin markets his favourite CDs of all genres, including one track from the Kirkintilloch Choir and features Joan Summers and Moira Anderson.

"The contribution of STV to drama is not shown by performances from the Theatre Royal........Scottish authors are thin on the ground, and their plays too often too thin altogether…
Thomson has assisted the Edinburgh Festival with a grant of £5,000 towards drama, and a similar grant to the new Scottish Repertory Theatres Trust chaired by Robert Kemp, which has assisted six companies so far.

"Religion – if the network programmes were adopted 60 per cent would be from the Church of England which has only a tiny membership in Scotland. It thus falls upon STV to see that the national balance of 7 Church of Scotland, 4 Episcopalian and other Protestants, and 2 Roman Catholic is maintained. STV must either do this or incur the wrath of the Kirk. (The balance became 5:2:2)

"Education ....is another matter of

ABOVE
Joan Summers *and Rai Purdy*

paramount importance in Scotland, and places a fairly heavy burden on STV. Associated-Rediffusion in England began educational programmes on independent television in 1957. STV took these programmes and made their contributions to them in a series in 1958-59 and will be producing a complete series in 1960/61. The numbers of schools taking such programmes is increasing, accelerated by the STV scheme of supplying and servicing suitable receivers and aerials at cost price and on a long term basis.

"Public Interest…….. STV co-operates

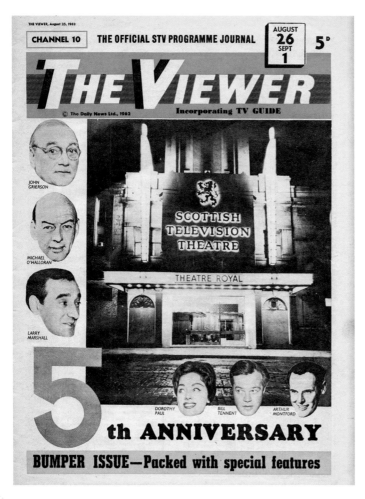

ABOVE
The Viewer, *1962*

RIGHT
The Beatles

with police and the Scottish Home Office by showing films on such matters as Polio, Litter and Clean Foods campaigns.

"Advertising ....Every form of participation is available to the advertiser. 10,000 visitors and potential clients have been accompanied in groups at the Theatre Royal. The proportion of local advertising is about 15 per cent."

Queuing up to get in

Each day queues stretched far down Hope Street to be the theatre audience of the *One O'Clock Gang* featuring Larry Marshall, Jimmy Nairn, Sheila Mathews, Brian Douglas, Charlie Sim, Marie Benson, Moira Briody, Dorothy Paul and joined by Fay Lenore, Gordon Mackenzie, Alistair McHarg, Peter Mallan and others. In the winter by the time each day's audience filed in the fog came in with them, and camera close-ups became essential. Guests included singers Cliff Richard, Shirley Bassey and many others promoting their own records, and actresses including Anna Neagle. In 1962 the Beatles joined the ranks when they appeared three times on *Round Up*, the magazine programme with the accent on youth, presented by Paul Young and Morag Hood, and scripted by Lavinia Derwent. These were amongst the very earliest TV shows of the four young men from Liverpool, who drove to Glasgow in their own car. Even the managing director went downstairs to the car park to get the Beatles autograph for his daughters.

Journalist Jack House presented *Whigmaleerie* in the afternoons, a programme of curiosities, and introduced the *Hogmanay Show* live from Glasgow Cross in 1957/58. A regular board meeting of the company was televised, warts and all, with Roy Thomson in the chair and Jim Coltart enjoying the contents of the cigar box. The producers thought the idea should not be repeated. In the coming years a play called *Blackhill* was produced based around the families living close to the mast.

The company produced *Top Hat, the Life Story of Jack Buchanan*, film and stage star in Britain and America. For this the sets constructed included a replica of the interior of the Brittania Panopticon Music Hall where the singer and dancer had started. For STV's own opening night in 1957 Jack Buchanan was determined to appear despite a terminal illness which few knew about. Complete with top hat and tails he sang *I Belong to Glasgow*.

On Saturday nights, and on Wednesdays, *Scotsport* showed filmed highlights of two top football games that day, all in black and white. Contracts were signed with the football authorities in England, Wales and Northern Ireland before the elusive Scottish Football Association finally gave live access to home and international matches here. *Scotsport* cameras were at Wembley Stadium six years before other commercial companies. By 1970 colour filming arrived, which was a blessing to sports televising, and later inventions of large electronic cameras allowed slow-motion replays.

By 1974 ITA had become the Independent Broadcasting Authority and asked from London a series of questions before a renewal of the licence, including whether there was a tendency to concentrate on the Forth/Clyde areas in Sport? To this the company replied:

> These are the areas where most of the best football teams reside. Other centres of football enthusiasm like Aberdeen and Dundee are outwith our area, (in Grampian TV's area.)

The next question from IBA was "Outside of football and golf we would regard your sports coverage as somewhat limited. This brought STV's reply:

> We are at a loss to understand your statement. We have covered – not from the network - Tennis, Racing, Athletics, Boxing, Motor Racing, Bowling, Speedway, Pigeon-racing, Curling, Ice Skating, Basketball, Badminton, Skiing, and Pony-trotting.

Magnus Magnusson chaired a weekly panel programme *Sense and Nonsense* with politicians and others discussing matters of the moment.

STV's lack of drama was first answered by a full length play by Perth Repertory Company appearing on the small screen on 30 January 1959. Perth had received some of the Trust funding created by Thomson. It was a romantic comedy *The Open*, the first programme from the huge Studio C and included film inserts from St Andrews golf

ABOVE
Miss STV, *1965.
Beauty contest, with
the Tommy Maxwell
Quartet.*

course. However the course was covered in deep snow which local volunteers cleared away from the scenes only to find ice covering the grass. The burgh council came to the rescue with a lorry full of sand to spread over it. The drama series included Robert Kemp's *The Highlander*.

A Licence to Print Money

To run the licence, which was in Roy Thomson's name, and to account for the advertising revenues and operating costs a company was created within the Thomson Organisation, with the new company informally adopting the name "Scottish Television." It became highly profitable straight away and its profits continued to exceed any other station per head of viewer. Thomson once quipped that his was *a licence to print money*. This famous phrase (uttered in Toronto) embarrassed ITA and riled the other commercial stations who thought that the eventual renewal of licences

would now have tougher conditions put on them all by ITA and its Director-General Sir Robert Fraser.

In one of his reports to the ITA board in May 1960, when responding to the Equity Union's concern about the need to engage more Scottish actors, Fraser refers to the company's **continued fabulous prosperity**. He was concerned whether there was, as the Act required "a suitable proportion of subject matter calculated to appeal specially to the tastes and outlook of persons served" despite the quota of programmes being fully met. Equity was advised to meet with the Scottish Committee.

Always with an eye to increasing STV's popularity, and his profits, Thomson saw the start that summer of a weekly hour-long programme of Scottish variety from the Theatre Royal, alternating each week with an Outside Broadcast variety programme from a seaside resort. Work proceeded on a fairly ambitious series of programmes about the British Commonwealth, for sale to the emerging Commonwealth nations. He suggested to ITA that his shareholding should reduce to 51 per cent by offering shares to individuals who lived in Scotland. ITA pondered over his motives, and did nothing.

The Scottish Advisory Committee gathered their thoughts about the balance and content of programmes, and ITA sent their Noel Stevenson to STV in 1961 to assess the situation which the Committee described as the need for more "Scottishness", less exporting and providing for the UK network, and the need to cater more for minority interests. In its view programmes were in a comfortable rut. Robert Fraser rebuffed the severity of their criticisms but he noted:

> The move of Thomson and Coltart to London has left a void, with too many matters referred to London …….and there is a belief that STV has been reduced to the status of a milch-cow in the Thomson estate.

Indeed the profits of STV helped Thomson buy prestigious newspaper groups in London. Fraser continued:

> STV has concentrated a perhaps undue amount of energy upon prestige programmes, some which can be sold abroad…..but this should be ancillary to production which is distinctively Scottish. In several respects, notably for instance, in school broadcasting – they have set an example which other companies have then followed.

School broadcasting, and its supporting book texts, was enthusiastically directed at Cowcaddens by Robert McPherson, Glasgow's Director of Education. Over 1100 schools in Central Scotland were provided with programmes for pupils up to 18 years old. For foreign language teaching, French plays were staged with actors being flown in from Paris. Fraser concluded "Over the last four years STV can well stand comparison with the other regional companies."

Noel Stevenson's assessment shows his colonial skills learned in Burma, where he had earlier been a Chindit during World War II, and his lecture skills gained at Glasgow University. He was aware of management friction within STV in Hope Street, and wrote "absentee direction (from London) plays its part, and often there is an over emphasis on cost criteria for productions."

"The critics are confused about distinctions between technical quality, production and design quality, costs, and subject matter. They may criticise popular programmes, as good as any on the network, but say they rarely watch them…They want more minority programmes, or greater design content, but simpler settings often work best.

BELOW
Talent shows *at the Lucky Diamond coffee bar*

"The One O'Clock Gang is in fact a very lively, happy and conspicuously clean frolic. Its chief comics, its quartet and singers compare well with those who appear on BBC or ITV network programmes. They also undertake a lot of good work in hospitals and old folks homes....There have been inserts including a 30 minutes series on the Scottish Regiments, the RAF and the Royal Navy. There has been a long series 15 minutes each on careers for the young, and on health issues. The critics, when pushed, say it does not appeal to a small proportion of people of high intelligence........

"Some critics complain of too much football on Scotsport....but it is the most enterprising and adventurous of all regional sports reports on ITV. Its reporting is clear, concise and apt, the film inserts are prolific and good (an average 3,500 feet of film is shot to provide a 10-15 minute film excerpt of a match.)

"Pattern of Programming .... here the critics have some cause for complaint.... Sure-fire hits have been stuck to too rigidly, new experiments are fewer and hesitant.... There is evidence that "external appeal" of local production which will sell well on the network or in the Commonwealth has a prior claim especially to the newly independent territories with expanding television services, in which the Thomson Newspaper Group is becoming even more deeply involved.

"It would be valuable to have the opinion of the Scottish Committee on for example the Commonwealth series. This has received a very good press..... and favourable attention from leaders in the Commonwealth. It has brought credit to STV and indirectly to Scotland. The question arises - is it better, in Scottish eyes, than a series on, say, Scottish art? In the last six months since meeting with Mr Hardy new programmes have been aimed to important minority audiences, for example, a series on Scots Law, in Fastand Folk, and in a series on music by Alexander Gibson."

Jim Coltart became Deputy Chairman and Noel Stevenson Managing Director, where he was joined in 1965 by Bill Brown's promotion to joint Managing Director. ITA sought details of widening the share ownership

BELOW
One Night Stand
each week for new bands

of STV, before they renewed Thomson's licence. He said that his holding could not reduce below 55 per cent "without serious harm to the wellbeing of the Thomson Organisation Ltd." 55 per cent of the company would now be owned by Roy Thomson who sold most of the remainder in 1965 to a few captains of industry and culture in Scotland who joined the board, including Dr Samuel Curran, Principal of the new Strathclyde University formerly the Royal College of Science and Technology. A quarter of STV staff also accepted the invitation to buy shares, as did the Scottish Trades Union Congress. Local programmes amounted to over 11 hours a week compared to the 9 hours required by ITA.

Scottish Opera and Francie & Josie

When Alexander Gibson started Scottish Opera in 1962 presenting operas at the King's Theatre, Bath Street, the first and largest commercial sponsor was Scottish Television. The company continued their support across Scotland, and in the commissioning of new operas for television.

A sketch, created by Stanley Baxter, from the *Five Past Eight Shows* in the Alhambra Theatre about the escapades and joys of two Tony Boys, was transferred to Cowcaddens, to become a television series starring Rikki Fulton and Jack Milroy in *The Francie & Josie Show*. The Tony Boys fashion had started in Italy, after the pseudo Edwardian fashion of "Teddy" Boys, and had tight bum-freeze jackets and trousers. "It was this look" recalls Stanley Baxter "I had to persuade Rikki was the "in" thing." He said "Where will we get an outfit like that?" I said "Oh we'll have to have it made at Maxwell Mann The Tailor." He said "Will we have to pay for them?" I said "I'm afraid so." It was the best investment he ever made!" It later returned as a theatre show in its own name. A monthly series of *The Rikki Fulton Show* was networked across Britain with burlesques and sketches including a parody of John Grierson's documentaries "This Wonderful World" renamed as "This Scunnerful World."

ABOVE
The Viewer Award
to Larry Marshall and Kay Rose, presented by Francie and Josie, watched by Bill Tennent

LEFT
Housecall
Isabel Begg (right), *with boxer Henry Cooper.*

ABOVE
The Viewer *cover
with Dorothy Paul*

BELOW
Dorothy Paul *sings
with trombonist
George Chisholm at
the piano*

In 1964 nation-wide strikes affected Britain's economy – resulting in fewer viewers and less advertising money - while public organisations at the same time became critical of BBC and the ITV companies. In bearding these criticisms Noel Stevenson sized up the opposition in a letter of May 1964 to ITA's Head of Information, Sir Harold Evans. Some extracts are as follows:-

"The women's organisations are concerned mainly about violent, sexy and "drinky" programmes and sweet advertising, the professional bodies seem to care most about "culture", advertising in general and so-called triviality.

"I have worked hard upon the Educational Institute for Scotland through the Educational Advisory Committee and succeeded through them in getting the EIS to reverse the opposition it expressed to the Pilkington Committee against an Educational TV service. Among Scottish teachers there is a considerable leftwing bias, and socialist-oriented attitudes towards all forms of advertising are common.

"Our churchmen seem to be most concerned about plays.
The medical profession has been much more tolerant towards us since we introduced "Post Graduate Medicine", but they still show great sensitiveness towards such things as tobacco advertising.

Catherine Wilson in the STV production of 'The Merry Widow' – Christmas 1976.

"There is not much I need say about the Press. As competitors for advertising we cannot expect them to boost us. I think on the whole we are fairly treated."

In the eight years from 1957 to 1965, when Thomson had total control, the income from advertising and sales totalled £35million and the profits sent to the Thomson Organisation in London reached a fabulous £13m. All this was from a start-up of £400,000, most of it a loan from the National Commercial Bank of Scotland. (In today's money this is equal to over £325m. profit from a £10m. investment.) From 1965 the business was now being run through a newly formed company Scottish Television Ltd. Lord Thomson was still chairman and the profits continued for a while.

Of course advertising reflected the ups and downs of the country's economy, weather and social interests. For instance there was a major change with the loss of cigarette advertising from August 1965, and a sudden cancellation of advertisements from the Gas, Electricity and Coal industries as a result of a cold snap in November and December.

ABOVE
Francie and Josie
Jack Milroy (right),
and Rikki Fulton,
1965

LEFT
Opera advert *for The*
Merry Widow, 1976

Continuing Success From Cowcaddens

S cottish Television's reports now became public, and the company described its progress at the end of 1965. Television was making its mark, and at the Royal it started Metropole theatre drama, medical education, children's serials, cartoons, cabaret and colour.

Of the 70 hours of broadcasting each week STV produced an average of 10 hours, networking companies 36, other regional companies 4, Independent Television News 4, and purchased film 16. A number of programmes produced by STV were broadcast by the Network and other regional companies, and some programmes were exported. Its balance of programmes was about the same as all the ITV areas, except that STV made a higher proportion of serious and drama programmes, and of sports programmes.

Informative programming of local origin from the Theatre Royal was welcomed by the majority of viewers, such as *Here and Now*, *The Commons Touch*, *Dateline Scotland* and two documentary series *Present Grandeur*, and *Vision on Scotland*. Political pro-grammes had to be self-balancing, and not partisan. The political editor James Gordon saw to all that before going off a few years later to start Radio Clyde,

when commercial radio was licensed after off-shore broadcasting had begun with pirate ships such as Radio Scotland in the Firth of Clyde.

Religious broadcasts from the Royal and outside were added to by *Quo Vadis*? where successful men and women from all walks of life were inter-viewed on their basic beliefs. STV was the first ITV company to transmit a re-ligious programme, *Clearway*, outwith

OPPOSITE
Hope Street *from Renfrew Street, 1960*

BELOW
Master control desk, *1971*

SIR WILLIAM BROWN

Champion of the Public

Bill Brown, as he is best known, joined Roy Thomson as STV's sales manager and rose to become the Managing Director in the 1960s and latterly Chairman. He twice served as the chairman of the ITV Federation, and was awarded the Gold Medal of the Royal Television Society. In commercial television he insisted upon public obligation as the highest sense of duty. A keen supporter of Scottish Opera, he was a member of its advisory council and joined the board of Scottish Opera Theatre Royal Ltd under the chairmanship of Gavin Boyd. On his retiral he became the chairman of the Scottish Arts Council. He was also a director of Channel Four television founded by Jeremy Isaacs, a fellow citizen of Glasgow and fellow pioneer of the best of TV programming.

Bill Brown, Gavin Boyd, Alexander Gibson and their families shared a bond of friendship, and avoided the limelight as best they could away from busy schedules of television, commerce and music. Bill Brown often said that just as Mary of Guise had the words "Mary Queen of Scots" written on her heart he had the words "Theatre Royal" written on his.

the normal Sunday period.

In association with the Glasgow Post Graduate Medical Board, STV pioneered specialised programmes for doctors on open television, and reported:

> The series "Post Graduate Medicine" has been widely seen throughout Britain and overseas, and the medical schools of other Universities are now also participating.
> The drama series based on the medical forensic work of Professor John Glaister was seen by 8 million people across Britain.

and STV continued:

> We have experimented with light entertainment series ranging from spectaculars to ceilidhs, small

groups to the Scottish National Orchestra, established artistes to new talent.

The Jimmy Logan Theatre Hour specially mounted by us at the Metropole Theatre, St George's Cross, has presented a series of Scottish plays providing enjoyment for viewers and employment for artistes in Scotland.

The series included *Mugs and Money*, and *A Scrape o'The Pen*, one of Graham Moffat's plays. Other regular shows were *Man Behind the Star*, *Theatre Royal*, *Scottish Television Music Hall*, *Fireside Ceilidh*, and the *Alexander Brothers Show*. *Scotsport* covered football, ice hockey, motor scrambling, sailing and golf; and the World Cup football match at Hampden Park between Scotland

and Italy was televised by STV to Italy, Belgium, Denmark, Switzerland, and West Germany.

In 1966 programmes from the network included *Emergency Ward 10*, *Coronation Street*, *This Week*, and *The Avengers*. Local programming continued *Festival Club* for the three weeks of the Edinburgh International Festival, which Thomson and STV supported each year; and started *Time out with Tennent* a series of 21 documentaries with Bill Tennent; and *Picture Palace* programmes on the Arts. The company's Arts Adviser was Emilio Coia who advised on educational, documentary and festival programmes.

The weekday programme for children *The Younger Set* was replaced by *Lesley* presented by Lesley Blair, a former station announcer "who shows great talent for talking to little children." Developing upon the *Quo Vadis?* programme *This is the Day* started, introduced by David Steel MP, a son of the manse, examining the pressing social problems of the day. Glen Michael's *Cartoon Cavalcade* also began and ran for a record breaking 26 years usually on Sunday afternoons for all the family. Some special editions were filmed out in the streets, and there were also *Christmas Cavalcades* and *Scotsports Cavalcades*.

TOP
Prime Minister Harold Wilson *being interviewed, 1966*

BOTTOM
The Islanders, *regular series, 1966*

A Song for Scotland competition, produced by Bryan Izzard, was held over the year to find new Scottish Songs, with hundreds of entries. The winners were *Loch Maree* written by R.D Ford and sung by Moira Anderson, followed by *For These Are My Mountains* written by James Copeland and sung by Peter Mallan. At New Year *A Show for Hogmanay* was fully networked and seen all over Britain. *Sounds and Sweet Airs* for St Andrews Day was shown in seven ITV areas, and Bruce McClure, trained by Margaret Morris, became Scottish Television's first (and only) full time dance director.

Eight plays were shown in the *Scottish Playbill* series, mostly one hour in length:

but in common with TV services all over the world we have the greatest difficulty in locating good scripts and scriptwriters.

..........in conjunction with Glasgow Citizen's Theatre we are seeking works, preferably by Scottish writers which are capable of production both in the theatre and in television, in the hope that the prospect of two outlets instead of one will stimulate the talent which we feel sure exists within Scotland.

To the regular programmes, including *John Grierson Presents*; *The Bill Tennent Show*; and *Eric Milligan's Cookery*, were added new successes in 1967 such as STV's first major children's serial in eight parts *The Flight of the Heron* by DK Broster, adapted by Moutrie Kelsall and starring Finlay Currie. Four full length plays were produced, the most ambitious being *Queen of Scots* written by Jack Gerson and Ian Stuart Black, with Ellen McIntosh as Queen Mary. Una McLean's own comedy show *Did You See Una?* had its first airing.

Australian pianist and accompanist Peggy O'Keefe and her trio started the first of many evening series including a *Date with Peggy* with singer guests; a daily 6pm series of *Today is…..* where John Toye or George Reid and a panel of VIPs combined the news with musical interludes connected to the topics of the day. A monthly series of *Night Club Night* was televised live from the Chevalier nightclub and casino in Sauchiehall Street fronted by Peggy O'Keefe and featuring guests including

Matt Monro, George Chisholm, Ronnie Carroll, The Dallas Boys, Kenny Lynch, Cleo Laine, Roy Castle, and Kenneth McKellar (in his first ever cabaret.) The newspapers wrote "This confection of light music captured the perfect mood for late night entertainment."

A series *Singing for our Supper* in opera and classical music was presented by Ian Wallace and had a marked effect on Scottish Opera's box office returns.

TOP
Charity Gala *co-presented by STV. Princess Margaret meets Bill Simpson, Alec Finlay next in line.*

BOTTOM
Peggy O'Keefe *with Ronnie Carroll and Sir Reo Stakis, left.*

STV sponsored the Scottish National Orchestra in Europe, and Scottish Opera's production of *The Soldier's Tale* at the Edinburgh International Festival.

During the year a colour film of the *Alexander Brothers Show* and guest

singers Ann and Laura Brand was made in Arran to gain colour experience. It was transmitted in black and white, colour signals (and sets) coming into general use from the end of 1969 onwards. The first major colour production was an eight-part serialisation of Sir Walter Scott's *Redgauntlet*, filmed on the shores of the Solway Firth and in the Theatre Royal. The company was also filming overseas for documentaries.

Modernising a nation

STV was playing its part in providing continuing education and in factual reporting on the political and economic changes facing the country. A second book was published describing Scotland as it stood and was developing, to serve as a platform for potential advertisers and to contribute to the commonweal. This was *Scotland: A New Look* by Geoffrey Credland and George Murray, and followed the first book which had become a standard work in some universities and an economic textbook in schools.

Two stalwarts of the company board from its beginning were stockbroker Charles McQueen who was a director of Howard & Wyndham Ltd, still with some theatre interests and now with major shareholdings in Britain's largest television production company – the Incorporated Television Programme Company Ltd. And the other was the industrialist Sir Ian Stewart, a President of the Institute of Engineers and Shipbuilders of Scotland and a director of the Thomson Organisation.

In 1965 one of the Clyde's largest shipbuilders, Fairfields, went bankrupt. Like much of British industry it was stuck in old methods and employee conflict. The Labour government, public

spirited investors and trade unions formed a new Fairfields Glasgow Ltd chaired by Sir Ian Stewart. STV's personnel department and others moved from the theatre to Govan, as did the Moral Rearmament gatherings. All involved brought in improvements to physical conditions at the yard, an end to strikes, and modern ways of planning and production.

ABOVE
Scotland, A New Look
1969

ABOVE
Sir Iain Stewart

RIGHT
Sean Connery *at*
Fairfields, 1967 for
The Bowler & The
Bunnet

OPPOSITE
(bottom)
All Kinds of Opera
Faust, with Vienna
State Opera and
Scottish Opera
Chorus, fully
networked.

Stewart invited Sean Connery to visit the yard to see what was happening, and could be made to happen to improve many industries, resulting in STV making a film in 1967 on location at Fairfields Shipyard with Sean Connery, equally enthused about the challenges, who charged no fees for

his six weeks there. The documentary *"The Bowler and the Bunnet"*, script by Cliff Hanley and directed by Connery, expresses the hopes and benefit of new attitudes to work and was networked throughout Britain, and shown at screenings in London for Labour MPs and Tory MPs. It is still available to cinema. Unfortunately the Labour government unexpectedly pulled the rug and rolled Fairfields into an Upper Clyde Shipbuilders group, larger but not lasting. Today the surviving shipyards of Fairfields Govan and Yarrows Scotstoun, now owned by BAE Systems, owe a lot to the Fairfields Experiment.

Across Britain TV services planned ahead for the changeover to colour in 1969/70 and the use of high frequency signals to improve the viewing picture. Lord Thomson explained:

> as a result of these major changes, studio and production facilities need to be reorganised and the present Theatre Royal site cannot accommodate the changes envisaged. Accordingly Scottish Television is seeking a site on which to build an entirely new television centre, work on which is expected to start before the end of 1968.

More changes

Changes in law came in to ensure no one person owned more than 25 per cent of a television company; this affected a number of stations including STV. In addition ITA's policy changed a few years earlier barring newspapers from owning more than 49 per cent of a station. Thomson's licence was due for renewal and ITA made it clear he would have to reduce his ownership to 25 per cent and that shares should be sold to people unconnected to the Thomson Organisation, with preference given to Scottish people and companies.

He asked ITA if he could sell 25 per cent to Sir Hugh Fraser junior, indicating he would appoint more new directors including Lady Fraser of Allander, widow of the legendary retailer Lord Fraser. He had not consulted the Fraser family but clearly Thomson was hoping a company could still be formed to jointly run the *Scotsman* and the *Glasgow Herald* even though the late Hugh Fraser had won the Herald after a bitter public takeover battle with the Thomson Organisation. ITA said no, pointing out that more newspaper ownership of television was frowned upon and also that the Fraser companies already held shares in Border Television.

In July 1968 STV shares were sold openly to the public for the first time, with a massive response, and were quoted on the Stock Exchanges. The few individuals who invested in 1957 were delighted to see their original shares become over 20 times more valuable!

Afternoon broadcasting was introduced across Britain, with STV's own programmes increasing by 3 and a half hours a week. During 1968 the melodrama of everyday life was the essence of the first of a "soap" series *High Living* in a block of flats named Caulton Court "somewhere in Central Scotland." A

six-play cycle was produced on the *Life of Robert Burns*, starring John Cairney (who then toured the world in Burns dramatisations, and other guises). STV commissioned a new opera *Full Circle* by Robin Orr, Professor of Music at

TOP
John Cairney *recites Tam O'Shanter, 1966*

Glasgow University and performed by Scottish Opera, as the climax to the second series of *Singing for our Supper*.

By now the crime fiction writer Bill Knox, who was STV's news editor, started his factual *Crime Desk* inviting viewers to come forward to help police solve some of the current crimes and mysteries. A regular insert in *Scotland Today* was an outdoor exploration of Scotland by the mountaineer Tom Weir.

By 1972 this became its own programme *Weir's Way*, and an islands series *Weir Aweigh*.

Orphaned

The next two years would bring even more changes than could be imagined. Most profound was the situation Scottish Television Ltd found itself in after Lord Thomson ceased to have full control. A few years later the Television Authority asked a series of questions including "In 1968 there were major changes at the Authority's request in the control of the company – what are your views since then." STV replied:

> The changes decreed by the Authority in 1968 liberated and at the same time orphaned STV. The provisions made by the Thomson Organisation for capital investment in colour and new buildings after 1968 were, as you know, withdrawn when STV ceased to be a subsidiary of Thomson. STV has undertaken these expenditures having no access to the reserves built up over the years and without the backing of a Group with financial strength in depth.

Adding to the woes ITA increased rentals to be paid from 1968 by all the commercial companies under renewed licences in what was seen partly as a vindictive response to Thomson's historical remark of a licence to print money. STV's rise was excessive and out of proportion to its revenue and population base compared to companies in England.

An advertising recession set in. There was little money for making new, quality programmes – the very thing ITA wished to encourage. At the same time STV drew attention to BBC competition in Scotland, with the Corporation designating Scotland as the biggest production centre outside London, with funds for 12 hours origination of Scottish work per week. 1969 just avoided making a loss and 1970 was a financial loss, for the first time ever. Plans for the new complex of studios on a new site were delayed. STV considered selling Theatre Royal for over £600,000 (possibly for a supermarket or carparks) and leasing new studios instead of buying them. ITA became sympathetic to their plight but help had to wait a few years for a national review when STV's rental was reduced by more than half, by almost £500,000 each year, making a more level playing field across Britain.

The creative side of programmes continued as best it could. In January 1969 at very short notice almost the whole of the journalist staff were deployed on the networked production of *The Ship* from the Clyde which told the story of building the new Cunard liner QE2 at Clydebank, its challenges and all its early difficulties. The programme was nominated for an Emmy Award. The discussion programme *Lion's Share* grew in stature and a weekly programme *Raw Deal?* was introduced dealing with viewers' complaints. STV

described it as a kind of Ombudsman of

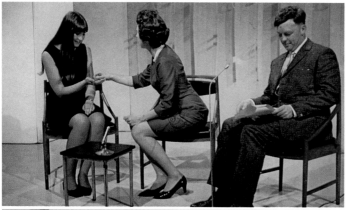

ABOVE
Glen Michael's
Cavalcade and Rudi

TOP
Young Scot, *1967*
Countess of Mar
congratulates
Euphemia Brand,
chairman Bob
Crampsey

TOP RIGHT
The Hilton Half
Hour
Ronnie Hilton and
guest Bernadette,
1969

It is vital to our future that the sale of colour sets should be encouraged in every possible way, and there is no doubt that programmes in colour are the most effective of all aids to sales.

The theatre went on fire at the end of the year destroying the stage with all its electronic equipment, and tragically a fireman lost his life. The firefighting foam reached the height of the Grand Circle. All transmissions switched to the Gateway studios, at additional cost, and for several months black and white was all that was possible. Studio A at the Royal was put out of action permanently but the small Studio B was brought back to use.

the Air. For the festive season three programmes were seen throughout Britain, *Cliff in Scotland*, *The Kelvin Hall Circus*, and the *Hogmanay Party*.

Colour through the air

Scotland's first colour TV studios opened in October at STV's Edinburgh base, the Gateway Theatre, connected to the Theatre Royal by a 45 mile landline. Sir Walter Scott's *Redgauntlet* was STV's first major colour production, and colour started on 13th December 1969. The company commented:

Into the 1970s

A television version was made of the 1970 Edinburgh Festival play by the Prospect Theatre Company of Boswell's Life of Johnston, and networked as *The Boswell and Johnston Show* the next year starring Bryan Pringle and Timothy West. Also televised was a new Scottish one act opera *The Undertaker* by John Purser, performed by Scottish Opera under Alexander Gibson. The company started its annual series of the STV Theatre Awards for distinguished work in the Scottish Theatre, the presentations being made by Lord Goodman, chairman of the British Arts Council.

As well as televising from the Royal the company published books including the *Scotsport Yearbook, One O'Clock Gang Book, Cartoon Cavalcade Annual* and a *Pocketful of Saturdays* by the Rev Nelson Gray. Support material and a record appeared for the Adult Language introductory Gaelic language course *Geagan Gaidhlig*. The first Gaelic programme *Highland Air* had started in the 1960s presented by John M Bannerman.

STV continued to give grants to many artistic bodies in Scotland and through the Television Fund "for the encouragement of the Arts and Sciences" all as required by the licence. Broadcasting hours were derestricted in 1972 and extended beyond 10 30pm to around midnight, with an eye to new advertising eventually, and school broadcasts moved to the morning. Thought was being given to establishing the habit of daytime viewing.

In 1972 work began behind the theatre on the new TV Centre and studios. Programme making continued to improve in range and quality. STV also took up shares in the newly formed Radio Clyde, with numbers of staff moving there, believing that:

a healthy radio company will foster

the public's and the advertiser's acceptance of commercial broadcasting as a permanent part of their daily lives.

ABOVE
Scotland Friday
Colin McKay awaits the studio preparation, 1974

It televised Scottish Opera performing Benjamin Britten's opera *A Midsummer Night's Dream* at the new McRobert Centre at Stirling University. *Scotch Corner* at 1pm each Wednesday starring Andy Stewart was networked across Britain. *Tobias and the Angel* by James Bridie was adapted by his playwright son Ronald Mavor and broadcast nationally. The light entertainment series *Showcase* with artistes of international reputation was well received.

STV became a main provider of golf for the ITV network, and *Scotsport* reached its 2,000 edition:

We invest large sums of money in football proportionately.... much

more than our colleagues in England…….. and during the year we joined with the BBC and the Scottish Football Association in paying for a major upgrading of the floodlighting of Hampden Park.

Colour filming of football in dark winter afternoons had been proving difficult.

Housecall presented by Isabel Begg became a regular weekly afternoon programme for everyone at home during the day. A second series of Kipling's *Elephant Boy* was co-produced in Ceylon with German and Australian companies, for networked children's hour. In schools broadcasting the *Time to Think* series was planned with the raising of the school leaving age in mind. *Play Fair* was a first series on community education, and in adult education *You Pays Your Money* was a guide to all aspects of insurance. *Fit to Last* focused on exercise and diet for a healthier way of life.

STV carried on making more religious programmes and documentaries than any other company in the ITV areas. *Late Call* was shown every evening from 1957 until interrupted in the last week of 1973 when a continuous run of 16 years was broken by the national emergency (due to national strikes and energy rationing) and the 10-30pm close-down being re-imposed. It resumed its slot afterwards.

The Stanley Baxter Scots Picture Show networked across ITV was a production by Stanley Baxter and STV. He was working in plays in Australia when STV phoned asking him to show on television some of his classic sketches from the Alhambra *Half Past Eight* shows. It was his first public return to Scotland for many years, and included such sketches as "The Lady from Kelvinside." Concert singers over the years included Kenneth McKellar, Moira Anderson and Peter Morrison.

Political journalism and current affairs investigations continued to be of high order from Cowcaddens including work by George Reid who would go on to be an MP, and then Presiding Officer of the Scottish Parliament. He was followed later by a similarly young Gordon Brown who also became an MP, then Chancellor of the Exchequer and

TOP LEFT
Dateline
Bill Tennent with Hughie Green and Kathy Kay, 1972

TOP
Showcase, *Julie Rogers, 1973*

LEFT
The Stanley Baxter Scots Picture Show, *1973*

now Prime Minister.

"A country which is on the move"

The Independent Broadcasting Authority sent out questions and comments in 1974 before the next round of licences. The first one put to STV was "it is occasionally observed that the undoubted potential within the company is not always fulfilled in what appears on the screen." The reply from STV starts with a quotation from the poet Robert Browning:

"Ah, but a man's reach should exceed
his grasp or what's a heaven for"
and continues:

This is a criticism which must apply to any broadcasting system worth its salt.

... there are always financial circumstances in which we operate...Our programme people complain from time to time that the resources tail wags the creative dog................ on balance a useful discipline.... More harmful to achievement has been the wide swings between good times and bad......... The need to spread the effort over the full range of programmes has produced fewer high peaks of performance than we would have wished........ We also feel that our better programmes go unnoticed in London.

Question: What ITV company has produced four operas for television, two of them specially commissioned?
We have raised our standards considerably in the last 10 years ... we now have modern first class studios...... and we have a country which is on the move.

One of the other IBA questions was "is Current Affairs and Documentary output becoming predictable?" STV's riposte starts:

We aim for flair and innovation, and are uncertain of the meaning of "predictable"

BELOW
Outside broadcasting *vans, 1972*

LEFT
New STV Studios
surround the Theatre

We suspect that the salvation of our country over the next ten years might lie in the reduction of conflict between the governors and the governed, between the classes, and between the generations.

Bill Brown reflected on what Scottish Television had achieved over the years, the development of its new Cowcaddens studios (officially opened by Princess Alexandra in December 1974, who would not have known there had been an Alexandra Music Hall just a few yards away!), budgets that had recovered, new equipment invested, and a width of programming even greater than before in all areas. Programmes were being exported to Australia, Belgium, Canada, China, France, Israel, Italy, New Zealand, Portugal and Spain. In his next public report he added:

As well as providing Scottish entertainment for our viewers, these programmes give employment to actors, singers, dancers and musicians which has been sadly reduced with the closure of so many theatres. We are providing more musician engagements than any other regional company, and more even than two of the major companies.

STV would soon screen live the Johann Strauss opera *Die Fledermaus* for Scottish Opera's opening of a magnificently restored Theatre Royal.

Restoring The Theatre Royal
By Public Demand

On the very day in October 1973 when Gavin Boyd of Scottish Opera launched his fundraising appeal for the theatre he got a phone call generously offering to meet the full costs of buying, restoring and converting the Theatre Royal to become the home of Scottish Opera (founded by Sir Alexander Gibson) and be the first national opera house in Scotland.

With elation and heart-searching he thought of the offer throughout the night and reluctantly next morning had to decline it – in order to let as many organisations and people as possible become involved. The donor's family continued (and continues) to be substantial benefactors to Scottish Opera and the Theatre Royal. Had the offer been accepted the theatre would be known by a most respected new name that of the donor's father, Lord Fraser of Allander, the retailing giant of Britain, owner of House of Fraser, Harrods of London and much more. The Lord Fraser of Allander Theatre was young Sir Hugh's proposal as a national gift in memory of his father. Soon after, the Fraser Foundation gifted the island of Iona to the nation as a lasting memorial.

Bill Brown of STV asked the opera company's advisory council in 1972 if they would be interested in the Theatre Royal when the television company moved out. A project committee was formed headed by businessman Gavin Boyd, which appointed the architectural firm of Arup Associates to examine the feasibility and likely costs. Arup had designed the Sydney Opera House. By 1973 the plans were ready and a deep breath was taken on how best to raise the money. A target was agreed of £3m, in today's money about £50m. The 1970s were to be difficult years for the country, never mind fundraising, with three-day working weeks, strikes and inflation rising to 25% a year. The Royal Opera Company in London had found a permanent home in Covent Garden after 1945 and now the next would be Scottish Opera with the opportunity of the Theatre Royal. The brochures of the time describe the excitement and the challenge:

ABOVE
Lord Fraser

OPPOSITE
Alex Gibson, *1975*

SIR ALEXANDER GIBSON

ABOVE
Alex Gibson *starts
Scottish Opera*

Born in Motherwell in 1926 Alexander Gibson became the most distinguished Scot in the world of music in the second half of the twentieth century. He made classical music and operas accessible to all. Following his studies at the University of Glasgow, the Royal Scottish Academy of Music, and in London, Salzburg and Siena, Italy he worked in London and Glasgow, including the BBC Scottish Orchestra. One engagement was as conductor of the Scottish (National) Orchestra in 1954 playing for the Glasgow Grand Opera Society at the Theatre Royal – a place he knew well as a boy attending operas. In 1957 he became the youngest music director and conductor of Sadler's Wells Opera in London, where he made his operatic conducting debut in 1952. He was appointed as the first Scottish principal conductor and musical director of the Scottish National Orchestra in 1959, a post he held for 25 years, longer than any other conductor to date, establishing an international reputation for the SNO.

Alexander Gibson founded Scottish Opera in 1962 while at the same time directing the SNO, and was responsible for its remarkable growth and artistic achievement. He continued as music director until 1987 when he became its Conductor Laureate and returned as a conductor many times. He was also principal guest conductor of the Houston Symphony Orchestra in the 1980s, and continued much of his operatic work in the United States. At Christmas 1994 he conducted Scottish Opera for the last time in Puccini's Madam Butterfly at the Theatre Royal, which fittingly was in the opening season in 1962 at the King's.

BELOW
Elmbank Crescent
*- Scottish Opera HQ
- staircase*

He was knighted in 1977, and became president of the Royal Scottish Academy of Music and Drama where, in his memory, the Alexander Gibson School of Opera opened in 1998 as the first purpose built opera school in Britain.

The four founders

The founders got together in 1961 when **Alex Gibson** decided it was time Scotland had its own resident professional opera company and not be dependent on touring companies from London. With three others the ball got rolling. **Richard Telfer** was a cinema and church organist, music teacher, and chorus master in Edinburgh and became its first company manager, and later it's archivist.

Ainslie Millar was a chartered surveyor, an amateur singer and the Scottish trustee of Sadler's Wells (known later as English National Opera) who regularly visited the Royal, King's and Empire theatres. He was elected a councillor on Glasgow Corporation, and through his good offices the Corporation in 1968 gave a long lease of the former Institute of Engineers and Shipbuilders building in Elmbank Crescent to be the Scottish Opera Centre, with offices, rehearsal rooms, and costume workrooms. He became chairman of the Royal Scottish Academy of Music and Drama.

Ian Rodger – the most erudite of lawyers, and a part-time lecturer at the University – was also a lover of music, theatre and opera. His wartime service in the 1940s ended appropriately in Venice! He created the Scottish Opera Society Ltd and linked to it an advisory council comprising the four founders, leaders of Scotland's main orchestras and music organisations and the managing director of Scottish Television. This was joined soon after by Scottish Opera staff delegates and elected councillors representing Scotland's cities and counties. By this there was formed an active bond with all parts of the country's social and civic life.

International and national

International and national singers were attracted. On a part-time basis the company produced 18 different new operas and five opera revivals in its first five years. The "Opera for All" group started touring to smaller towns throughout Britain, and "Opera for Schools" also started. In 1966 the chairman Robin Orr reported

> We have a record number of 36 principal singers, more than a third of whom are Scottish; a Scottish Opera Chorus of 40 under chorus master Arthur Oldham; and eight dancers by arrangement with Glasgow Theatre Ballet Ltd.; with the Scottish National Orchestra, and its Scottish Opera Chamber Ensemble.

It was soon presenting between 10 and 12 different operas each year in its extensive touring in Britain, to which was added a number of continental tours.
Unsolicited opinions in the Press were included in the Theatre Royal fundraising brochures of 1973:

The Financial Times
At its best Scottish Opera is unsurpassed by any other opera company in Western Europe.

Opera Magazine
This company is at present the best ensemble in the country. There is an unmistakably corporate feeling about the whole enterprise that one just does not find at the moment in London.

The Observer
To cross the Border on an operatic mission is to be reminded that the continuing progress of this remarkable young company is perhaps the most important single development in the field of British Opera since Covent Garden first received a public subsidy after the war.

TOP
Richard Telfer

MIDDLE
Ainslie Millar

BOTTOM
Ian Rodger

RIGHT
Work in Progress
*Peter Hemmings,
Gavin Boyd, and Alex
Gibson*

RIGHT
Work in Progress
*Peter Hemmings,
Gavin Boyd, and Alex
Gibson*

BELOW
Inspection
*Dame Eva Turner
inspects the changes
with Gavin Boyd and
Peter Hemmings*

Chairman Robin Orr:
The Theatre Royal project represents a unique opportunity to provide a permanent opera house in Glasgow. Scottish Opera has acquired an international reputation within a remarkably short period of years, but I do not know of any other major company which, for want of a home theatre, is obliged to give most of its performances on tour, under conditions which are inevitably variable and difficult as well as uneconomic and artistically hazardous.

For a fraction of the cost of a new building Scottish Opera and its devoted public could enjoy the lasting benefits of a first-class opera house in the city which has contributed so staunchly to the development of the company.

General Administrator Peter Hemmings:
The possible acquisition of the Theatre Royal would enable Scottish Opera not only to present half, instead of a quarter, of its performances in its home town, but would also provide a stage for visiting

companies under the Arts Council banner, none of whom have been to Scotland in recent years, eg Royal Ballet, Royal Shakespeare Company, National Theatre, London Festival Ballet, Sadler's Wells Ballet etc.

The idea is to provide in Glasgow a theatre which is as near ideal for opera as possible. Most important of all is that it should have a staff both backstage and front-of –house who know and like the needs and habits of operagoers; stage staff who are used to heavy scenery and quick scene changes, barmen who actually enjoy intervals, box office staff who understand why *Traviata* houses are better than *Turn of the Screw* houses. Give the staff decent facilities and space and theatre-going becomes a real pleasure again.

Discussion has already taken place with the Scottish Theatre Ballet of a winter season of opera and ballet every night for about four weeks. An integrated repertoire of opera, ballet and drama (perhaps from the new Scottish National Drama Company) could be given in the Theatre Royal so that Mondays were regular drama nights, Tuesdays regular ballet nights, Wednesdays regular opera nights etc.

Architects Arup Associates:
The acoustics are ideal for opera and the slightly longer reverberation time on stage should ensure a

LEFT
Up She Goes!
Gavin Boyd helps the Lord Provst place the canopy grill

fine acoustic for the singers. …………the Theatre Royal auditorium has remained unchanged since Charles Phipps second design. The auditorium is generous and yet intimate. It promises a superb acoustic and the Victorian Renaissance which is still in very good condition can be realised together with the restoration of the spaces and the bars around it to make a home of real distinction for Scottish Opera.

Theatre Campaign chairman Gavin Boyd:
To secure in Scotland the future of professional opera, performed to international standards, Scottish Opera is setting out to raise £3m within the next 18 months - to purchase, restore, re-equip and

GAVIN BOYD

Of his generation Gavin Boyd was regarded as the best corporate lawyer in Scotland. As well as founding the legal firm of Boyds with his father he was the adviser to Hugh Stenhouse when the insurance broking firm of Stenhouse grew to be the world's largest. He was one of the masterminds behind the Hunterston Development Company deep-water port on the Clyde. In 1971 he became chairman of Stenhouse Holdings, and later a director of Scottish Television.

When they were boys and unknown to each other at the time, Alexander Gibson and Gavin Boyd were both taught to play music by Wilfrid Emery the organist at Glasgow Cathedral. While a student at Glasgow University he enjoyed classical music and choral singing. A keen supporter and funder of Scottish Opera he became a board member in 1972, when Stenhouse Holdings agreed to meet any deficits of the company, headed the Theatre Royal Campaign Executive and was the founder chairman of Scottish Opera Theatre Royal Ltd from 1973 to 1988, after which he remained a director. He became Chairman of the Court of the University of Strathclyde.

ABOVE
New Start
STV's Lewis Hynd hands the Theatre keys over to Gavin Boyd, Chairman Robin Orr looks on

endow the Theatre Royal and make it Scotland's first national opera house.

Currently Scottish Opera has a schedule of 107 full company performances in 10 major cities in and out of Scotland and another 14 by its smaller company and 50 by its subsidiaries Opera for All and Opera for Schools. Today while Glasgow is the company's spiritual home, lack of theatre availability is one of the main reasons why 80 per cent of its performances are given in other cities.

The company needs a theatre, a permanent home in which it can cater for its large, regular audiences, improve the standards of production for touring and contribute even more to the quality of the balanced life offered by Scotland to its inhabitants and to those it seeks to attract. It needs a theatre of a size and character which will ensure that the best possible talents of the opera world are attracted to perform with Scottish Opera. Presently it is rare to find a full time company of international standing which does

not have a theatre of its own. Such a base would provide facilities for longer seasons, a wider repertoire, and greater convenience for a larger public to choose and budget for its opera-going. Opera – the most complex and complete of the performing arts – needs space, time and a well-established headquarters if it is to flourish. From this base Scottish Opera would continue to tour on at least the same scale as that of today.

Financing the Project is envisaged in three stages
1.   £1m from industry and commerce from the appeal starting in October 1973
2.   An equivalent Grant from the State
3.   £1m from trusts, private foundations and private individuals with a public appeal starting in May 1974.

The government has made it clear to arts organisations that if they wanted increased financial support from the State they had to demonstrate that they were doing everything in their power to raise money privately. In other words, self-help before State-help.

It was hoped that a third of the money

ABOVE
Auditorium *restored*

LEFT
Roof chandelier *and arch detail*

RIGHT
Foyer *wih Royal Charter in corner*

OPPOSITE
Staircase
(top) *with portrait of Sir Alex Gibson* (bottom) *looking to foyer and grand circle landing*

could be a reserve for future development or enhancement. All the fundraisers were members of the appeal committee or staff of Scottish Opera and the Scottish National Orchestra, there were no paid fundraisers. The then Prime Minister Edward Heath gave a guarded welcome to the project in 1973, and the incoming Labour Government early in 1974 had financial problems and could give no firm commitment to a grant, although generally supportive. However the next General Election campaigning of September 1974 brought a promise after a visit to the theatre from the Conservative leader Edward Heath of a government grant if they were returned to power in October. Two weeks later the sitting Labour Government announced that they would provide one million pounds to match the money raised to date in the Campaign. The public appeal brought responses from thousands of individuals with donations from 50p to many hundreds of pounds. The appeal continued for several years. Gavin Boyd said that many donors contributed "as an affirmation of national pride."

STV sold the theatre to Scottish Opera for £300,000 and Scottish Opera Theatre Royal Ltd got the keys in October 1974. The directors of the new company were Gavin Boyd (chairman), Adam Bergius, Bill Brown, Ian Chapman, Ainslie Millar, Sandy Murray, and Ian Rodger. Building work started right away, and was completed one day early in October 1975 just before the first show. Sir Robert McAlpine & Sons were the project planners and contractors (appropriately the firm started in Glasgow in 1869 when William Glover brought the name Theatre Royal to Hope Street.) They and the subcontractors had only a year to carry out all the work. An article in the McAlpine house magazine in 1975, about the planning for the physical work, had it that the solution to completion on time was a simple one. Everyone involved merely had to work a 48- hour day!

To Bill Brown's chagrin it was discovered that the theatre title deeds did not include the public house at the Hope Street corner. It had never been owned by STV! Now called the Top Spot it started in 1869 as the Theatre Royal Vaults, then Thomson's Theatre Royal Dining Rooms, changing to the Camel's Head and then the College Bar. The restoration plan was to use the ground floor of the pub to create a large new theatre entrance and foyer and change the use of the upper floors. As a result the only major change from the project plans was in January 1975 when the Top Spot was omitted altogether.

A few years later Scottish Opera

Scottish Opera

Tuesday 14 October 1975

Scottish Opera
Chairman: Robin Orr CBE
Artistic Director: Alexander Gibson CBE
General Administrator: Peter Hemmings
Director of Productions: Peter Ebert

presents a

**SPECIAL INAUGURAL
PERFORMANCE**

to mark the opening of the Theatre Royal
Fanfare for the Theatre Royal
by Robin Orr

Die Fledermaus
by Johann Strauss

Theatre Royal
Glasgow

ABOVE
Opening Night
*Programme in
original Howard &
Wyndham style*

RIGHT
Gibson *and Lord
Provost McCann*

started.

Opening Season

The restored Royal was seen by millions on its opening night 14th October 1975 when Scottish Television televised live the whole of Johann Strauss' comic opera *Die Fledermaus*, and Radio Clyde broadcast it in its entirety. An edited version was seen in eight other Independent Television areas. The evening included an opera cabaret inserted into the stage production. Scottish Opera's production director Peter Ebert appeared on stage at the interval and spoke for all - "Well, we made it!"

At 6pm that evening on the new main staircase between the stalls and the circle Mrs Peter McCann, the Lady Provost, unveiled the full size portrait of Sir Alexander Gibson painted by the Queen's Limner in Scotland, David Donaldson. A few minutes later the audience, who had balloted for tickets, was admitted and began to wander round the theatre to see all that was new. All 1550 seats were sold out. Their way in the foyer and staircase was, and is, illuminated by grand chandeliers from the Marlborough function rooms in Shawlands. In 1987 the company added to the foyer a bust of Sir Alexander Gibson specially commissioned from the sculptor Archie Forrest.

The opening season ran from October to February with Scottish Opera presenting ten operas, twice as many as any previous Glasgow season of the company and around four times as many performances. The ten operas

bought the Top Spot from its owners Glenvey Blending and ran it as a public house and catering base – but it ran at a loss. STV then used it as a staff social club, until it finally closed. The entire rebuilding of the Hope Street corner site from basement to roof was achieved in 1993, and declared open by actor Bill Paterson, which is when the Café Royal

were *Otello, Hermiston, Ariadne on Naxos, Cosi fan Tutte, The Golden Cockerel, Die Fledermaus, A Midsummer Night's Dream, Don Giovanni, Madama Butterfly* and *Falstaff*. Gibson restated the company's artistic credo:

> to present the best works in the repertoire liberally interspersed with the unknown and the contemporary. And to present them to a high standard since only then will we attract and maintain an audience which knows what is good for us and for them.

The public was invited to take out a subscription series of tickets and come to the theatre on a Tuesday, Wednesday, Thursday or Saturday. Discounts of up to 30 per cent were available if a full series was booked. British Rail offered a travel and theatre seat subscription from towns as far away as Ayr, Edinburgh and Perth at a price no higher than the normal theatre seat price, and a snack was provided for the journey. Bus parties received a 50 per cent grant towards the coach hire. Subsidised parking was arranged with National Car Parks in Hope Street. Single seat prices ranged from 50p to £6.50. The theatre was alive and back to full business.

The architects Arup Associates described their work in the 1975/76 edition of Scottish Opera's magazine:

> Although our aim was to conserve and restore the Victorian

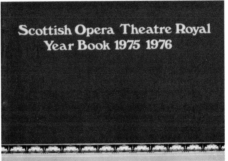

ABOVE
Subscription Brochure
10 operas for the price of 7

LEFT
Year Book, *1975/76*

Renaissance splendour of the old building, elsewhere we have torn the building apart and refitted it in such a way as to be worthy

WHAT THE PAPERS SAID

GLASGOW HERALD

Tonight the curtain will rise on a great Scottish achievement. Scotland will have its first opera house and Scottish Opera will have a permanent home worthy of its considerable artistic reputation.

Once under way the delights of this coming season of opera in Glasgow should provide ample encouragement to potential benefactors. In an era when artistic patronage is increasingly seen as a Government function it is refreshing to observe individual enterprise. Indeed the example set by Scottish Opera in vigorously promoting its cause to the eventual benefit of everyone is one which could be usefully copied by other groups in the arts and other leisure fields.

SCOTSMAN

Not only does the theatre promise to be the answer to every Scottish operagoer's dream with its rich intimate colour-scheme of brown and beige and gold, and its close relationship between stage and audience; but the voices project tellingly and truly, so that every word of the company's lively new translation of the operetta Die Fledermaus came over.

SUNDAY TIMES

The ascent of Scottish Opera from its modest beginnings in 1962 to its triumphant occupation of the handsomely restored Theatre Royal, Glasgow, forms one of the brightest pages in Britain's post-war artistic annals. Self-help, patriotic enthusiasm, efficient planning and sheer hard work – all have played their part in this inspiring success story.

THE TIMES

Music and spoken dialogue sounded clear, resonant and vivid; the acoustics appear well judged not least because the orchestra pit extends backwards below the stage, allowing room for a sizeable band without fear that singers will be swamped.

THE OBSERVER

The theatre is in the main admirably suited to its new role. The pink, brown and gold colours and delicate plasterwork of its late nineteenth auditorium are lively, warm and welcoming, and the strongly circular sweep of its balconies brings a feeling of intimacy and closeness to the stage. Unlike, for instance, the London Coliseum, this is a house which will accommodate Mozart as well as Wagner. The general balance between the orchestra and the stage is excellent…….

OPPOSITE
(top)**Auditorium**
postcard
(bottom)**Ceiling** *and balconies*

MUSIC WEEK

The company's achievement in raising the money and opening the theatre, not only on time but a day in advance, cannot be underrated. The new showcase will provide the most modern

▼

△

of theatre facilities, and some of the best acoustics in Europe. It is likely that recordings will not be long in coming.

FINANCIAL TIMES

By means of intelligent planning, energy, discernment and guts, Scottish Opera in the 13 years of its existence has won a place among Europe's leading companies. One thing has been lacking – a permanent base. Now one exists in the form of the Theatre Royal in Hope Street, Glasgow.... recently occupied by Scottish Television. In a remarkably short space of time it has been expertly converted and restored as a well-equipped modern opera house with an old-style auditorium. Although a few stair carpets and coats of paint were missing, the opening took place on schedule this week, in a last-minute aroma of scarcely dry plaster and builders' dust, with a special performance of Die Fledermaus followed the next evening by Verdi's Otello.

A handsome home they have made of it ....The side boxes with Corinthian columns, the circle fronts with Renaissance-style plasterwork are surprisingly delicate and elegant. The colour scheme of chocolate brown and beige with touches of kingfisher blue and subdued gilt is extraordinarily pleasing – comfortable, warmly festive, not gaudy.

DAILY TELEGRAPH

No wonder the chorus of Scottish Opera sang "Vittoria" so ecstatically in the first act Otello in Glasgow last night for they were taking part in the most significant evening for opera in Britain since Glyndebourne opened in 1934.

While Edinburgh and Manchester have been talking for years about opera and getting nowhere, in Glasgow the enthusiasts formed a company, built a reputation and now, after only 13 years, have bought and restored the Theatre Royal and have made it into a highly attractive opera house as the company's permanent home.

SUNDAY TELEGRAPH

Pleasant as were the opening performances of Scottish Opera in its new home – the reconverted Theatre Royal, Glasgow –nothing on stage was quite as bold as the company's long-term subscription plan. All ten operas in the current scheme are offered on an inclusive subscription at reduced prices which bring the best seats down from £6.50 to £4.50. The lowest price works out at a ridiculous 35p. Though not offered by other British companies, such a scheme is a mainstay of Continental houses (and of the Metropolitan in New York), and invites an advance pledge of public support which Scotland's company strongly deserves.

The first comedy played in the new house was an unintentional one. Alerted by a drum-roll Tuesday's first-night audience rose to their feet in anticipation of the National Anthem, only to sit down when finding their ears assailed by Robin Orr's ugly fanfare. But the Fledermaus that followed was enough to restore good humour, and Wednesday's Otello was equally auspicious. Wet paint might still be smelt in the theatre, but there was polish on the productions.

of the great tradition created by Scottish Opera. The fly tower has been completely re-equipped with new fly galleries, loading galleries, safety curtain and all the necessary stage equipment and machinery. A new, flat, stage has been designed with a large cantilever providing an orchestra pit which will take one hundred players. A band room, together with changing rooms and lavatories has been included at this level for the orchestra.

The whole of the auditorium has been carefully restored (and galleries strengthened). The rear of the house has been virtually rebuilt to give the Opera Company and Principals dressing rooms, a green room, rehearsal room, lavatories and showers

In the reconstruction of the front of the house, sufficient of the structure has been demolished to expose Phipps' original design which allowed the Auditoria to flow into

LEFT
Proscenium *plaster detailing*

RIGHT
Side Boxes *and more rich plasterwork*

the rear and side circulation spaces with direct access at bars to all the levels. One of the biggest design problems was that of the foyer. Space was very limited and yet it was essential to provide a generous feeling as people entered the Opera House. We hope this has been achieved by a total reconstruction of this area providing a very high space into which the public enters, with a staircase to the south of the main entrance hall rising within this volume.

Research in some depth was carried out into decorations and colour schemes for the restored Theatre Royal. Although red and gold is a very traditional approach to the interior of an Opera House, the Victorian French Renaissance style has many fine examples where shades of brown and gold, highlighted by other colours have been used very successfully. Various shades of cream and brown have been used for the painting of the restored fibrous plaster work. This has been highlighted with the use of blue and orange in certain areas of the decoration. The seating is in brown with a brown decorated carpet and above the dado rail, a William Morris brown and gold wallpaper is used. All the light fittings, chandeliers, bar furniture and bar fittings are in brass and bar joinery in deep mahogany.

The original orchestra pit could hold 40 players and now held 100. The new Fly tower was built with steel galleries, replacing the wooden ones, and new flying machinery installed. Much of the original flying machinery appeared to date from 1895. There had been 50 three line hemp hand lines with most of the sets having dyed strands to indicate the different lines, and relying on man-handling from the fly gallery. Twelve counterweighted sets had been added over the years. All new lines were now counterweighted.

A continental atmosphere
Peter Hemmings wrote in the company magazine of:

> …….. the immediate reaction of enchantment when patrons enter the auditorium bolstered by later experience of the unique relation-ship between the audience and the stage. Because of the very deep overhang above the orchestra pit, the gap between the front row of the stalls and the front of the stage is unusually small. This also prevents the orchestra swamping the voices and facilitates a good homogeneous balance of voice and orchestra. Certainly conductors enjoy the feeling of close control and producers and lighting direc-tors the subdued visual impact of the orchestra.
> Back stage accommodation is well arranged given the labyrinthine nature of old buildings that have

OPPOSITE
Renaissance *splendour*

RIGHT
David Jackson
*with his daughters at
a Victorian Eveming,
1980*

The theatre's directors planned the Royal to be the home of

1. Scottish Opera
2. The Scottish Ballet
3. Scottish Theatre

In the 1970s there was a prospect of a Scottish National Theatre company being formed to perform new and traditional plays. The Citizen's Theatre company in Gorbals had a question mark over its future and even a possibility it would go into a projected Concert Hall in Sauchiehall Street. With all this in mind The Scottish Theatre Ballet dropped the word "theatre" to avoid possible confusion with a Scottish Theatre company.

been added to and the fittings and furniture have proved robust.

Front of house heating and ventilation teething problems still abound and the bars are unequal to the unique Glasgow pressure. In spite if this, many unexperienced patrons have remarked on the uncommmonly "continental" atmosphere of the theatre – an impression deliberately aimed at and surprisingly achieved with the limited space available.

What did it cost? During 1975 inflation still galloped along and some changes were required once the condition of the building fabric was fully known. The final cost was £2.8m which includes the purchase price. The Government's grant was increased to 50 per cent of the total.

David Jackson - Manager

David Jackson became the first manager and Royal Charter licensee under Scottish Opera wings. In the 1950s he was a salesman in a gent's outfitters and in the evening a stage hand at the Alhambra Theatre. He met his wife at the Alhambra – she was a dancer there – and he decided to try to get in on the television scene in London. He worked in theatre instead and was also a cinema manager for six years, then box office manager at Covent Garden. In the summer of 1975 he worked part-time to set up Scottish Opera's box office, after studying new theatre systems in America, and was appointed full time manager.

Staff were recruited with experience of dealing with the public; office and customer services organised; uniforms chosen for the usherettes, barmen,

LEFT
**Sir Alexander
Gibson**

RIGHT
Gavin Boyd

Cartoons by Malky

LEFT
Die Fledermaus

RIGHT
Cabaret *inserted in
the production, with
kilted Bill McCue and
David Ward*

commissionaires; facilities checked for disabled members of the audience; fire precautions and insurance arranged. To go with the Victorian décor the front-of-house staff wore Victorian-style uniforms.

Guided by its chairman Gavin Boyd

it was decided that the lowest opera seat price, always up in the gods, would never exceed the price of a packet of cigarettes. Today a ticket price of £9 or £10 is more than a packet of cigarettes of some £6.

Scottish Opera at Home

W hen the lights dimmed and the curtain rose the theatre sparkled again with the gold highlights of the auditorium. The singing and playing sparkled too. The Glasgow Herald wrote: "Brilliant singing at the Royal."

Sir Alexander Gibson and his staff ensured that in each of the seasons of the theatre year there would be at least one classical opera, one of the twentieth century and one of the less-known new ones. Popular operas merited revival, often with new styles of production, scenery and costume. Audiences seek spectacle, good voices and vibrant music from their opera company in their theatre. Performances increased and audiences grew further. The theatre opened with three of the world's best directors working there in Anthony Besch, Peter Ebert and David Poutney. More would follow.

Photographs of some of the many operas produced at the Royal since 1975 are shown on the following pages. Principal singers, guest singers, choruses and orchestral players performed to the highest levels of music - and acting. For a number of years the company had the use of a ballet troupe from Scottish Ballet. The number of separate operas grew to around 14 each year by 1980/81, settling to around 9 productions annually. Production sponsors increased in support, including banks, insurance companies, investment institutions, oil, energy and commercial firms.

Scottish Opera   Theatre Royal
October 15 1975

Using the theatre

The acoustics are first class throughout the auditorium, while the presence of pillars for the galleries does restrict views in a few areas. The best seats for viewing are often the dearest ones, while ironically the best of the excellent acoustics are to be heard in the cheapest seats – high in the Balcony and Upper Circle – because of the architecture of the building. Extra uses became possible linked to the operas. Fortnightly Lunch & Listen sessions were started about the opera in the theatre with speakers

ABOVE
First Day Cover

OPPOSITE
Expectation

discussing its music, plot or preparation. Evening Foretalks started. A series of Masterclasses started with the help of Sean Connery's Scottish Educational Education Trust, including a Masterclass by Tito Gobbi, and by Sesto Bruscantini.

Visiting opera companies were able to perform again at the Royal, including English National Opera and Glyndebourne. The first overseas company was Stuttgart Opera presenting *Boulevard Solitude*.

Tennent's Brewery sponsored Promenade series, firstly *The Magic Flute*, and the following year *Macbeth*. The stall seats were removed, making a promenade area for 650 people at 50p each, and the circle and other seats remained, selling at £1 to £5. Suppers on theatre evenings could be pre-

booked at the Top Spot but for very long operas such as the *Mastersingers of Nuremberg* special catering was made for the first intervals: hot and cold suppers served for £1.50, cold suppers for £1.50 or pizzas at 50p in the 2nd circle, and selections of sandwiches in the gods for 20p, with house wine available in all parts, and coffee and gateaux in the main foyer. For £6 the public was invited to a Scottish Opera Stage Party to meet the artistes and musicians and enjoy the bars, buffets and cabaret, with the whole theatre in use including the stage.

For younger folk at holiday times the company's Opera for Youth presented their versions of the *Merry Widow*, and *Hansel & Gretel* – a glove puppet performance. At Christmas time a Family Package of tickets was introduced for

ABOVE
Die Meistersingers
1976

OPPOSITE
(top) **Gibson**
conducts dress rehearsal
(bottom) **Otello**
1977

Theatre Royal Glasgow

THE
PURVES PUPPETS

Presents

NESSIE
The Loch Ness Monster

A tale of the Highlands

Saturday 9 April 1977

THEATRE ROYAL GLASGOW

Scottish Opera Theatre Royal Ltd.
Chairman: Gavin Boyd, CBE
General Administrator: Peter Hemmings
Theatre Manager: David Jackson

An original play by Jill and Ian Purves

THE CHARACTERS

3 CRAWS	who sat upon a wa'.
HUGHIE McDHUI	a laddie from Drumnadrochit.
MAIRI GLENGARRY	a Highland lass.
NAGGIE McCRAGGIE	her nasty aunt.
SPIKE	a little hedgehog.
AULD JOHNNIE URQUHART	the friendly ghost of Castle Urquhart.
AH SI YOO	a Japanese diver.

Haggises, thingummyjigs, tattie bogles, whigmaleeries, etc., etc., and of course—

the one and only NESSIE!!!

THE STORY

Act 1

Scene 1. Hughie's old car breaks down near Loch Ness, and he has to spend the night in Castle Urquhart where a mysterious light is shining.

Scene 2. Inside the Castle. Hughie falls asleep while the spiders enjoy themselves. Then he meets Spike and sees Mairi who is hiding from her nasty Uncle. Someone very STRANGE is helping her! Spike takes Hughie to meet Nessie.

Scene 3. Nessie's Secret Cave. Far below the Castle where Loch Ness flows into the caves, Spike and Hughie wait for Nessie and see the funny creatures who live there. Nessie appears and explains her problem—the Yellow Submarine is coming!

Scene 4. At the bottom of the Loch, in the deep dark waters, Nessie plays hide-and-seek with the Yellow Submarine which is always trying to catch her. Nessie wins again!

I N T E R V A L

Act 2

Scene 1. The bell-tower of the Castle. Mairi sings happily, feeling safe from her uncle, Naggie McCraggie. But he finds her hiding-place and Spike and Hughie have to rescue her in the nick of time.

Scene 2. In Nessie's Cave, the Haggis Pipers are practising hard. Spike brings the news that Naggie is caught in the bell-tower. There is a grand celebration and Nessie makes a plan to get rid of Naggie for good.

Scene 3. Back in the Castle, Mairi is ready to escape, but Naggie makes a final effort to stop her. Then Nessie's plan goes into action. What's that? Wait and see! Naggie is driven away for ever, and they all live happily ever after.

BEHIND THE SCENES

PRODUCTION AND DESIGN	Jill and Ian Purves.
MANIPULATION	Jill Purves, Graham Moodie, Ian Purves.
VOICES	Jill Purves, W. F. Purves.
COSTUMES	Heather McDowall.

NOTES

We suggest that parents and teachers read part of our synopsis to younger children before each act.

Ice cream and orange squash will be on sale during the interval.

You are invited to meet the puppets after the performance.

Theatre Royal Glasgow

RADIO CLYDE

Tuesday 24 May 1977
7.15 p.m.

presents

Children's Art Festival

OPERA—BALLET—DRAMA

THEATRE ROYAL GLASGOW

Scottish Opera Theatre Royal Ltd.
Chairman: Gavin Boyd, CBE
General Administrator: Peter Hemmings
Theatre Manager: David Jackson

TAG
THEATRE ABOUT GLASGOW

presents

Poverty, Plague and Pestilence

POVERTY, PLAGUE AND PESTILENCE was presented to second and third year pupils in Glasgow schools in February.

Devised by Christine Redington, the programme is an historical documentary about life in Glasgow from 1820, concentrating upon urban development and public health. It includes poetry, music movement and song, and has been enjoyed by both pupils and teachers:

"Even our stiff and cynical academic third-year were forced to laugh and join in the fun . . ." St. Gerard's Sec.

"I am full of admiration for a most hard-working cast as well as a splendid script which clearly rammed home many points to the children in the audience. . . ."
History Adviser

The show is directed by Christine Redington, and the members of the company are:

Mary-Ann Coburn, Murray Ewan, Martin Head, Anne Myatt, Bob Sendall.

INTERVAL

SCOTTISH BALLET WORKSHOP

presents

Chance Dancing

Written and Directed by Sue Weston
Designed by Terry Jacobs

1.	Do You Wanna Dance	Company
2.	Pavan	Chris Blagdon, Susan Cooper, Serge Julien, Judyth Taylor
3.	Masque	Company
4.	Extract from LA SYLPHIDE	Chris Blagdon, Susan Cooper, Serge Julien, Hilary Clark
6.	C'est La Vie	Company

All dances choreographed by Sue Weston except for LA SYLPHIDE (Choreography: August Bournonville) staged by Julie Haydn, Choreologist for The Scottish Ballet.

Chance Dancing is presented by the five dancers of Scottish Ballet Workshop—the educational and experimental dance group of The Scottish Ballet. The aim of the group is to take dance into schools and cultural centres. In schools an adaptation of this Chance Dancing programme is presented together with practical sessions where interested people are able to experience creative movement with the dancers.

Musician	The Scottish Ballet
Barry Jobling	Chairman: Robin Duff
	Artistic Director: Peter Darrell
Lighting	Administrator: Robin Anderson
John Watts	
Costumes made by	Scottish Ballet Workshop
Clare Mitchell	Director: Sue Weston
	Manager: Michael Throne

The Scottish Ballet acknowledges financial assistance from the Scottish Arts Council and Regional Councils of Scotland.

SHORT PAUSE

SCOTTISH OPERA FOR YOUTH

presents

The Pied Piper of Hamelin

A one Act Opera for Principal Baritone, Young Persons' Chorus, Piano and Percussion Band

Music—Peter Nayler
Libretto after Browning's Poem by Beryl Ashburn

The Pied Piper	Alan Oke
Conductor	Stewart Robertson
Piano	Peter Nayler
Producer	Ann Baird
Production Team	Marie Louise Cumming
	Gordon Hunter
	Jim Railton
Designed	Alex. Reid
Costumes made up by	Marilyn Apps
Piper's Costume	Tom Robson

Chorus of TOWN COUNCILLORS, TOWN PEOPLE and CHILDREN from ST. ROCH'S SECONDARY GLASGOW, HERMITAGE ACADEMY, HELENSBURGH AND MERKSWORTH HIGH, PAISLEY.

Scottish Opera for Youth would like to thank the Schools concerned for their enthusiastic co-operation.

Scottish Opera gratefully acknowledges the assistance of the Calouste Gulbenkian Foundation in the commissioning of this work.

The Golden Cockerel – for every seat bought at the normal price the adjacent same-priced seat could be bought for a school child for £1. In the 1980s bargain prices were set for Saturday matinees with a 15 per cent discount and up to 25 per cent off for senior citizens, the unemployed, children, teenagers and students.

In the 1960s Scottish Opera became the first opera company in Britain to create Opera for Schools, known then as Opera for All, connecting with schools and local communities. In 1971 it became the European pioneer of opera-in-education, working with the school authorities. With the Theatre Royal this continued with schools being bussed in to see the theatre at work and for secondary students and community groups to see how the opera they have been studying is brought together on stage, and unwrapping the production secrets from behind the scenes. For primary schools the children are involved in a mix of song, movement, puppetry, and costumes as the company's workshop is toured around the country. An original score is written around topics being taught at school, and for communities often an opera is developed by themselves about their own lives or surroundings and has the participants usually asking for more, and wanting to see a theatre – which they do by coming in to see a main company performance.

ABOVE
Madame Butterfly
Gibson's favourite

OPPOSITE
Programme Styles
1977
(left) *Nessie, the Loch Ness Monster*
(right) *Children's Art Festival*

In the early 1990s the Royal joined the Doors Open movement pioneered by Glasgow where on one weekend of the autumn the public could wander round all parts of the building to see how things happened on stage, behind it and above, and usually ending with a short concert by the orchestra. Up until 2005 the company's education staff helped plan and co-ordinate any visiting company to the Theatre Royal who had education support activities to offer, including national drama and dance.

To spread the news of the restored theatre and its music the company and the Scottish Trades Union Congress held their own midday Workers Playtime on an operatic note, starting at Chrysler in Linwood with excerpts of *La Boheme* played by the orchestra under Gibson and sung by Bill McCue and others. Government Minister Frank McElhone said:

We are taking opera to the shop floor. People these days have so much leisure time, this is a way of giving them an interest. It is our plan to take opera round the works and shipyards on Clydeside.

TOP
Queen Elizabeth
awaits Fiddler on the Roof
1979

MIDDLE
Backstage
with manager David Jackson, and director Peter Ebert, left.

BOTTOM
Arrival
Gavin Boyd escorts the Queen, and Mrs Kathleen Boyd greets the Duke of Edinburgh

OPPOSITE
(left) **Eugene Onegin**
1979
(upper right)
Ernest B Hood
painting of Puccini's Manon Lescant
1982
(lower right)
Tosca
1980

Venues included Volvo at Irvine, BP Grangemouth, Evening Times at Albion Street, British National Oxygen at Polmadie, and Strathclyde Regional Council in their Charing Cross offices. Scottish Opera singers also created small groups who performed sometimes in the Royal and usually in smaller venues; such as Music Box (with Linda Ormiston and Donald Maxwell) and in a later decade Opera on a Shoestring (with Christina Dunwoodie, Graeme Danby and Scott Cooper).

Fundraising continued for the theatre and its Endowment Fund, from special concerts to lottery tickets (with prizes from 50p to £1,000 – the equal now of £10 to £20,000); from hiring out the theatre for events (and some weddings) and the public monthly meetings of Glasgow Chamber of Commerce, which always had a musical entertainment and buffet lunch; fashion shows and musical serenades; to an evening auction of fine paintings, porcelain, and sculpture, conducted by Christie's. and preceded by an informal musical performance. Gala Concerts sponsored by the Friends of Scottish Opera took place usually on Sundays with singers Isobel Buchanan, Linda Grey, Dennis O'Neill, Benjamin Luxon and others. Strathclyde Regional Council hosted *A Strathclyde Evening* in 1983 to welcome the Confederation of British Industries' Conference to Glasgow. The company performed under Gibson, and others included Mary Sandeman, Fulton McKay and Strathclyde Police Pipe Band. All raised money and all brought

ABOVE
Having a break!
Gibson and Billy Connolly, who was in Die Fledermaus, 1978.

LEFT
STV Advert
1983

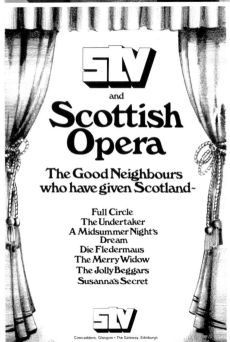

people to the theatre.

Tradition continued of the Royal playing its part in raising money for charity. Examples involving the orchestra and artistes of Scottish Opera are - an International Variety Gala called *Stage for Age* in aid of Help the Aged which included Randy Crawford, Andy Cameron and David Copperfield; a

OPPOSITE
Egisto
1982

Concert for Paul in aid of Cancer Research which was an evening of song, dance, music and poetry compered by Bill McCue; a Gala Glasgow Premiere performance of the company's latest *Pearl Fishers* for Action Research for Crippled Children as part of the 1981 International Year of the Disabled People. Scottish Ballet and Scottish Opera held a joint Gala Evening where all proceeds went to the new Prince and Princess of Wales Hospice. Verdi's *Requiem* was performed in 1989 in aid of those affected by the Lockerbie Air Disaster, the soloists being Jane Eaglen, Linda Finnie, Jorge Pita, and Willard White.

For the stage

Scottish Opera performers, Scottish Ballet performers, and crew now benefited from having their own theatre. Rehearsing by the orchestra and singers now took place in the same acoustics as the public performances. Extra space helped produce top quality work; up to two weeks of rehearsal in theatre before opening, modern changing rooms, showers, lockers, space for all scenery and wardrobe requirements, ample space for productions to get-in and get-out backstage. The scenery and props for ten different operas could be stored at the back of the stage and moved to position with ease at the changeover each day.

Benefits of the Royal also included the stage being a flat floor – a great help to dancers (traditionally theatres had raked stages). There was new lighting equipment and computerised lighting control, all very state of the art for 1975. The lighting desk was upgraded to the latest "Galaxy" in 1985. The company's technical workshops for sets and scenery now moved from Finnieston and Woodlands to new premises in Springburn built by the Scottish Development Agency. Over the next

TOP
Rigoletto
Costume designs
1979

MIDDLE
Scenery Workshop

BOTTOM
Wardrobe at Work
2007

OPPOSITE
(top left)
L'Elisir D'Amore
1980
(top right)
Cosi Fan Tutte
1981
(bottom)
Death in Venice
1983

decades scenery evolved from wood and canvas to using steel and fibreglass. The need for a first class scenic artist has never gone away, in fact they have been increasingly asked to create that "new look" for designers. Scottish Opera continues to be very well served in this department by Kelvin Guy.

Right from the start Scottish Opera made a name for the excellence of its costumes and wardrobe workroom, guided greatly by costume designer Alex Reid, from Perth, who supervised its development and was in demand in Britain and America. The theatre meant more productions and performances, needing even more costumes and their maintenance and alteration.

Today the company has the largest wardrobe in Scotland with over 10,000 items in the store-rooms, and hundreds of wigs, all made to a high standard and for a long life of wear. The costume-makers are experts in theatrical dress-making and tailoring. Turning out anything from a Savile Row style suit to an elaborate 18th century dress, all made to fit the individual performer – and made to a strict deadline. The creations are for all of the company's productions, from small touring shows with only a few singers, to main-scale operas with 50 or 60 performers on stage (more for Carmen!), each of whom may have 2 or 3 costumes.

In the 1990s a new Scottish Opera Production Centre was specially designed and opened in Edington Street, off Garscube Road (on the site of the former Port Dundas Electricity Generating Station). This houses the workshops for making sets and scenery, rehearsal space, stores, and the wardrobe

TOP
A Decade of Scottish Opera Design
Exhibition brochure
1981

MIDDLE
Candide
costume designs

BOTTOM
Wardrobes
wait their turn

OPPOSITE
(top left)
The Magic Flute
1981
(top right)
Carmen
1986
(centre left)
The Rise and Fall of the City of Mahagonny
1986
(centre)
Gala Concert
Sir Alexander Gibson and Dame Kiri Te Kanawa
1985
(centre right)
Il Seraglio
1982
(bottom)
Barber of Seville
1985

Scottish Opera on Classics for Pleasure

CFP 40217 RICHARD STRAUSS
DER ROSENKAVALIER
SCOTTISH OPERA/GIBSON

CFP 40246 MOZART
DON GIOVANNI
SCOTTISH OPERA/GIBSON

CFP 40252 VERDI
UN BALLO IN MASCHERA
SCOTTISH OPERA/GIBSON

CFP40276 LEHAR
MERRY WIDOW
SCOTTISH OPERA/GIBSON

£1.25

The MAKROPOULOS Case

Leoš Janáček

La Bohème

Giacomo Puccini

SCOTTISH**OPERA**

The Marriage of Figaro

OTTISH**OPERA**

nkavalier

Richard Strauss

Billy Budd

ABOVE
**The Orchestra of
Scottish Opera**
well travelled

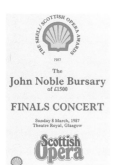

ABOVE
John Noble
singing competition

RIGHT
Fundraising
*Carmen (Emily
Golden) accepts
sponsorship cheque at
Bridgeton Cross
1985*

department – which many regard as the best designed in Britain.

Orchestra notes

Scottish Opera performed with its regular orchestras depending on the seasons and diary commitments - the Scottish National Orchestra, also directed by Sir Alexander Gibson, the BBC Scottish Symphony Orchestra, the Scottish Baroque Ensemble for smaller operas under its leader Leonard Friedman, the Scottish Chamber Orchestra which graduated from the Baroque Ensemble, and the Scottish Philharmonia. After making their name by playing for the company the Scottish Chamber Orchestra decided to move away from opera and play only concerts and tours.

At this point Gibson decided to form a Scottish Opera Orchestra, advertising for players and auditioning in Glasgow and on the Continent. The new full-time orchestra of 52 players was born in 1979 under its first leader Angus Anderson. Small groups are formed to support opera touring to small and medium size venues, and for chamber opera performances. These have included in the initial years the Anderson String Trio and the Paragon Ensemble.

The orchestra's rehearsal halls of the past include the Dalintober Hall in Morrison Street, the former Highlanders Institute, the Moir Hall of the Mitchell Library, and now in Woodside Halls at St George's Cross. Rehearsals start about 3 to 4 weeks before the 1st night and the singers and chorus join them at the theatre about 2 weeks before 1st night.

25th Anniversary of Scottish Opera

In June 1987 the Silver Jubilee of Scottish Opera was celebrated with a Royal Gala performance of *Madam Butterfly*. Poet and historian Maurice Lindsay wrote on the occasion:

By the highest European standards, Sir Alexander's triumphs were outstandingly memorable – particularly in the earlier years, before the cult of the ego-trip producer infested the international operatic stage – his Ring, his Rosenkavalier and his Trojans, to name only a few. Thus Sir Alexander Gibson, often overcoming difficult local circumstances, has, it seems to me, contributed more to the honour and glory of music-making in Scotland than anyone else in our performing cultural story. I am therefore proud to have been invited to join my voice to the sound of the applause which will undoubtedly ring round the Theatre Royal when he makes his appearance to conduct the Silver Jubilee performance of Madam Butterfly.

In the same month the Silver Jubilee Butterfly Ball took place. The stall seats were removed and the stage extended fully into the auditorium for dancing and cabaret to the music of Scottish Opera Orchestra, Humphrey Lyttleton and his Jazzmen, Terry Lightfoot and his Band, and the Highfield Reel Band. Three restaurants were set up in the festooned theatre, and breakfast served in the wee small hours in a marquee in the car park. The following evening a Silver Jubilee Concert completed the celebrations with singers led by Dame Janet Baker and Charles Craig. The profit from the Butterfly Ball of £70,000 created a record for any single charity evening in Scotland. In today's money over £300,000.

John Mauceri succeeded Gibson as music director, becoming the first American conductor to head an opera

ABOVE
John Mauceri, (*right*) *kilted at the Butterfly Ball, 1987, with producer John Lawson Graham and soprano Patricia Hay*

house in Italy or Britain. He brought with him a full range of European operas and music from across the Atlantic. He conducted the first complete recordings of Scottish Opera productions – *Street Scene, Regina*, and *Candide* - and a special performance of *Candide* was taped for television. In the first two decades in the theatre the company continued to commission new operas including *Confessions of a Justified Sinner* by Tom Wilson, words by John Currie, based on the writings of James Hogg; *Mary Queen of Scots* by Thea Musgrave; and *Friend of the People* by

RIGHT
Princes Square
celebrations
1990

David Horne, words by the Liberal MP Robert MacLennan, based on the life of the democrat and public reformer Thomas Muir of Huntershill.

Cultural Capital of Europe 1990
In March 1990 the Royal hosted the International Gala, to open Glasgow's year of celebration as the first city in Britain to win the accolade of Cultural Capital of Europe, with an evening of international ballet and the Scottish Opera Orchestra and Chorus. Verdi's *La Forza del Destino* was premiered by

the company at the start of nine operas for the year. Another special production was *Les Troyens* near the end of the year.

Another summer Royal Gala Concert was organised, this time the 30th anniversary of Scottish Opera – one of the main sponsors was the theatre's caterer Billy MacAneney, owner of the Baby Grand and other restaurants. In 1993 the corner building in Hope Street was rebuilt and redesigned behind its façade. Additional funders appeared this time from the National Foundation for Sport and the Arts, and Glasgow Development Agency. On the ground floor a bar restaurant was created – the Café Royal – with a new box office at the Cowcaddens corner entrance. The main entrance foyer was expanded northwards into the café area, using flagstones similar to the foyer flagstones. In 1975 the flooring stones were chosen to be the same as those in opera houses in Venice – essential there when the canal waters rise and flood the entrances! Hospitality suites were created on the first floor – the Charter, Gibson and Boyd Rooms – and a new suite of offices built on the top floor. The basement was built anew with a fully fitted restaurant kitchen.

Around this time the theatre was attracting between 200,000 and 250,000 people a year. The number of performances totalled about 220 – of which 100 were by Scottish Opera and Scottish Ballet, and 120 by visiting companies. (Sir) Richard Armstrong had now joined as music director, coming from

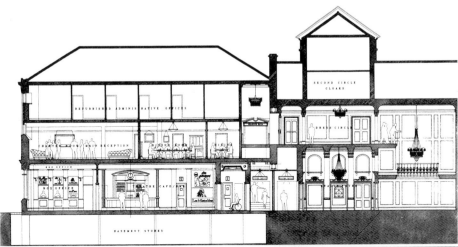

LEFT
Hope Street
Corner building
1993

Welsh National Opera.

In 1997 the auditorium was refurbished with the National Lottery adding its funds for the first time. Seating was renewed, in turquoise blue upholstery, and the orchestra pit extended again, this time into the auditorium. Audience lighting was changed to a 1930's styling. The Victorian plasterwork received new coats of cream and gold, and the walls painted a cherry red.

The mid 1990s witnessed the board and directors of Scottish Opera leading attempts to merge with other artistic bodies, although there was no compelling need, nor priority, to do so. Some hoped it would result in a giant body that could not be unfankled later. Discussions in secret to merge Scottish Opera Orchestra and the BBC Scottish Symphony Orchestra into a National Orchestra for Scotland were met with amazement by the players. After much negotiation the players in both orchestras voted unanimously against such

LEFT
(top)
Dress Circle Bar
(middle)
Box Office
(bottom)
Charter Room

RIGHT
(top)
Cafe Royal
(top right)
Looking down Hope Street
(bottom)
Cafe Royal Bar

OPPOSITE
(top)
View from Stage
(centre left)
Der Rosenkavalier
2006
(centre right)
Flying Ropes
(bottom left)
Madame Butterfly
2007
(bottom right)
Stage Control Desk

moves. Today they thrive artistically in front of their respective audiences - the Orchestra of Scottish Opera in the Royal and other theatres in Britain as well as St Andrews-in-the-Square for concerts; and the BBC Scottish Symphony Orchestra in its new home in the City Halls. The Scottish Ballet Orchestra is a third orchestra which continues well in its performing for ballet across the country. It would have closed as a victim of the thirst for merger.

The company board and directors continued to invest effort in a merger with Scottish Ballet. After a period of financial stability Scottish Opera started a significant trend of loss making in the direction and control of operatic production. As the century ended the number of opera productions remained eight or nine a year.

The Scottish Ballet
at the Theatre Royal

10th-21st January
THE NUTCRACKER-
Tchaikovsky

22nd-25th March
New Ballets by-
Cat Stevens
Ian Anderson (Jethro Tull)
Syrinx and Chilliwack

27th March-1st April
SWAN LAKE
Tchaikovsky

Elaine McDonald and Graham Bart
in Scottish Ballet's production of SWAN LAKE

The Scottish Ballet

The Scottish Theatre Ballet started in Glasgow in 1969 and its first show in the restored Royal was *The Nutcracker* in December and January, and followed in spring 1976 by a busy season of the premiere of *Mary, Queen of Scots*, as well as *Tales of Hoffman, Giselle, La Ventana, La Sylphide*, and then *Paquita, La Fete Etrange, Pax de Quatre, Three Dances to Japanese Music, Le Carnaval, O Caritas, Jeux*, and *The Lesson*.

The nucleus of the new company came from England's Western Theatre Ballet, formed in 1957 in Bath. It was invited to Scotland with its artistic director and choreographer Peter Darrell; one half of its members making the move (the other half going to Manchester.) Robin Anderson, the new company's general administrator in Glasgow noted that in the 1960s:

> the then novel idea of having a ballet company based outside London proved too difficult and the Western company moved to London and based itself on Sadler's Wells Theatre, where as well as its own performances, it was responsible for the artistic direction of the Sadler's Wells Opera Ballet. The company's first contact with Glasgow was in 1960 when in an effort to hold the small company together throughout the year they appeared in Howard & Wyndham's spectacular pantomime

A Wish For Jamie in the Alhambra where Darrell was the show's choreographer.

The move to Scotland was to fill the vacuum caused by Margaret Morris's move south for a time following the death in 1961 of her painter husband JD Fergusson, who was also the art director of the Margaret Morris Movement schools in Britain and overseas. From her Celtic Ballet college and dance

ABOVE
Tales of Hoffman
1979

OPPOSITE
Scottish Ballet *advert*
1977

RIGHT
Peter Darrell

studio theatre in Blythswood Square performances had been staged in the Royal and in many smaller venues nationally from 1940. It was the first Scottish dance company to visit America. In 1960 she renamed her company the Scottish National Ballet, after a suggestion from Stewart Cruikshank of Howard & Wyndham, performing in

BELOW
261 West Princes Street *opens* *1979*

Pitlochry Festival Theatre and Howard & Wyndham theatres in Scotland and England. At the end of the decade dancers trained by her joined the new company under Peter Darrell, as did members of the Glasgow Theatre Ballet led by Catherine Marks (who had been a principal dancer with the Anglo-Polish Ballet, a choreographer for Howard & Wyndham, and dancer with Margaret Morris), and others from schools in the east and north of Scotland.

Darrell introduced dramatisation into dance, and made it available across Scotland and Northern Ireland, and also toured in England. Overseas touring was to Switzerland, Australia, New Zealand and Spain, and from 1976 this extended to Portugal, France, Italy, Greece, Cyprus, Malaysia, China, Hong Kong, America and Australasia again. Before going to Australia in 1974 the word "Theatre" was dropped from its name – perhaps to avoid confusion with a new drama company being planned, the Scottish Theatre Company. In its first ten years the number of dancers increased from 20 to 48, and the company established its own dance scholarships. The Scottish Ballet shared premises with Scottish Opera in Elmbank Crescent on a grace and favour basis until 1979 when it bought and converted its own building at 261 West Princes Street as its headquarters, which was opened by Queen Elizabeth the Queen Mother. The new rehearsal studios and facilities were the largest and best equipped of any major company in Britain at the time. A few years later, on ground adjoining, a new Studio Theatre was built for small performances, later known as the Robin Anderson Theatre. Seating 450, this was the first purpose built dance space in Scotland.

Photographs on the following pages show some of the performances at the Theatre Royal. The company now enjoyed all the benefits of a home theatre, a very large stage, ample space in the wings, and modern backstage services. Dates for performing became suitable for the company and audiences alike. With the Royal restored there was a phenomenal growth in interest in dance, both in the works of Scottish Ballet – whose World Premieres were staged in the theatre – and in visiting companies. The opening of the Royal also saw an expansion of the company's educational work, beyond schools, and by starting its long running series of "Prelude to the Ballet." This spread the gospel and its repertory by visiting community halls, Miners' Welfares and British Legion clubs – illustrating in dance, word and film the conventions of ballet and the training of dancers involving a presenter, a pianist and a female dancer. A Prelude presentation was even made while on one of British Rail's new high speed trains.

Audiences enjoy productions when dancers, choreography, music and décor are all in balance. The major classic ballets prove the most popular, attracting large audiences of up to 90 per cent, while middle-of-the-road style dance attracts audiences of around 60 per cent and only a fraction attend

TOP
Programme
1979

MIDDLE
Queen Elizabeth the Queen Mother, *with chairman Robin Duff meets David Ashmole, dancer in Tales of Hoffman*
1979

BOTTOM
Princess Margaret *meets dancers after Roneo & Juliet*
1982

OPPOSITE
(clockwise from top)
Othello, *televised,
1982*
Giselle, *1976*
**Mary Queen of
Scots**, *1976*
Napoli, *1986*
Cheri, *1980*

THIS PAGE
(clockwise from top)
Le Carnaval, *1976*
La Fete Etrange, *1976*
Such Sweet Thunder,
1979
**Three Dances to
Japanese Music**,
televised, 1980

The Scottish Ballet

The Scottish Ballet

Theatre Royal Glasgow
1983-84

The
Sco
Bal

Tales
Hoffm

Theatre Royal, G
26th-30th May

THIS TOUR IS SPONSORED BY
THE GLASGOW HERALD.
GLASGOW
HERALD

CARMEN

The Scottish Ballet

Napoli

The Scottish Ballet

Photo: Bill Cooper

CHÉRI
LE SPECTRE DE LA ROSE
SYMPHONY IN D

THEATRE ROYAL GLASGOW
TUES 20 MAY to SAT 24 MAY
SPRING TOUR 1986

Subsidised by the Scottish Arts Council

ANNA
KARENINA

The Scottish Ballet

IN ASSOCIATION WITH
THE SCOTSMAN

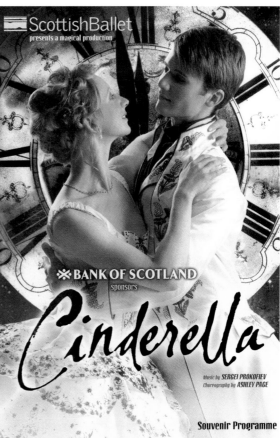

OPPOSITE
Programmes
(clockwise from top)
Carmen, *1985*
Romeo & Juliet, *1984*
Tales of Hoffman,
1987
Anna Karenina, *1993*
Spring Tour, *1986*
Napoli, *1986*

THIS PAGE
(left)
Offenbach, *2000*
(right)
Cinderella, *2006*

Top
Swan Lake, *1995*

Bottom
Nutcracker, *1993*

Opposite
(top)
Romeo & Juliet, *1990*
(bottom)
The Snowman, *2001*

ABOVE
Scottish Ballet Orchestra *gather on the staircase*

RIGHT
Sponsorship
Council leader Pat Lally with a sponsorship cheque for Carmen (Christine Camillo)

experimental and shorter works. The Scottish Ballet Orchestra is usually in the pit. It was formed in 1976, led by Clive Thomas. The company has commissioned a number of new scores over the years, all premiered by the Scottish Ballet Orchestra including *Cheri*, *Peter Pan*, *A Midsummer Night's Dream* and *Aladdin*.

In 1983 the Dance School of Scotland opened at Knightswood

School pioneered by Scottish Ballet and Strathclyde Regional Council, and is the first public school in Britain to have dance in its main educational curriculum. The founder director Peter Darrell died in 1987 and was succeeded by the Russian-born Galina Samsova. In 1997 the American-born choreographer Robert North became artistic director, and today the company is led by Ashley Page.

Cultural Capital of Europe 1990
On 2nd March 1990 the Queen declared Glasgow's celebration year open at a civic reception held in the City Chambers. That evening the inaugural performance was the *International Dance Gala* at the Theatre Royal, with the Duke of Edinburgh as guest of honour, and opening with a Fanfare by the band

ABOVE
Cinderella
2005

of the King's Own Scottish Borderers. In all there were eleven dances of which six were British premieres and two were World premieres, performed by The Scottish Ballet and guest artistes from Paris Opera Ballet, La Scala Milan, Bolshoi Ballet, Spanish National Ballet, New York City Ballet and the Royal Ballet, Covent Garden. The first was the British premiere of *Scotch Symphony* choreographed by the Russian-born George Balanchine in 1952 following a visit to Scotland that year with his newly created New York City Ballet.

Ballanchine was impressed by the grandeur of the landscape and by the massed Scottish regiments at the Edinburgh Military Tattoo and set his work to the music of Mendlesohn's romantic symphony. He had moved to Britain and joined the Ballet Russes until it collapsed at the end of the Twenties. For several years before he emigrated to America he staged dances for the *Cochran Revues*, headed by Charles B Cochrane.

Scottish Ballet is also the first dance company in Europe to offer live audio description for the visually impaired. In 2009 the company plans to be in its new rehearsal space and studios being built next to the Tramway on the city's south-side at Albert Drive.

The Scottish Theatre Company and Other Galaxies

Manager David Jackson set the scene well for the third leg of the Royal's new life, and a national acting company was born to tour Scotland.

Visiting companies soon came on a regular pattern, from the National Theatre in London's South Bank, the National Shakespeare in Stratford-upon-Avon, to Sadler's Wells Royal Ballet and the Harlem Dance Theatre. For national drama the new Scottish Theatre Company started in Glasgow in 1980, with its first productions in 1981. The theatre's diary gave priority to Scottish Opera, Scottish Ballet, and the Scottish Theatre Company. To all this was added a wide range of shows and events from folk music to jazz, starting with Stephane Grappelli; musicals to concerts; children's shows to charity galas.

As an example the bill of fare in 1980/81 included Mary O'Hara, Richard Stilgoe, Sheena Easton, Gerard Kenny, Denis Waterman, Pitlochry Festival Theatre, Louden Wainwright III, Whirligig Theatre, Ballet Rambert, D'Oyle Carte Opera Company, Syd Lawrence and his Orchestra, Malcolm Sargent Carol Concert, Gala Concert in aid of the Italian Earthquake Fund, National Theatre Company, Sadler's Wells Royal Ballet, Vanessa Ford drama, Mike Harding, King's Singers, Larry Norman gospel rock, Save the Children Gala starring Ronnie Corbet, Royal Scottish Academy of Music & Drama, and a subscription series of eight Sunday night concerts by the Scottish Chamber Orchestra. Calum Kennedy revived the *Five Past Eight Show* starring Dickie Henderson, Vince Hill, Allan Stewart,

The cast of Mr Gillie

From left to right — front row: Anne Kristen, Tom Fleming, Una Ailsa Macnab.
Back row: John Grieve, Michael Elder, Leon Sinden, Ian Wallace and Colin Gourley.

ABOVE
The cast of Mr Gillie
Tom Fleming at front
1984

OPPOSITE
Ane Satyre of the Thrie Estaites
1986

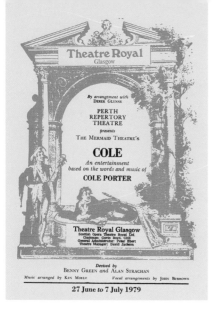

Theatre Royal
Glasgow

By arrangement with
DEREK GLYNNE

PERTH
REPERTORY
THEATRE

presents

THE MERMAID THEATRE's

COLE

*An entertainment
based on the words and music of*
COLE PORTER

Theatre Royal Glasgow
Scottish Opera Theatre Royal Ltd.
Chairman: Gavin Boyd, CBE
General Administrator: Peter Ebert
Theatre Manager: David Jackson

Devised by
BENNY GREEN *and* ALAN STRACHAN
Music arranged by KEN MOULE · *Vocal arrangements by* JOHN BURROWS

27 June to 7 July 1979

Theatre Royal
Glasgow

BILL KENWRIGHT
by arrangement with
MICHAEL CODRON
presents

KATE · GEORGE
O'MARA · SEWELL
in

NIGHT
AND DAY

by TOM STOPPARD

Theatre Royal Glasgow
Scottish Opera Theatre Royal Ltd.
Chairman: Gavin Boyd, CBE
General Administrator: Peter Ebert
Theatre Manager: David Jackson

with

ROBIN SACHS · JOHN WHITE · MARK HEATH
HONEYBOY KEITH WILLIAMS · HUGH SULLIVAN

Directed by EDWARD DE SOUZA · *Designed by* CARL TOMS

16-21 June 1980

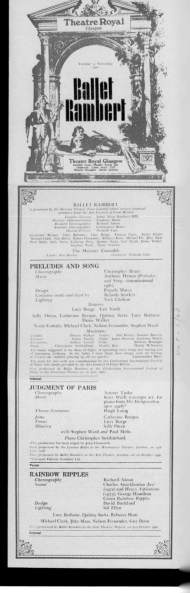

Theatre Royal
Glasgow

Tuesday 11 November 1980

Ballet
Rambert

Theatre Royal Glasgow
Scottish Opera Theatre Royal Ltd.
Chairman: Gavin Boyd, CBE
General Administrator: Peter Ebert
Theatre Manager: David Jackson

BALLET RAMBERT

PRELUDES AND SONG

JUDGMENT OF PARIS

RAINBOW RIPPLES

THEATRE
ROYAL
GLASGOW

WHAT EVERY
WOMAN
KNOWS
BY J.M. BARRIE

Scottish
Theatre
Company
DIRECTOR: TOM FLEMING

THEATRE
ROYAL
GLASGOW

Chairman: Gavin Boyd, CBE
Theatre Manager: David Jackson

Exclusive Fox Limited
presents
THE NEW VIC THEATRE
in

THE NIGHT
THEY RAIDED
MINSKY'S

adapted by
Jamie Reid

15-18 SEPTEMBER 1982

The New Vic Theatre Company and the Theatre
Royal gratefully acknowledge financial assistance
from the Scottish Arts
Council, Strathclyde
Regional Council and
Glasgow District Council

FOR THE NEW VIC THEATRE

Theatre
Royal
Glasgow

Hope Street, Glasgow G2 3QA
Chairman: Gavin Boyd, CBE
Theatre Manager: David Jackson
Box Office Tel 041-331 1234
Open Monday to Saturday 10am-8pm
(7.30 pm performance days)
Instant credit booking 041-332 9000

Tickets £3.50-£4.00
Children, students, senior citizens
and parties of 10 or more – ½ off

25-27 May
evenings at 7.45pm

Scottish
Theatre
Company
Director: Ewan Hooper

cast includes:
John Grieve
Roy Hanlon
Peter Kelly
Phyllis Logan
Fulton MacKay
Jonathan Watson
Jan Wilson
John Young
Paul Young

Director: Bill Bryden
Settings: Hayden Griffin
Costumes: Deirdre Clancy
Lighting: Andy Phillips

CIVILIANS
by Bill Bryden

The Scottish Theatre Company receives financial assistance from the Scottish Arts Council

JAMIE THE SAXT

A Historical Comedy
by Robert McLellan

Ron Bain
Joseph Brady
John Buick
Sheila Donald
Michael Elder
Colin Gourley
Roy Hanlon
Sally Kinghorn
Edith Macarthur
Phil McCall

Michael Mackenzie
Ron Paterson
Lloyd Quinan
John Shedden
Bill Simpson
Leon Sinden
Gerda Stevenson
Alan Watters
John Young
Paul Young

12-15 May, 24-29 May

The Theatre Royal, Glasgow
The Scottish Theatre Company

Directed by Tom Fleming Designed by Adrian Vaux Lighting by Robert Bryan

7.15 pm Tickets £1.60–£5.20 Full details of prices and concessions from the Theatre Royal Box Office Hope St. Glasgow
Tel. 041-331 1234 Instant Credit card bookings on 041-332 9000

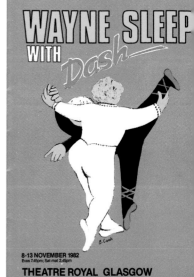

WAYNE SLEEP
WITH Dash

8-13 NOVEMBER 1982
Eves 7.45pm; Sat mat 2.45pm

THEATRE ROYAL GLASGOW

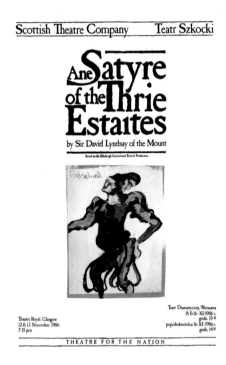

LEFT
Let Wives Tak Tent
1981

RIGHT
Ane Satyre
Programme
1986

BOTTOM
Ane Satyre
on stage

OPPOSITE
(top left)
Cole, *1979*
(top centre)
Night and Day, *1980*
(top right)
Ballet Rambert *(full length), 1980*
(centre left)
What Every Woman Knows, *1986*
(centre)
The Night They Raided Minsky's, *1982*
(bottom left)
Civilians, *1981*
(bottom centre)
Jamie the Saxt, *1982*
(bottom right)
Dash, *1982*

Dana and many more from July to September 1980.

Jackson computerised the Box Office in 1981 and reported that the ticket subscription series for Scottish Opera and for Scottish Ballet were very popular. These were now being applied to other companies including the Scottish Theatre Company and the Scottish Chamber Orchestra. A mixed Ballet subscription was created for a season of four companies, as was a return visit of D'Oyle Carte with six productions. The Scottish Ballet and the National Theatre operated linked ticket schemes giving a discount to those who subscribed to both.

The Scottish Theatre Company

By 1980 the new Scottish Theatre Company had been formed with its first director the actor Ewan Hooper,

from Dundee, and later joined by theatre administrator Ruari McNeill. From its offices and rehearsal space in the Otago Street warehouse formerly used by Red Hackle whisky, and on occasion also used by Scottish Ballet, it set out its policy of presenting Scottish and International classic drama, and

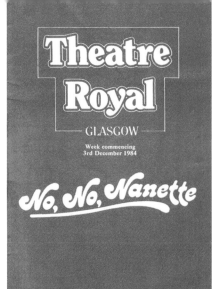

Theatre Royal
GLASGOW
Week commencing
3rd December 1984

No, No, Nanette

Tim Rice and Andrew Lloyd Webber's

**Joseph
and the Amazing
Technicolor Dreamcoat**

Theatre Royal Glasgow
Scottish Opera Theatre Royal
Chairman: Gavin Boyd, CBE
Theatre Manager: David Jackson

THEATRE
ROYAL
G L A S G O W

'ALLO 'ALLO

The Blockbuster MGM Musical now on Stage!

**SEVEN BRIDES
FOR
SEVEN BROTHERS**

♪ *Bless Your Beautiful Hide* ♪
♪ *Wonderful Wonderful Day* ♪ ♪ *Spring, Spring, Spring* ♪
♪ *Goin' Courtin'* ♪ ♪ *Sobbin' Women* ♪ **and many more**

Production by Michael Winter

"*A glorious romp....handclapping effervescent energy.... dazzling dancing....a colourful and breathtaking production*"

Theatre Royal
GLASGOW

THEATRE
ROYAL
G L A S G O W

EVITA

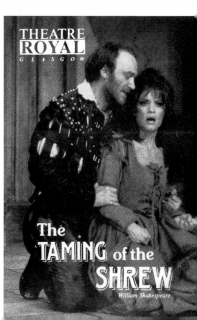

THEATRE
ROYAL
G L A S G O W

**The
TAMING of the
SHREW**
William Shakespeare

LEFT
5 Theatres of the World, *1990*

RIGHT
1000 Airplanes on the Roof, *1989*

BELOW
Coriolanus, *1991*

of commissioning new plays, to audiences throughout the country. Its first production was in 1981 with Moliere's *L'Ecoles des Femmes* adapted into Scots by Robert Kemp as *Let Wives tak Tent*, headed by Rikki Fulton.

The Scottish Theatre Company presented at the Royal, and smaller venues in Glasgow, and toured until 1987- mainly under the direction of Tom Fleming, the successor to Hooper. After appearances at the Edinburgh Festival, and the Royal, *Ane Satyre of the Thrie Estaites* written by Sir David Lyndsay in the 16th century opened the International Theatre Biennale in Warsaw in 1986, to wide acclaim and government recognition. This was the first time the classic had been seen in another country and it represented British Theatre at the Biennale. It was also the largest company of Scottish actors ever to perform in

another country. The text was adapted by Robert Kemp, with music by Cedric Thorpe Davie. *The Thrie Estaites* is rightly described as the cornerstone of all Scottish theatre, a mighty satirical pageant of the human condition and of the body politic. However, despite the company's plays being well attended, and its ability to attract sponsorship, the vision of Ewan Hooper, Ian Cuthbertson, Andrew Cruickshank, Ruari McNeill and others was brought to an end by the continuing indifference of the Scottish Arts Council.

The Theatre Royal became a venue of the annual *Mayfest*, from its start in 1983; which was city-wide and soon became the second largest arts festival in Britain.

Cultural Capital of Europe 1990

International drama featured in the

OPPOSITE
(top left)
Five Past Eight, *1980*
(top centre)
No, No, Nanette, *1984*
(top right)
Joesph and the Amazing Technicolor Dreamcoat, *1984*
(centre left)
The Theatre's *'Allo 'Allo float won the Trophy for Best Overall Entry in the Lord Provost's Procession, 1986*
(centre)
'Allo 'Allo, *1986*
(bottom left)
Seven Brides for Seven Brothers, *1985*
(bottom centre)
Evita, *1987*
(bottom right)
The Taming of the Shrew, *1988*

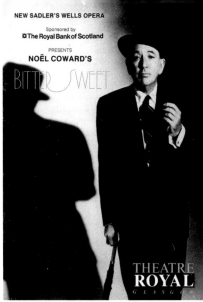

NEW SADLER'S WELLS OPERA

Sponsored by
✿ The Royal Bank of Scotland

PRESENTS
NOËL COWARD'S

Bitter Sweet

THEATRE
ROYAL
GLASGOW

ONEGIN

BALLET BY JOHN CRANKO FROM ALEXANDER PUSHKIN

STUTTGART BALLET · THEATRE ROYAL GLASGOW

THEATRE
ROYAL
GLASGOW

SINGLE
SPIES

by ALAN BENNETT

THEATRE
ROYAL

THE
COTTON
CLUB

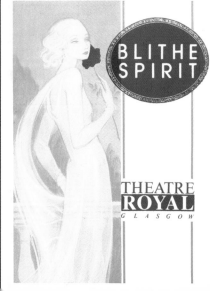

BLITHE
SPIRIT

THEATRE
ROYAL
GLASGOW

THEATRE
ROYAL
GLASGOW

Stewart Macpherson presents
The Original Stage Musical

Phantom
of the Opera
by Ken Hill

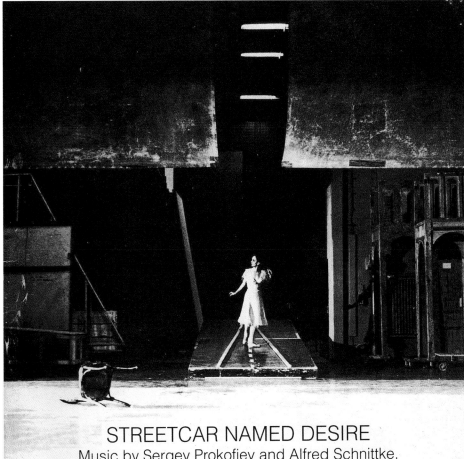

STREETCAR NAMED DESIRE
Music by Sergey Prokofiev and Alfred Schnittke,
Ballet by John Neumeier after Tennessee Williams

Theatre Royal Glasgow . Stuttgart Ballet

LEFT
Streetcar Named Desire
1990

theatre's repertoire with the ground breaking *5 Theatres of the World* when a group of companies from Hungary, Indonesia, Russia, Japan and Sweden performed in five weeks of the summer. Among them they offered no less than eight British premieres of work and covered European classical traditions, epic Russian drama, and non-Western forms such as the Indonesian gamelan and Sankai Juku's Butoh techniques. Live simultaneous translation was provided for the performances from Hungary, Russia and Sweden. Public workshops and talks were held in the theatre.

In the 1980s and 1990s the national subsidised drama and ballet touring companies came each year, and the galaxy of other artistes included:-

OPPOSITE
(top left)
Bitter Sweet, *1988*
(top right)
Onegin, *1990*
(centre left)
Single Spies, *1990*
(bottom left)
The Cotton Club, *1991*
(bottom centre)
Blithe Spirit, *1991*
(bottom right)
Phantom of the Opera, *1991*

THEATRE ROYAL GLASGOW

DEATH OF A SALESMAN

UNITED WE STAND

10 February 1949 **10** CENTS

First Performance in New York

by ARTHUR MILLER

piaf

THEATRE ROYAL GLASGOW

THEATRE ROYAL GLASGOW

ROYAL LYCEUM THEATRE COMPANY

WITH ANDY GRAY
DIRECTED BY KENNY IRELAND

A **Midsummer Night's** Dream

by William Shakespeare

"Gray is a scream."
John Linklater, The Herald

MON 15th - SAT 20th NOV 1993

ON SALE NOW
041-332 9000

THE APOLLO PLAYERS

CHESS

THEATRE ROYAL GLASGOW

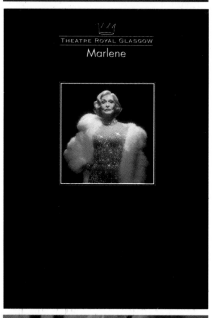

THEATRE ROYAL GLASGOW
Marlene

Sailing Into Town For 2004
One Week Only
Commencing 19th April, 2004

THE APOLLO PLAYERS

ANYTHING GOES

Theatre Royal
Hope Street, Glasgow

Booking Hotline 0141 429 6006

THEATRE ROYAL GLASGOW

DECEMBER 2006 -
MAY 2007

PHONE SALES
(Mon - Sat, 10am - 8pm)
0870 060 6647 (bkg fee)
www.theatreroyalglasgow.com

SWAN LAKE
ON ICE

Tue 23 - Sat 27 Jan

THEATRE ROYAL GLASGOW

MATTHEW BOURNE'S
CAR MAN
BIZET'S CARMEN RE-IMAGINED

comes to Glasgow

Tue 11 - Sat 15 Sep

APRIL 2007

PHONE SALES
0870 060 6647 (bkg fee)

THEATRE ROYAL GLASGOW

MAJOR
INTERNATIONAL
HIT MUSICAL

WEST SIDE STORY

SCOTLAND'S BROADWAY

APRIL -
DECEMBER 2008

PHONE SALES
0870 060 6647 (bkg fee)

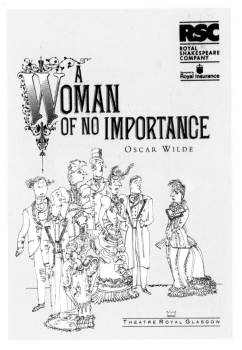

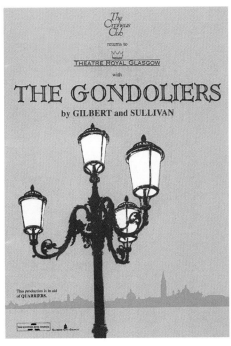

LEFT
A Woman of no Importance
1992

RIGHT
The Gonodoliers
1997

Moira Anderson, Isobel Buchanan, The Corries, George Chisholm, Kelly Monteith, Dave Brubeck, Elaine Page, Bonnie Langford (as Peter Pan), The Drifters, The Chieftains, Buddy Rich, Nancy Wilson and Brook Benton, Jack Jones, Peggy Lee, Band of HM Royal Marines, Tony Bennet, Billie Jo Spears, George Melly with John Chilton's Feetwarmers, the Red Army Ensemble, Rowan Atkinson, Fascinating Aida, Andy Prior, Marti Webb, Wayne Sleep. New York City Ballet, Rambert Dance, Stuttgart Ballet, Moscow Classical Ballet, Netherlands Dance Theatre, National Ballet of Latvia, Glyndebourne Opera, and the Vienna Boys Choir. Billy Connolly, David Essex, Barbara Dickson, Dave Allen, Charlie Pride, Elaine Delmar, Hue & Cry, Nina Simone, Humphrey Lyttleton, Carol Kidd, Chris Barber, Martin Taylor, Gerry Mulligan, the BBC Big Band, Barry Humphries and Hank Marvin. Janet Suzman, Prunella Scales, Albert Finney, Timothy West, Anthony Quayle, plays by the Compass Theatre company and the Oxford Stage company. The Reduced Shakespeare company (all 37 plays in 97 minutes!) Musicals including Show Boat, Evita, Marlene, Phantom of the Opera, and The Blues Brothers. For children the Purves Puppets were frequent performers, Flying Tortoise, Roald Dahl's Big Friendly Giant, Enid Blyton's Noddy, and The Singing Kettle.

OPPOSITE
(top left)
Death of a Salesman, *1992*
(top centre)
Piaf, *1993*
(top right)
A Midsummer Night's Dream, *1993*
(centre left)
Chess, *1994*
(centre)
Marlene, *1997*
(centre right)
Anything Goes, *2004*
(bottom left)
Swan Lake on Ice, *2007*
(bottom centre)
The Car Man, *2007*
(bottom right)
West Side Story, *2008*

Into the 21st Century

New versions of Wagner's Ring cycle of operas started the new millennium with *Das Rheingold*, *Die Walkure*, *Siegfried*, and *Gotterdammerung*, as did Mozart's *Magic Flute* and Puccini's *La Boheme*. Scottish Ballet's *The Snowman*, *Aladdin*, *Romeo & Juliet*, and *Carmen* also packed the house. Visits from national drama companies in England became fewer as they considered their futures.

Unfortunately, in the few years to 2000 the Scottish Opera board and management incurred large losses on opera preparation and production, with costs overrunning. Opera losses continued and spiralled further in the new century. As a result more than half of the company's employees lost their jobs including the full time chorus, stage and technical staff. No main scale opera was performed for a period. Fortunately Scottish Opera Orchestra continued to fly the flag with a series of concerts - from their St Andrews Square venue and elsewhere. Each year their Children's Classics Concerts take place in the Glasgow Royal Concert Hall and in other cities. They play for the City of Glasgow Chorus in the City Halls, with recordings being made, and for the Dundee Choral Union. The annual Burns Festival at Culzean and Ayr is another calendar feature.

Educational and medium-scale touring activity also kept going. Opera at the Royal resumed with four productions a year, half the normal. Hopefully Scottish Opera will restore itself to eight operas a year to meet the demands of the audiences for good singing, music and stagecraft. Glasgow has many entertainment venues and competing attractions. Lately the Royal Concert Hall has hosted more operas and ballets by visiting companies. The growth of cheap flights regularly takes thousands away for days and weekends to other destinations, including dropping in on London or Italy for a range of operas. They also bring tourists inwards. Compared to the brave days of Sir Alexander Gibson more of the

LEFT
Sir Alexander Gibson *in the foyer*

OPPOSITE
Hope Street *looking towards the National Piping Centre*

RIGHT
Foyer *ticket window*

period of 25 years from 2005. Much like Howard & Wyndham, they manage a large circuit of theatres in Britain and can arrange a bounty of touring plays and shows. To help ensure the Royal is open and used Glasgow City Council agreed to continue its financial help to attract visiting companies, and a larger sum each year towards the building, often to meet new standards of health and safety and building regulations.

The opera company's quest for empire mergers was also brought to an end. Under a fully independent board and a new artistic director Scottish Ballet is thriving once more, with large audiences at its Theatre Royal performances.

Glasgow City Council, the successor to Glasgow Corporation and Strathclyde Regional Council, continues to support the theatre and its uses (as they do with the King's which the Council owns and is also leased to the Ambassador Group). Another long-time friend is Historic Scotland, the national conservation agency, which helps buildings of historic and architectural importance. These sources add to fundraising by Scottish Opera.

country's commercial and professional firms are owned by international companies with headquarters outside Scotland which may make the raising of sponsorship problematic, but the prizes are for the asking. Annual programmes restored to eight or nine operas and longer seasons reach more audiences, generate greater vibrancy and meet the community aspirations of sponsors.

Recent productions continue at the high level of quality demanded by its audiences. In 2007 the Italian born Francesco Corti was appointed as the fourth music director in the company's history.

Open doors again

Scottish Opera leased out the management of Theatre Royal to the Ambassador Theatre Group for a

The Head of Hope Street

The Royal sits well at the head of Hope Street. Its doors open to a wonder of anticipation, a place of entertainment. Its walls echo the applause of generations, laughter and lilt, enjoyment and stimulation. The theatre continues as it started, except there is no pantomime on stage, no silent films, and no circus. Its bill of fare is opera, ballet, drama, light entertainment, dance, talks and workshops for all ages. And as many novel activities as the creative management and the city would like to see.

Cowcaddens today

Most of Cowcaddens' tenements are demolished. Multi-storey flats and motorway pillars point skywards. The city's Theatre Royal continues where it started. *A New and Magnificent Theatre* said James Baylis in 1867. *A public meeting place of friends* said the Evening Citizen in 1957. *A home for Scottish Opera and an opera house for Scotland* said Gavin Boyd in 1975.

If James Baylis could return he would recognise the Head of Hope Street – but wonder where the Royal Arcade had gone - and remember his site and some of the interior. If Michael Simons could return he would recognise most of the city centre and nearly all of his theatre. The Royal's neighbours today are the Royal Scottish Academy of Music and Drama across the road at Renfrew Street. McConnell's Building is across Hope Street and busy with its residents and restaurants – the Council restored it in the 1970s after threatening to demolish it for road widening, and it was considered for rehearsal space for Scottish Opera. Round the corner is the very modern Alexander Gibson Opera School. On the other side of Cowcaddens is the former Cowcaddens Church in McPhater Street now restored as the National Piping Centre, and its

ABOVE
Main Entrance
2008

hotel, thanks to the initiative of Oona Ivory who was also a director of The Scottish Ballet, the Theatre Royal, and the Music Academy. It too had been looked at earlier as rehearsal space for Scottish Opera. Behind the theatre the former television studios are being built upon with new offices, shops and flats now that Scottish Television has moved its nest to Govan.

In the Theatre Royal the curtain, *that old-fashioned mechanism*, continues to rise.

Encore

Theatres-Royal in Glasgow before 1867

ALSTON STREET from 1764
Glasgow's magistrates were not keen to have a permanent theatre in the royal burgh; there were some very large wooden ones and smaller penny geggie booths around Glasgow Green, but Baillie John Miller, after whom Miller Street is named, had no compunction. He owned the area around Grahamston Brewery just across the boundary of the royalty which was St Enoch's Burn where now sits Mitchell Street known then as the Malt Dubs. He sold land to the promoters of Glasgow's first main Playhouse theatre, in Alston Street named after his son-in-law James Alston.

John Jackson – no relation to manager David Jackson 200 years later – was invited by five wealthy Virginia and West Indies merchants William McDowall of Castle Semple; William Bogle of Hamilton Farm; John Baird of Craigton; Robert Bogle of Shettleston; and James Dunlop of Garnkirk to come from the Canongate Playhouse in Edinburgh to help open a theatre in Glasgow, which he did at Alston Street in 1764 installing a colleague Mr Beatt as manager. The theatre was designed and built by the architect John Adam. In due course John Jackson became the lessee and manager in 1780. Shortly after that, fire engulfed the building. Theatres and fires seemed to go together. The building was insured for £1,000 but the premium had not been paid; however the Sun Fire Office generously gave a present of £300 towards the loss. It was not rebuilt and

the remaining walls were refitted and used as the South West Granary. Much later the streets in Grahamston became the underground arches to Central Station.

DUNLOP STREET from 1782
Looking for new premises Jackson met with Robert Barclay, a writer (lawyer) and an "Admiral Depute for the River and Firth of Clyde" (whose country mansion of Capelrig at Newton Mearns still exists.) Barclay sold him a plot of his land at the new Dunlop Street, formed

ABOVE
Alston Street Playhouse
the tallest building above, off Argyle Street

RIGHT
Queen Street Theatre Royal
to the right of the view

from the grounds of the mansion belonging to Provost Colin Dunlop one of the Tobacco Lords.

Opening on 11 January 1782 the THEATRE ROYAL was built with a sandstone front and an interior supported by iron columns which could accommodate almost 2,000 customers on wooden forms. Each month Jackson alternated the performing companies with his Edinburgh Theatre Royal and other theatres in the country, and actors from the London stage. It is thought he purchased Letters Patent from the magistrates to have the sole right to present "legitimate drama using the spoken word" in the town, giving him a monopoly over others.

To the north of the theatre he built a house for himself and his family. "It had a small flower-garden in front, with an alcove, and honeysuckle trained up part of the walls". It survived until 1852. To the south he had more ground which he sold to William Craig & Son, architects, who were probably the theatre architects. A new street connecting Dunlop Street back to Stockwell Street was named "Jackson Street" in his honour. He was enjoying success in his profession, and he moved permanently to Glasgow in 1788. The Garrick Hotel opposite the

theatre and the Bucks Head Hotel at the top of the street, were among the favourite lodgings for performers and playwrights.

However by 1791 Jackson was bankrupt, ousted from the theatre, but returned in 1799. Over the next few years the theatre was not busy, and no longer fashionable, even with an extension of the auditorium in 1802. A powerful and luxurious rival appeared in Queen Street.

QUEEN STREET from 1805

The city was continuing to move westwards. Walter Neilson, a market gardener and merchant, bought some riggs of land at Back Cow Lone and led the initiative with other merchants to set out plots to form Queen Street and the large elegant mansions which followed. William Cunninghame of Lainshaw, one of the most prosperous of the Tobacco Lords, took three plots for the site of his mansion in 1770 (which was incorporated in 1827 into the new Royal Exchange and is currently a Gallery of Modern Art). To the north of his mansion was ground which was a market garden of fruit, vegetables, pear, apple and other trees. When the tenancy of this ended in 1801, and the two thatched cottages demolished, the site was bought from the Council for a new theatre paid for by public subscription, the committee of merchants responsible being Laurence Craigie, John Hamilton, Dugald Bannatyne, William Penney and Robert Dennistoun.

The Corporation sent a petition

to Parliament in February 1803 for a patent for the theatre:

> That the City of Glasgow has of late been much extended and enlarged and beautified, whereby the number of wealthy and opulent inhabitants has much increased; and it has become expedient to provide for their amusement and that of the nobility and gentry of the neighbourhood, a public theatre or playhouse, for acting tragedies, comedies, operas, and other performances of the stage, under proper rules and regulations; therefore pray that leave may be given to his Majesty to issue letters patent.

Designed by the city's leading architect David Hamilton, the new Theatre Royal opened on 24 April 1805 and was "Unequalled out of London".

The new building in its Adam style and splendour accommodated 1500 people and had six Ionic columns on the front, Corinthian columns in its main vestibule, an elliptical *spectatory*, three galleries and a proscenium gilded to resemble a picture frame. For a time there was a wooden building connected to it to house panoramas. John Jackson convinced the committee he should be the first manager.

Jackson was now totally exhausted and died a poor man in 1806. A series of new managers took over and in 1807 the Glasgow Herald wrote:

> The superior excellence of the

present company of the Theatre Royal is manifest from the number and respectability of the audience. We have no hesitation in saying that we bear off the palm from every provincial theatre in the kingdom.

Popular artistes included Julia Glover, Charles Macready, Edmund Kean, Mr & Mrs Charles Kemble, Mrs Howard and Mrs Wyndham. Whenever Kean appeared the house was full to overflowing and 250 additional seats were added in the wings and onstage. The premiere of the national opera Rob Roy took place in Queen Street in June 1818 starring W H Murray before it went on tour round Scotland.

Performances attracted the rich and not so rich patrons (there was a riot in 1818 when ticket prices were increased, requiring the Militia to be called to restore order). On the 18th September the same year the theatre became the first in Britain to have gas lighting, with the announcement that:

> The Grand Crystal Lustre of the front Roof of the Theatre, the largest of any of that time in Scotland, will, in place of the Wicks and the Candles and the Oil Lamps, be *"Illuminated with Sparkling Gas."*

A reviewer wrote:

> every seat in the boxes up to the double and triple tier was at once engaged, the spacious pit was crammed to suffocation, the first,

second, and third galleries had not an inch of standing room to spare. The house presented a most brilliant appearance. Nearly every citizen of wealth or repute was present with his family. The signal was given. The green curtain of the stage was raised. Then the band struck up the National Anthem, the audience joining in the chorus. The gas, as if by magic, made its first "evolutions" to the astonishment of all, leaving some of them to fancy that they had been ushered into a new world – a perfect Elysium on earth.

The programme that night consisted of Mozart's *Don Giovanni* by a company of Italian artistes under the baton of Mr John Corri. Scene painters included Alexander Nasmyth, who had added to his fame through his portrait of Robert Burns, and later David Roberts who wrote of his arrival in 1819:

This theatre was immense in its size and appointments - in magnitude exceeding Drury Lane and Covent Garden.

But it was eventually the Dunlop Street theatre that became busier - partly because the old building now had two operators in it, one upstairs and one downstairs, and partly because of the high rental cost of operating the Queen Street theatre.

In 1829 this beautiful theatre in Queen Street was burned to the ground following a rehearsal. The theatre cost £18,000 but was insured for only £5,500 and the materials of the actors and manager were not insured. It was not rebuilt. The manager Frank Seymour made off with the £1,000 proceeds of a Relief Ball and went to Belfast. He returned in October the same year as manager of the newly built YORK STREET theatre, claiming he had the right to the Letters Patent. Over a year later that theatre closed (it was too far from the town centre and the Dunlop Street theatre made certain that all shows came to it first).

DUNLOP STREET....... Again

Jackson's family and co-proprietor Francis Aitken of Liverpool sold the theatre by auction in 1807 to Andrew Thomson who owned one of the mansions in Queen Street. He soon converted the basement into a warehouse for West Indies produce and then to a coach works, letting out the upper part for theatrical shows, circuses, boxing and public meetings. But interest in the theatre, drama clubs and concert halls was not diminishing. Scene painters were used to attract attention. John Knox taught drawing and painting in his artist studio at 40 Dunlop Street, including scene painting by three young friends Daniel Macnee, Horatio McCulloch and William Leitch, who later became the art master to Queen Victoria and her expanding family for 20 years.

Andrew Thomson sold out in 1822 and Jackson's theatre became known as the CALEDONIAN THEATRE operated by a series of managers including Frank Seymour before he moved off to the Queen Street theatre, and the basement as the DOMINION of FANCY operated by the energetic and flamboyant actor John Henry Alexander who triumphed and won over the whole building which he extended. He restored the name THEATRE ROYAL and built anew in 1830 with his architect William Spence. He bought the Letters Patent and was enjoying his success. In 1839 he built new again (opening in March 1840), this time in the grand manner by the eminent Spence with statues adorning the façade, including Shakespeare, David Garrick, and of course a statue of Alexander himself, as well as the classical muses *Thalia* (comedy) and *Melpomene* (tragedy). This was the first public commission of the sculptor John Mossman. The theatre had a pit, two galleries, dress boxes and upper boxes, and was 70 yards long, 50 feet high and 50 feet wide. The interior was complete with chandeliers and the fronts of the boxes painted with scenes from William Shakespeare and Sir Walter Scott.

Damaged by more fire in 1840 and a false alarm in 1849 (when sixty five customers died in the panic, mainly from the upper galleries) Alexander always rebuilt, but the last tragedy and its consequences haunted him and he expired in 1851. He "left a large fortune" which included the theatre valued at £20,000, houses and other properties in Dunlop Street worth over £6,000 and shares in the Western Bank, but his widow Elizabeth was sequestrated in May 1858 following the financial collapse of the Western Bank because of these shares (shareholders did not then enjoy limited liability) and most of her inheritance passed into the hands of the liquidators of the bank.

PRINCE's THEATRE-ROYAL West Nile Street

Glover & Lind: Lumsden & Wylson

The ageing WH Murray of Edinburgh sent Glover to London to settle terms for the Swedish singing star Jenny Lind to tour Scotland; which he did, but for himself, not Murray.

She performed in "The Daughter of the Regiment" at the Theatre Royal Glasgow, Edinburgh and Perth in the autumn of 1848. Seat prices were as high as 31 shillings, ten times the normal for best seats, Afternoon performances were slightly cheaper. In the two nights in Glasgow she sang Donizetti's *La Figlia de Regimento*, and Bellini's *La Sonnambula*. Clearing a record £3,000 he started his own theatre with the additional encouragement of a dedicated patron of the arts James Lumsden, stationer and publisher whose warehouse was in Dunlop Street, (Lumsden was a founder of the Royal Infirmary and Clydesdale Bank, and had become Lord Provost). Glover leased from him a large hall erected in 1847 for the exhibition of dioramic pictures by the brothers Daguerre at 100 West Nile Street which the building's architect James Wylson redesigned as The Prince's Opera House known better as the PRINCE's

ABOVE
Jenny Lind Jug
*potted by J & M.P.Bell,
Glasgow Pottery*

Encouraging New Theatres

Government in the 18th century, especially under Prime Minister William Pitt the younger, continued to be nervous of allowing free speech on stage to crowds of people, thoughts of sedition kept them awake at night. Demands for democracy and voting reform grew especially after the independence of America, and France's overthrow of its royal hierarchy. Following the Reform Act of 1832 a Select Committee of the House of Commons met that year and recommended the abolition of the theatrical monopoly which Letters Patent or Royal Charters had brought about in controlling "legitimate drama". Abolition eventually took place in Scotland and England under the Theatres Regulation Act 1843.

There was now free trade in theatres and a great expansion in the number of new permanent buildings. However new scripts continued to be sent in advance to the Lord Chamberlain's office, and could be censored. This was to continue until the 1960s.

THEATRE-ROYAL. It accommodated 1400 people and had a wing attached containing the Green Room, property room, wardrobe and dressing rooms. The interior decorations included festoons of fruit and flowers, medallions, and panels containing groups of children. These were in white, picked out in gold, with pale blue backgrounds in the panels, and the fronts of the tiers rose-colour.

Glover opened on 15 January 1849 with the opera *Giselle*, followed by a vaudeville of the *Imperial Guard*, and a

Right
Prince's Theatre Royal
became Hengler's Cirque, West Nile Street

ballet company. Its playbills advertised "during the Summer Season Bonnets may be worn in the Dress Circle." The North British Daily Mail, Glasgow's first daily paper, stated:

> we know of no theatre which ladies can visit with such comfort, propriety and freedom from annoyances as the Prince's, Glasgow.

James Wylson wrote papers and books on architectural matters including in 1848 "Remarks on workmen's houses in town districts with plans, elevation, details, and descriptions of the Lumsden model dwellings for the working classes, now erecting in Glasgow at New City Road." He also wrote "The Mechanical Inventor's Guide" in 1859, and major contributions to the Architectural Publication Society's Dictionary.

The building was on the east side of West Nile Street facing along West

Regent Street. It was advertised as being at "West Nile Street & Buchanan Street." The Glover family home at the rear had windows facing Buchanan Street, on a lane which gave public access to the theatre. Later the family moved to West Regent Street and then to Great Clyde Street.

It was also the first theatre outside London to have seated stalls separate from the pit. Sam Bough was chief scene painter and Edmund's half brother Howard Glover was the musical director. Mrs Edmund Glover continued in charge until 1863, when it was converted to become Hengler's Circus until their move twenty years later to Wellington Street.

Designers and scenic painters were very artistic and could also be pragmatic. Glover noted in his diary on Saturday 27th December 1856 of his conversation the other day with Bough:

showing me over the flies when he said I was well insured it would be a good job if the place burned down. My reply was 'Don't talk so, Mr. Bough, God forbid I should ever see that day'. I am led to remark this from previous observations made by Mr. Bough. Morning performance £45. At night £54.3 - narrow escape of the theatre being burnt to the ground. Saved by me and the blessings of God - strong suspicion of a certain party. Gas rod turned in batten. NB. See and have hose ready.

In addition to Glasgow he had managed the Dunfermline Theatre Royal, and the Paisley Theatre Royal in Moss Street, and appeared with his family and mother Julia Betterton in the Adelphi Theatre on Glasgow Green in its first year 1843. It burned down in 1848.

DUNLOP STREET......finally

Alexander's manager Mr Simpson continued the Theatre Royal Dunlop Street until he retired a year later in 1852, when Mrs Alexander decided to lease it to Edmund Glover the elder son of Mrs Julia Betterton Glover who had made her Glasgow acting debut in 1807 in the Queen Street theatre. By 1840 Edmund Glover had become the leading actor in WH Murray's Edinburgh Theatre Royal, being paid 3 guineas a week. He and his wife Elizabeth, experienced actors themselves and lessees of the Prince's Theatre in West Nile Street, were now in charge of the Theatre Royal.

Edmund Glover was an actor-manager, dancer, pantomist and swordsman whose repertoire at both theatres focussed on the great classical plays, pantomimes, and operas (although he noted these "do not make so much profit because of the larger expenditure.") At the Royal and the Prince's the same management team was used, including a Mr Houghton who is charmingly described as the "Treasurer and Superintendent of the Audience Department."

Edmund Glover is credited as creating in Glasgow "perhaps the very best stock company of actors and actresses ever gathered together in

Scotland."

Glover opened his Theatre Royal in Dunlop Street on 3rd October 1852 with Italian opera, including three of the greatest singers Giulia Grisi, Mario, and Liugi Lablanche; subsequent weeks had plays, and at the end of the year he staged his first pantomime there *The Great Bed of Ware*. As well as the actors and actresses of the day who trod the boards in the old Royal, the novelist Charles Dickens appeared on two occasions, at the invitation of Glover, to read from his works.

Many of Edmund Glover's Diary entries are about the tribulations of his large Victorian family, - he assisted many relatives, the theatre widow Mrs Alexander, and theatre staff - as well as the ups and downs of theatre life. On the upside he writes on 31st December 1853 "So ends year. Cleared £3,000 over my own salary" and two years later on 3rd November "Elizabeth and I on General Fund of company, should be £800 a year each."

Edmund Glover expands again

In December 1858 he also opened the Theatre Royal Greenock at a cost reported at £8,000, designed by the architect Joseph Potts of Port Glasgow and Sunderland. Situated in West Blackhall Street it held 1600 customers, with entrances similar to the Dunlop Street theatre and with a black and white marble floor. The façade even had niches for statuary, and the proscenium had Corinthian columns, the newspapers declaring:

> The decorations are white and gold and the ornamentation extremely chaste and elegant. The fronts of the boxes are adorned with scrolls, alternated by medallions, containing groups of figures in bas relief on a blue ground.

Glover bought ground next to his Greenock Royal and opened the Western Concert Hall, designed by architect William Spence, with a grand concert in May 1860, seating 700 customers. When the Theatre Royal Dunlop Street was demolished three of its statues were erected in the niches at the Greenock theatre. It continued to be owned by the Glover Trust until 1896, eventually coming under the management of Alex

RIGHT
Theatre Royal
Dunlop Street
1855

Wright, one of the Dunlop Street team. The Greenock press wrote:

> Tragedy, comedy, opera, burlesque, pantomime, concert, have all been put before the public during the thirty eight years……...great actors and actresses have trod the boards of our theatre. Sir Henry Irving has played in it at a salary of £2 a week, and in later years with his world famous impersonation of Hamlet has packed it with people at double prices.

It changed its name later, in 1908 it was the Hippodrome Variety Theatre, and closed in 1923 to make way for road-widening. The statuary was put on display in the town's Auchmountain Glen.

Moving on

Aside from theatres his recreation was painting seascapes and country scenes, which continue to sell today. On 24th October 1860 the pioneering Edmund passed away at 23 Gayfield Place, Edinburgh the residence of Mr & Mrs Robert Wyndham, where he had gone from his cottage in Luss to recover from an illness. Extracts from the Testimonials at the time are in Chapter 3.

Mrs Elizabeth Glover continued as lessee of the Royal and held the Letters-Patent. She was aided by Charles G Houghton the manager and treasurer, and by her elder son William who also pursued his own passion for painting.

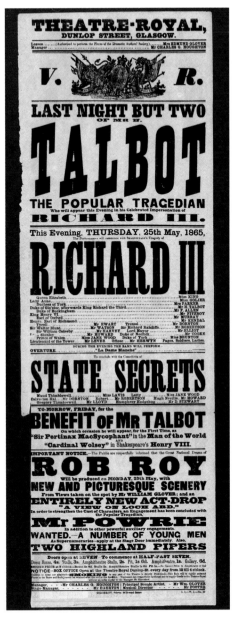

LEFT
Theatre Royal,
Dunlop Street, playbill 1865

On the last night of the pantomime *Blue Beard* in January 1863 the theatre was damaged by fire, but using most of the £3,400 from the Norwich Union Insurance Co. it was rebuilt behind the facade and open again at the end of the year, together with workshops at nearby

Moodie's Court. During the 12 months of rebuilding the Theatre Royal performances took place in The Prince's Theatre.

With Glasgow and its suburbs now having a population of 460,000, an increase of 100,000 since the 1850s, the townsfolk were increasingly concerned over the slum conditions and overcrowding of the old streets and wynds surrounding the Saltmarket and the High Street. Under the City Improvements Trust started in 1866 the Council planned to have housing constructed elsewhere and to rebuild the old areas. The quickest "improver" was the arrival of the railways. The Glasgow & South Western Railway and the Caledonian Railway each had city terminals on the south-side of the Clyde and were looking to cross the river. As part of the railway plans the Theatre Royal was bought by compulsory purchase by the City of Glasgow Union Railway (owned by the two giant companies), finally closing its doors on 28 May 1869, and being demolished.

The Glover Trustees lodged their claim for compensation, about equal to 9 years future profits totalling £27,000. After arbitration the amount decreed in their favour was £11,798, being three years profit together with over £2,000 for the loss in value of props and machinery.

The railways crossed the Clyde over the new viaduct at Hutchesontown in 1870 and swung into a temporary Dunlop Street Station, clearing away streets and houses below. St Enoch Station was erected in 1876 and the luxurious St Enoch Hotel three years later. After a century of use the station and hotel became the site of today's St Enoch Shopping Centre.

Theatre Royal's Owners and Lessees

Owners from year	Lessees/Managers from year
1867 James Baylis	1867 James Baylis
	1869 William Glover & George Francis
1870 Baylis Trust	
1877 Yuille & Rae Messrs McClures and Hannay	
	1878 William Glover
1879 Mrs Margaret Anderson Trust	
	1880 Marie Litton
	1881 Charles Bernard
	1884 Fred Sydney
	1885 Edward Lee Knapp
1886 Richmond Trust (*daughter of Mrs Anderson*)	
	1887 William Thomas Rushbury

1888 James Howard and Fred Wyndham
    (*funded by Michael Simons and the
    Richmond Trust*)
	1888 James Howard and Fred Wyndham

1895 Howard & Wyndham Ltd (*created by Michael Simons*)	1895 Howard & Wyndham Ltd
1957 Scottish Television	1957 Scottish Television
1975 Scottish Opera Theatre Royal Ltd	1975 Scottish Opera Theatre Royal Ltd
	2005 Ambassador Theatre Group Ltd

HOWARD & WYNDHAM EPILOGUE

We have read of the fashions and many changes of entertainment over the years since the Royal began. The seismic change above all was the arrival of television, which closed down a majority of all theatres in Britain from the 1950s onwards. With good fortune, and paradoxically, it was television which saved the Theatre Royal. But what happened to Howard & Wyndham?

Into the 1960s Howard & Wyndham Ltd continued its theatre activities, with its *Five Past Eight Shows*, Summer Revues in England, and especially the pantomime spectaculars such as a *Wish for Jamie*, *A Love for Jamie* and *The World of Jamie*, which toured Scotland and England. It started making films, including *The Promise*, a romantic war drama set in Leningrad, starring Ian McKellen and Susan Macready. Film production proved very costly and the company needed to find substantial money.

Stewart Cruikshank's successor as chairman from 1965, the company's managing director Peter Donald (of the Aberdeen entertainments family), wrote to all shareholders and announced in public in 1966 that although the company was profitable there was only room for one live theatre in each city where they operated and they could not compete with the civic theatre movement which received Arts Council subsidies. The same month it sought planning permission to redevelop the sites of their six theatres in Scotland and the North of England. The chairman suggested that in some redevelopments it may be possible to have a small theatre built as part of a new complex.

During the furore that followed, and campaigns to save the theatres, it sought the support of the Arts Council to keep open the Alhambra, the King's, and the Edinburgh King's Theatre. At the same time the company bought property next to its Alhambra to make a large street block available for redevelopment.

While the company sought a full price for the sites it was open to selling to city councils at a lower price. Glasgow Corporation bought the King's in Bath Street in January 1967, and Edinburgh Corporation bought the King's Theatre in that city in 1969.

In January 1969 Peter Donald declared that colour television was a fresh threat to theatres. The Citizens Theatre continued to have its own difficulties and, for a second start, looked for a new site. He suggested it would be possible to save the Alhambra if the Citizens moved into the King's and his company managed the Alhambra. The Alhambra was so well equipped by the company that even all the dressing rooms had showers, (unheard of elsewhere in Britain) and the dressing rooms could open to two levels allowing artistes to enter at the top of a grand staircase on the stage. The revolving stage and the moving orchestra platform, which could rise over the stage and at the stage front, were features seen in Las Vegas and occasionally in Paris.

However in March 1969 Glasgow Corporation decided not to buy the theatre, it had chosen the King's although popular preference was for the Alhambra. Despite a public petition with 500,000 signatures the Alhambra was sold to a property developer in January

1970 and demolished in 1971. Scotland's largest quality theatre and one of the best equipped in Europe was no more.

During 1970 the Cruikshank, Beaumont and Donald families sold their controlling shares to Ralph Fields of the USA. He came from generations of showbusiness playwrights and producers, and an aunt was the lyricist Dorothy Fields who wrote some 400 songs for Broadway and Hollywood. In the 1970s the company's remaining theatres, all in England, were added to by buying theatres in Oxford and Bath, and its active production company continued to produce pantomimes. However due to a number of factors and changing

THEATRE ROYAL
GLASGOW

MESSRS HOWARD AND WYNDHAM LTD
Managing Director: Stewart Cruikshank

KING'S THEATRE
GLASGOW

MESSRS HOWARD AND WYNDHAM LTD
Managing Director : Stewart Cruikshank

ALHAMBRA THEATRE
GLASGOW

MESSRS. HOWARD & WYNDHAM LTD.
Managing Director - Stewart Cruikshank

habits, including the spread of television, the ease and economy of travel abroad taking people off to sunny climes, and the fact that touring large productions had become un-economical, many of Britain's largest theatres were gone by the 1970s. The company's last big commercial tour was My Fair Lady. The Royal Ballet and the National Shakespeare Company came on tours subsidised by the Arts Council, who insisted on low ticket prices, insufficient to pay for the theatre. At the end of the 1970s its final theatres were sold to city councils - Manchester Opera House, Liverpool Royal Court, Oxford New Theatre and Bath Theatre Royal. The contract management of theatres owned by others also came to its end.

In order to continue, the company obviously needed to have other business activities. In February 1971 it had acquired, from an American cinema magnate, W. H. Allen & Co. Ltd., UK book publishers, (whose book list included recreational and film books and show-business biographies – Margot Fonteyn, Marilyn Monroe, Jimmy Young, and the Beatles' Biography among others.) And in 1975 the company purchased Ciro Pearls Limited which operated 105 retail jewellery stores stretching from San Francisco to Vienna. W H Allen was sold to the Virgin Group in 1987 and in 1990 the Ciro Group was sold to its management. This was the end of Howard and Wyndham as an operating business, Ralph Fields selling his shares in 1990. It became a private investment company and based itself in the Caribbean tax haven of the Cayman Islands when it came off the public register in 1995; one hundred years after Michael Simons started it at the Theatre Royal.

ACKNOWLEDGEMENTS

Thank you

Many in Britain, Australia and America have helped with information and illustrations. In writing the story of the Royal I have been inspired by the vision and ability of the late Gavin Boyd, Bill Brown and Ian Rodger in restoring the theatre in 1975. Contributors who kindly shared their knowledge include the late Ian Rodger, Kathleen Boyd, John Lawson Graham, Allan Campbell, Peter Hamilton, Morag Chisholm, June Caunce, Robin Anderson, James Hastie, Ruari McNeill, Martin Reid-Foster, Nigel Reid-Foster, Robert Glover, Bill Glover, Joan Schugel, Ernie Glover, Graham Simons, Tony Simons, Vivien Heilbron, Khirstine Baylis Johnston, Bill Baylis Thomson, Harry Dick-Cleland, Mathew Lloyd, John Short, Stanley Baxter, Fay Lenore, Herbert Donald, Ralph Fields, Michael Moss, Blair Scott, Russell Galbraith, Ferdi Coia, Frank Morris, Tom Carbery, Tony Currie, Peggy O'Keefe, Gordon Irving, John Hepburn, Ian Hepburn, Roy McLachlan, Paul Iles, Paul Maloney, Anna Wilson, Cameron Smith, Ian Johnston. My wife Jean is due a medal, even while escaping to the golf course or supporting our large family on both sides of the Atlantic.

Glasgow University Library Special Collections, Glasgow University Business Archives, Mitchell Library, Glasgow City Archives, Strathclyde University Library, Dundee University Archives, Edinburgh City Library, National Archives of Scotland, Royal Commission on the Ancient & Historical Monuments of Scotland, Lodge Montefiore, Glasgow, Royal Faculty of Procurators of Glasgow, Royal Glasgow Institute of the Fine Arts, Scottish Jewish Archives, Scottish Television, Scottish Opera, Scottish Ballet, Scottish Screen, Ambassador Theatre Group Ltd., Newcastle City Library, Victoria & Albert Theatre Museum, London, Guildhall Library, London, National Archives, Kew, London, California Art Gallery, Laguna Beach, USA.

Photographs

Many of the photographs are from private collections.

Others have been kindly made available as follows :

Page numbers are shown, and where relevant :
b = bottom, c = centre, l = left, m = middle, r = right, t = top

Edinburgh Central Library
91

For Further Reading and Viewing

www.theglasgowstory.com
excellent site created by Glasgow University and Glasgow City Council

www.scottisharchitects.org.uk
architects and architecture 1840-1940

www.arthurlloyd.co.uk
about theatres in Britain

www.theambassadors.com/theatreroyalglasgow
what's on at the theatre

The Second City	Charles Oakley	1975
Glasgow	Irene Maver	2000
Scotland : A New Look	Geoffrey Credland and George Murray, published for Scottish Television	1969
Scotland's Splendid Theatres	Bruce Peter - but beware of old misinformation	1999
Scotland and its Music Hall 1850-1914	Paul Maloney	2003
The Glasgow Stage	Walter Baynham Theatre Royal, Dunlop Street and Queen Street	1892
Music Hall Memories	Jack House	1986
Kings, Queens and People's Palaces	Vivien Devlin An Oral History of The Scottish Variety Theatre 1920-1970	1991
The Good Auld Days - Entertainers from Music Hall to Television	Gordon Irving ..with clear gazetteer of Scotland's theatres	1977
Roy Thomson of Fleet Street	Russell Braddon	1965
After I Was Sixty	Lord Thomson of Fleet	1975
It's A Curious Story	Cordelia Oliver The Tale of Scottish Opera 1962-1987	1987
Scottish Opera	Conrad Wilson The First Ten Years	1972
Alex	Conrad Wilson The Biography of Sir Alexander Gibson	1993
A Ballet for Scotland	Noel Goodwin The First Ten Years of The Scottish Ballet	1979